CONTESTING COMMUNITIES

EMILY BARMAN

Contesting Communities

The Transformation of Workplace Charity

STANFORD UNIVERSITY PRESS

STANFORD, CALIFORNIA 2006

Stanford University Press
Stanford, California

Printed in the United States of America
on acid-free, archival-quality paper.

Library of Congress Cataloging-in-Publication Data

Barman, Emily.
    Contesting communities : the transformation of workplace
charity / Emily Barman.
        p.   cm.
    Includes bibliographical references and index.
    ISBN 0-8047-5448-9 (cloth : alk. paper)
    ISBN 0-8047-5449-7 (pbk. : alk. paper)
        1. Employees—Charitable contributions—United States.   2. Charities—United
States.   3. Fund raising—United States.   4. Community—United States. I. Title.

HV91.B26 2006
361.8—dc22

                                                                    2005037278

Original Printing 2006
Last figure below indicates year of this printing:
15   14   13   12   11   10   09   08   07   06
Typeset by TechBooks, New Delhi, in 10/14 Janson.

Contents

Tables and Figures

Acknowledgments

This book would not be possible without the participation and goodwill of a great many people, and I would like to take this opportunity to thank them all. I am very grateful to those individuals in the arena of workplace charity whose cooperation and helpfulness allowed me to gather data on this topic. Thanks to the leaders of the United Ways in San Francisco and Chicago for permitting me to study their organizations and to the staff and volunteers at these two organizations for courteously and unfailingly answering my questions and tolerating my observation of their daily work lives. Thanks also to several members of the staff of the United Way of America who kindly took the time to meet with me and provided me with access to their own research. I also wish to thank representatives from other participants in workplace charity, including the National Committee for Responsive Philanthropy, the National Alliance for Choice in Giving, and the Environmental Support Center, who gave me a sense not only of their own organizations but also of the larger dynamics and history of workplace charity. My gratitude also goes to the staff of local and national Alternative Funds across the nation for talking with me and/or responding to my survey.

Funding from the Aspen Institute's Nonprofit Sector Research Fund, the National Science Foundation, and Boston University provided support for the research and writing of this project. I presented earlier drafts of chapters at meetings of the Association for Research on Nonprofit Organizations and Voluntary Action; the American Sociological Association; Boston University Workshop on Organizational Theory and Economic Sociology; Indiana University Center on Philanthropy and Aspen Institute Doctoral Seminar; MIT-Sloan School of Management Organization Studies Group Seminar Series;

National Alliance for Choice in Giving Biannual Conference; the Park Ridge Center for Health, Faith, and Ethics; Rational Choice Mini-Conference; University of Chicago Culture, History, and Social Theory Workshop, and University of Chicago Graduate School of Business Organizations and Markets Workshop. I also presented earlier versions of parts of the book to audiences at the departments of sociology at the University of Chicago, Ohio State University, Emory University, University of Wisconsin-Milwaukee, University of Arizona, and University of Illinois, Urbana-Champaign. I am indebted to all those who made valuable criticisms and suggestions.

This project has benefited from the intellectual attention and engagement of several individuals. I thank Andrew Abbott, Eleanor Brilliant, Mark Chaves, Susan Eckstein, Joseph Galaskiewicz, Andreas Glaeser, Julian Go, Kristen Gronbjerg, Alya Guseva, Virginia Hodgkinson, Mary Ellen Konieczny, Edward Laumann, Michael Lounsbury, Heather MacIndoe, Daniel Monti, Susan Ostrander, Steven Rathgeb-Smith, Polly Rizova, Laurel Smith-Doerr, Marc Steinberg, and John Stone for discussion and comment on various versions of this project. The departments of sociology at the University of Chicago, Harvard University, and Boston University all have served as fruitful settings in which to pursue my work. I am grateful to Daniela Florea and Masayo Nishida for their terrific assistance in gathering and sorting data.

Along the way, I have been supported by my family. My parents, Roderick and Jean Barman, seasoned academics themselves, have provided both emotional and intellectual sustenance. My brother and sister-in law, Rod Barman and Dom Bajard, ensured that I kept my eye on the practical issues really at stake in this analysis. This book is dedicated to Julian Go, my dearest friend and my husband.

CONTESTING COMMUNITIES

CHAPTER I

The Question of Community

Community can be the warmly persuasive word to describe an existing set of relationships, or the warmly persuasive word to describe an alternative set of relationships. What is most important, perhaps, is that unlike all other terms of social organization . . . it never seems to be used unfavorably, and never to be given any positive opposing or distinguishing term.

— RAYMOND WILLIAMS *1983:76.*

On a rainy and cold morning in downtown Chicago, a workplace campaign was taking place at one branch of the city's municipal government. In a darkly lit basement room, employee coordinators sat with coffee and donuts in hand, listening to a series of speakers present their pitches for charitable contributions. Each speaker represented a different fundraiser, each seeking to gather donations from workers. One after the other, the speakers introduced themselves and then gave an impassioned case for why their organization deserved funds. A representative from the Black United Fund of Illinois began; he encouraged African-American employees to give in order to help others in their community across the state. He was followed by a representative of the Illinois Women's Funding Federation. She employed the same discourse of donors' assisting others in their own community, but she emphasized the importance of women aiding women. Next, a speaker from an international development organization stressed the plight of the poor and disadvantaged abroad, emphasizing that "we are all interconnected," even if we don't personally know those in need. The next speaker, the representative of a progressive social fund, began by conceding that a gift to her charity could not help as many people, but she noted that the problems, and their solutions, were the same right here at home. Finally, it was the turn of the United Way™ representative: this young woman made a plea for the cause of the community – "of people just like you and me right here in Chicago." Having presented their appeals, the representatives distributed flyers and asked the employee coordinators to return to their respective offices and encourage their fellow workers to donate, to "give from the heart."

So began the first stage of a quintessentially American phenomenon – the annual appeal for charitable contributions in the workplace. In the fall of each year, thousands of such fundraising drives take place across the country. With the consent of management, employees make a commitment to have a percentage of their pay regularly deducted for charitable purposes. Their gifts are taken by their employer directly from their wages or salary and given in a lump sum to a pledge processor, which then distributes those funds to selected nonprofit organizations. This form of philanthropy is called workplace charity.

Giving by workers constitutes one of the primary fundraising efforts in the nonprofit sector. Workplace charity provides an important vehicle for altruism: almost one-half of individual givers have said that they made charitable contributions because they were asked to do so at their place of work (Hodgkinson and Weitzman 1994). Taken together, employees' donations comprise a considerable source of philanthropic resources. In 2001 alone, workplace giving totaled over $4.1 billion (National Committee for Responsive Philanthropy 2003; United Way of America 2004), constituting one of the single largest pool of private funds for the nonprofit sector (Salamon 1999).[1]

Yet, workplace charity is undergoing some significant changes. The campaign that I described above is not the only way in which workplace charity has taken place. To the contrary, it looks very different from those campaigns that took place in the past. For much of the twentieth century, the United Way has held a monopoly over workplace charity.[2] A gift at work meant a gift to the United Way, and donors had no choice in how their contributions would be dispersed. The United Way distributed employees' donations based on what it perceived the needs of the local community to be. Thus, the United

Way was the sole collector, decision maker, and arbiter. Its monopoly meant that only those nonprofit organizations affiliated with the United Way could benefit from funds gathered in the workplace (Seeley, Buford, and Junker 1957; Brilliant 1990).

By contrast, in some cities across the nation, the United Way today faces rivalry from other federated fundraisers, such as those described above. These Alternative Funds, as they are often called, are coalitions of nonprofits gathered together for the sole purpose of collecting workplace donations.[3] They solicit contributions for a variety of particularistic identities and interests, including minority and ethnic concerns, health research, the environment, and women's issues. Their presence alongside the United Way in workplace campaigns expands the scope and the targets of charitable giving while reconfiguring the entire field of workplace charity. Donors gain the ability to direct their contributions to issues and organizations of their own choice, the United Way loses its monopoly, and a wider variety of charities serving a broader assortment of recipients can benefit from workplace donations.

The goal of this book is to examine the presence of competition over donations in workplace charity. How and to what extent has this shift occurred? And what are its implications for individual giving in the workplace, for nonprofit organizations, and for intermediary fundraisers? Although a number of scholars and observers have noted the rise of Alternative Funds in workplace charity, these questions have yet to be addressed fully (Wenocur, Cook, and Steketee 1984; Brilliant 1990; Hall 1992; Salamon 1999; Perlmutter and Kramer 2001). This book, based upon original research on workplace charity, is the first to theorize and account for the appearance of Alternative Funds and to specify their consequences for charitable giving and for nonprofit organizations. In so doing, this book contributes to a better understanding of the contemporary face of workplace charity and, by extension, the nonprofit sector.

Two central themes guide the chapters to follow. The first has to do with when and where Alternative Funds have arisen, how they compete with United Ways, and how United Ways have responded to them. Although there has been a historical shift in workplace charity from the United Way's monopoly and toward the emergence of Alternative Funds, the shift has only been partial. On the one hand, the growth of Alternative Funds is striking. Across the United States, 160 Alternative Funds raised over $200 million in 2001, representing an increase in total revenue of over one-third from 1996 to 2001 (National Committee for Responsive Philanthropy 2003). On the other hand, Alternative Funds have not spelled the end to the United Way's monopoly of workplace fundraising in most places. There are Alternative Funds in some cities but not others, and the United Way has been able to retain dominance in many locales, although not all. One of my goals is to explain this variation and specify its implications. What accounts for the emergence of Alternative Funds? Why have they appeared in some cities rather than others? What have been the consequences of their formation for the structure of workplace charity and the distribution of workplace gifts?

The second theme of this book is how these changes in workplace charity relate to larger questions concerning community and the nonprofit sector in American society. What is meant by community has increasingly come into question in both the academic realm and the popular press. Some observers have decried the loss of community, claiming that the processes of modernity have resulted in a decline in collective affiliation and sentiment among individuals. By contrast, rather than seeing community as disappearing, other scholars have emphasized the appearance of a new vision of community, based on novel types of belonging.

My analysis of the case of workplace charity offers one window into this debate. For as we will see, the different fundraisers competing for control in workplace charity represent very different visions of community. The United Way gathers donations in the name of a local community of place, whereas Alternative Funds solicit contributions for particularistic communities of purpose. These participants in workplace charity advance their own specific conception of community in order to state their mission, to achieve legitimacy, and to garner resources and support. Therefore, at stake in the struggle to control workplace giving is not just a rivalry between nonprofit organizations; instead, in question is what *kind* of "community" should be the proper target of charitable activity and hence reap the benefits of giving in the American workplace. In this sense, to track the struggle over workplace charity is also to track a series of contests and conflicts over the meaning of community. As a result, the debate over community is recast. Rather than probing whether or not community has declined in American life, this book examines the organizational representation of different visions of community in one social setting and asks whether and how one form of community comes to be privileged rather than another.

This chapter proceeds by providing an overview of the debate over community. The case of workplace charity is then introduced and located within the question of community. Incorporating a discussion of the data and methods employed in this study, the chapter concludes with a summary of the arguments presented in the book.

Conceptions of Community

Within the social sciences, the debate over community has arisen out of two different and fundamentally contrasting perspectives on community. These theoretical frameworks diverge not only in how they define community but also in how they measure it – resulting in fundamentally incompatible assessments of the health and vitality of civic life. As I show, however, the case of workplace charity allows for the examination of how these changing conceptions of community intersect and play out in contemporary American society.

Although there is no set agreement on the definition of community, the first body of literature on community holds the assumption that community exists when certain structural characteristics are met. I call this conception a *community of place*. Community occurs when residence in a common locale results in shared sentiments and goals among members (Hillery 1955; Bell and Newby 1971; Williams 1983; Weiss and Friedman 1995; Putnam 2000). Community, at the most basic level, entails place; it refers to a locality, bounded space, a limited geography (Park 1959; Suttles 1972; Hummon 1990).[4] The physical location of individuals within this common place entails propinquity, which refers to the nearness and proximity of individuals – in space, time, and in social relations (Tonnies 1957).

Place and propinquity generate a web of interactions among residents, another important structural prerequisite of community. These networks must be of a specific type for community to emerge. Individuals' relationships must be dense and long-term, instead of dyadic and temporary, and they must be moral or "affect-laden," rather than instrumental or exchange-oriented (Durkheim 1970[1897]; Williams 1983; Paxton 1999).[5] A community based on locale and social ties must also produce a community of the mind. Members must embrace a common good: a set of shared values, ideals, and expectations that exist outside the specific and oft divergent interests of individuals. This common faith is reinforced by common narratives, collective ways of doing, and a communal history (Bellah et al., 1987; Selznick 1992).[6]

The presence of community provides benefits to both its members and to the social collectivity as a whole. Individuals gain support and assistance as they pursue their own goals (Coleman 1988). In turn, the presence of shared networks and meanings further solidifies social connectedness, generating intensified feelings of trust and reciprocity (Etzioni 1995; Astin, Sax, and Avalos 1999; Paxton 1999). As Tocqueville (1844:117) noted, "Feelings and opinions are recruited, the heart is enlarged, and the human mind is developed only by the reciprocal influence of men upon one another." The existence of social bonds, also called social capital (Putnam 1993, 1995, 2000), is perceived to induce higher rates of public goods, such as volunteering, charitable donations, and associational participation.

At the same time that social scientists have proffered this particular vision of community, many have also bemoaned its loss in contemporary society.[7] As a result of the forces of urbanization, industrialization, and migration, community has been and is in a state of decline. The transition to modernity entails a turn from shared sentiment to instrumental rationality and the individual pursuit of self-fulfillment (Riesman 1950; Tonnies 1957; Durkheim 1964[1893]; Weber 1978, Lasch 1979, 1991; Habermas 1989; Putnam 2000). The loss of social ties of a dense and affective nature results in a breakdown of mutual trust and reciprocity, and without a sufficient supply of social capital, social groups are unable to pursue and achieve their common goals (Wirth 1938; Stein 1960; Bellah et al. 1980; Putnam 2000). Some scholars have tied the loss of community to a specific set of measurable outcomes, such as suicide, political participation, economic development, and crime (Durkheim 1970[1897]; Etzioni 1995; Paxton 1999).

A second group of scholars has been more sanguine about the possibilities for community in contemporary society. Rather than viewing modernity as a retreat from community, these authors conceive modernity as consisting of the emergence of new social groups – the development of new opportunities and mechanisms for individual membership and for collective action (Webber 1963; Fischer 1984[1976]; Bender 1982; Calhoun 1994; Minkoff

1997; Schudson 1998; Wuthnow 1998; Wellman 1999; Brint 2001). "Community...has rarely disappeared from societies. It has been transformed" (Wellman 1999:20).

What then characterizes this emergent conception of community? These social scientists maintain an understanding of community as the existence of individual understandings of and beliefs in a larger social entity, but identify a different set of social processes by which it has emerged, supported by a new theoretical framework. Although the forces of modernity have made difficult the existence of a structural vision of community, they have also produced new modes of collectivity, what I call *communities of purpose*. The New Social Movements of the 1960s and 1970s generated new sources of identification, based on race, ethnicity, gender, sexual orientation, physical disability, and other characteristics. Similarly, the postmodern era has expanded the bases of self-understanding beyond residence and/or class to individuals' interests and hobbies (Bellah et al. 1980; Harvey 1989). These communities of purpose are made possible by new communication technologies, mass media, and new transportation systems, which allow for the maintenance of social networks without the necessity of place and propinquity (Webber 1963; Fischer 1984[1976]; Wellman 1979, 1999; Anderson 1983; Giddens 1991; Rheingold 1993; Wuthnow 1994, 1998; Cerulo 1997).

To make sense of this form of community, a new theoretical framework has emerged. In this approach, the interpretive – rather than the structural – dimension of community has been emphasized. Community is based on meaning: the collective imaginings of members with a shared characteristic or interest (Cohen 1985; Gamson 1992; Lamont 1992; Wellman 1999). Drawing their inspiration from classical sociologists, scholars have focused on the ways in which individuals employ symbolic boundaries to create similarities and differences (Durkheim 1954[1912]; Weber 1978; Bourdieu 1984).[8] "Symbolic boundaries" (Lamont 1992) or "social closures" (Weber 1978) are the lines that include and define some people, groups, and things while excluding others (Epstein 1992).

Thus, community is generated from a shared sense among members of the "we" and the "they," of an inside and an outside, and of association and disassociation. These social borders serve a dual purpose: they not only mark the commonalities of a group but also intensify them by emphasizing their inherent distinctness from others (Taylor and Whittier 1992:111). To generate and maintain those shared lines of inclusion and exclusion, an interpretive community is dependent upon the production of a collective identity among members – common vocabularies, symbols, and practices (Lamont 1992).

In all, an interpretive model of community provides a more promising picture of the state of community. Although place and propinquity still matter, they no longer offer many individuals an "overall template of social and personal identities" (Calhoun 1994:11). By drawing on a new theoretical framework for community, this literature highlights novel sources of social collectivity and new ways and modes in which we are coming together. This new conception of community continues to provide individuals with opportunities for participation in collective life.

The presence of communities of purpose complicates our understandings of community and raises new topics for investigation. This body of scholarship suggests that community is not in decline, as had previously been posited, but rather is expanding in meaning and form. By recognizing the multiplicity of meanings of community in contemporary society, these authors pose a new set of more difficult but also more fruitful questions for empirical research. Rather than examine how and why community is disappearing, instead the challenge becomes one of determining how these competing understandings of community are being realized across different arenas of social life.

Workplace Charity and Community

In the nonprofit sector, no single organization represents the traditional conception of a community of place more than the United Way. Fittingly once called the Community Chest, the United Way solicits and distributes workplace contributions in the name of the local community. Since the 1910s, the United Way has held annual campaigns in cities and towns to solicit contributions. It has distributed this revenue to member agencies within the health and human services, such as the Salvation Army, the Boy Scouts, the YMCA, and others (Brilliant 1990). To legitimate its place between donors and recipients, the United Way frames its role as ensuring the health and well-being of the local community. Over the last two decades, however, the United Way has experienced a sharp decline in support. For some observers, the demise of the United Way serves as empirical confirmation of the thesis of community decline (Hall 1992; Haider 1997).

At the same time, the United Way has faced the emergence of rival fundraisers oriented around a different vision of community. These new organizations, typically called Alternative Funds, are coalitions of charities, each possessing a specific purpose or mission. They seek to compete alongside the United Way for individuals' donations in the workplace. Alternative Funds symbolize the growth in America of communities of purpose, some new and others of long standing in the nation's history. Overall, these United Way rivals represent strikingly different and varied conceptions of community, emphasizing a multiplicity of identities and interests. These interests include minority and ethnic rights, health research, environmentalism, women's rights, social action, international development, and others. The rise of Alternative Funds has been remarkable. First appearing in the late 1960s, 160 Alternative Funds were in existence across the nation by 2001, raising about $220 million.

With the emergence of Alternative Funds, the meaning of community in workplace charity has been both complicated and expanded. As federated fundraisers, both the United Way and Alternative Funds embody and enact community by allowing donors to make contributions based on their collective affiliation and by generating resources for nonprofits that assist a particular group. The presence or absence of the United Way and Alternative Funds in workplace charity matters because it affects the flow of resources – determining to whom donors can give and, concomitantly, which recipients can receive funds.

The task of this book is to determine the origins and implications of these contrasting conceptions of community as they have played out in this one key site of the nonprofit sector. The book commences by investigating how the United Way historically equated workplace charity with the local community. It then asks how and when Alternative Funds, representing communities of purpose, have emerged in workplace charity. Although many of these social groups and movements have appeared periodically over the nineteenth and twentieth century in America (Lears 1991; Calhoun 1995), Alternative Funds began to form in the field of workplace charity only a few decades ago. I examine why and how these expanded understandings of community did not appear in workplace charity until the 1970s. The book next analyzes the consequences of the entrance of Alternative Funds into workplace charity. It delineates how competition over community has played out in practice and how these outcomes have affected individual givers, federated fundraisers, and the flow of workplace donations.

In addressing these queries, this book advances the existing literature on community. Typically, scholars have focused on one type of community or another. Some have focused on the declining centrality and relevance of community based in place (Bellah et al. 1987; Putnam 1993, 1995, 2000; Skocpol 1999; Keller 2003). Others have examined how communities of purpose are realized across various social sectors, including the political (Berry 1997; Reid 1999; Schudson 1999), the economic (Goode 1957; Kuhn 1970; Gieryn 1983; Van Maanen and Barley 1984), and the religious (Roof and McKinney 1987; Wuthnow 1988; McRoberts 2003). Within the nonprofit sector, similar attention has been given to the emergence of these new collectivities, such as organizations oriented around children's rights, the feminist movement, and the environment (Hawes 1991; Freudenberg and Steinsapir 1992; Taylor and Whittier 1992; Ferree and Martin 1995; Minkoff 1995).

Yet, this literature on community has yet to investigate how different understandings of community, based on place and purpose, intersect with each other. Instead, research has focused solely on one conception of community or another. This emphasis on a singular notion of community is reflected in the debate over community, in which scholars have asked simply whether or not community is in decline. They have presupposed only one kind of community – a community of place, thereby overlooking a new, interpretive conception of community and how it both affects and is affected by communities of purpose.

Through the case of workplace charity, this book examines what happens when contrasting notions of community are co-present in one social setting. Specifically, it focuses on how organizations engage in contestations over community. Although community can take a variety of forms, including the existence of individual-level networks and the growth of informal groups, this book focuses on the organizational dimension of community. Organizations matter to our understanding of community because community is both embodied and enacted by organizations. For one, organizations are the sites in which community is realized. Organizations are formed when individuals and groups come together to pursue or further the goals of their community, whether it be local and place-based or derived from a shared identity or interest (Tocqueville 1840, 1844; Nisbet 1953; Habermas 1989; Putnam 2000). Nonprofit organizations are "communities made manifest" (Smith and Lipsky 1993). Organizations also enact community: they fundamentally contribute to the success and survival of a community. Organizations are the means by which social collectivities obtain resources, locate new members, distribute cultural models of belonging, and influence the political, economic, and domestic sectors of society (Cohen 1985; Foley and Edwards 1996; Minkoff 1997; Polletta 1998; Boris 1999; Frumkin 2002). As Minkoff (1995:2) notes, "Formal organizations, not abstract collectivities, are given a voice."

Hence, the study of nonprofit organizations in workplace charity provides a window into the question of community. The book asks how changing understandings of community in American society have unfolded in this one site of the nonprofit sector. Does the case of workplace charity embody the thesis of community decline? That is, does the demise of the United Way constitute the dominant narrative of workplace charity? Or, have Alternative Funds come to re-define the meaning of community in workplace charity? How do competing conceptions of community play out within this one arena of the nonprofit sector?

Drawing from an analysis of workplace charity across different cities and over the last three decades, I find that a new vision of community, based on a shared purpose, is not simply replacing or eliminating the traditional vision of community. The story told here is not one of a gradual and smooth transition from one model of community to another, but rather one of contestation and conflict between different organizations, holding different understandings of to whom donors can give and which recipients should receive donations. The United Way and Alternative Funds pursue and defend their own specific vision of community in order to garner resources and establish legitimacy. In all, I argue that the debate over community should be understood not as the decline or survival of "community," but as an ongoing competition between different conceptions of community.

This rivalry, moreover, is playing out in different ways across different sites (localities). I examine the presence of Alternative Funds across locales, finding that they have become dominant in some types of workplaces, but are largely absent in others. They participate in workplace campaigns in some places, but the United Way has retained its monopoly in many others. Even when Alternative Funds are present, their implications for the local field of workplace charity vary dramatically. In only a small number of cities have Alternative Funds successfully legitimated the presence of communities of purpose in workplace charity. In San Francisco, for example, the field of workplace charity has been reconfigured around new conceptions of community. In other cities, a traditional conception of community has dominated. In Chicago, although the local United Way faces rivalry from Alternative Funds, workplace charity remains equated with a place-based model of community.

The book's second task is to account for these divergent outcomes in the logic of community across locales. The book asks why a community of place has retained dominance in some cities, but has been replaced by a particularistic community of purpose in others. Although community matters because it shapes resource flows between donors and recipients, I find that neither donors' demands nor recipients' needs matter. Instead, these contrasting outcomes result from organizational contestations within institutional constraints. Although the United Way and Alternative Funds are capable of employing proactive maneuvers to pursue legitimacy and revenue, they are also limited by cultural understandings held by a specific set of key actors within the local field. All organizations are subject to institutional pressures – socially constructed rules and regulations in the larger world – that convey legitimacy (Meyer and Rowan 1977; DiMaggio and Powell 1991).

In workplace charity, the institutional environment is driven by the local business community and its shared beliefs and understandings of philanthropy. Local business leaders hold a model of how corporate philanthropy should look and operate (McCarthy 1987; Hall 1992; Abzug 1996). These charitable understandings vary across locales: cities tend to possess a "distinct climate of giving" (Useem 1988:83) among its corporate elite that affects the amount and scope of firms' donations (McElroy and Siegfried 1986; Galaskiewicz 1991; Burlingame and Young 1996; Sinclair and Galaskiewicz 1997).

However, the local climate of giving possesses implications beyond the charitable behavior of firms themselves. These models of philanthropy matter because they establish the legitimacy of different conceptions and organizational forms of community within workplace charity. Firms act as gatekeepers: they decide which nonprofits will participate in their employees' fund-raising drives. They do so by extending their own models of philanthropy to their workplace campaigns. Different models of philanthropy possess differing degrees of elective affinity with different conceptions of community. Hence, both Alternative Funds and the United Way face varying amounts of accommodation or antagonism on the part of local corporate elites. These fundraising organizations are restricted in their ability to solicit donors by gatekeepers' decisions.

The institutional composition of the local field, however, cannot fully account for differences in conceptions of community across locales. Although workplace fundraisers may face institutional constraints, they are able to strategically react to them in ways that maximize their own interests. By emphasizing the responsive capabilities of organizations, I contribute to and expand upon a theoretical perspective called strategic choice (Child 1972; Oliver 1991; Alexander 1996, 1998; Oakes, Townley, and Cooper 1998). Both Alternative Funds and United Ways engage in tactical moves to gather legitimacy and to garner resources in a crowded environment. These moves take two distinct forms. Due to the presence of gatekeepers in workplace charity, these fundraisers engage in a contest over the matter of entry to workplace sites. They employ a range of tactics, ranging from the formal to the informal, to gain access to workers' contributions. Once permitted to solicit donors' gifts, these organizations strive to obtain charitable contributions from individuals. Here, their tactics vary in nature from the symbolic to the substantive.

In all, the debate over community in workplace charity is resolved based on processes that scholars have not typically emphasized to explain the status and meaning of community in contemporary society. Neither the support of individuals nor the needs of recipients matter much here. We might expect that donors' wishes would be significant drivers of the logic of community in workplace charity, but the affinity of givers to a particular vision of community has little to do with why one form of community prevails over another. We might also anticipate that the demand for services would be relevant, but the actual needs of the local population do not determine whether a community of place or of purpose comes to structure workplace charity. Instead, the book shows that it is the intersection between the institutional environment and the strategic maneuvers of organizations that explains variation in definitions of community. By examining this interaction of institutional culture and nonprofits' responses over time, we can understand why different conceptions of community become dominant in some places and not others.

Along the way, this book incorporates a concern for other changes that have occurred within workplace charity, the nonprofit sector, and larger society. As I discuss in later chapters, the structure and dynamics of workplace charity have been influenced not only by the rise of Alternative Funds but also by other historical developments. As the federal government has altered its flow and distribution of resources to nonprofit organizations, the role of workplace charity in local communities has been reexamined both by the United Way itself and by other actors in the field. As the economy has been restructured away from manufacturing and toward the provision of services, corporations have altered their understandings of the viability of and the need for employee fundraising. And as the nation has becoming increasingly ethnically and racially diverse, firms have adopted a new management ideology based around the recognition of difference. We will see that these changes have not only played a role in how contestations over community are resolved across locales but they also have possessed separate and distinct implications of their own for the meaning and structure of workplace charity.

Data Collection and Analysis

The book employs a historical and comparative perspective. Although other scholars have discussed the presence of Alternative Funds in workplace charity, they have tended to employ anecdotal evidence and/or to consider the case of workplace charity in a small sample of cities (Brilliant 1990; Hall 1992; Oster 1995; Lauffer 1997; Salamon 1999). This book contributes to but also moves beyond those studies by examining the consequences of competition for workplace charity both across time and across place. By employing this approach, it is able to make evident the underlying processes and conditions that have allowed both for the growth of Alternative Funds and for their implications for workplace charity across locales.

To make my argument, I employ both quantitative and qualitative data. For a historical perspective on workplace charity, I examined a variety of primary and secondary sources that identify the formation, methods, and spread of the United Way. In addition, the study draws from secondary research on workplace charity, including newspaper and magazine reports, scholarly accounts, archival research, and data generated by participants in the field.

To assess the state of workplace charity across locales, I make use of a survey of Alternative Funds that I conducted to identify the scope and nature of their formation and organizational practices. In the book, I employ the statistical method of logistic regression to analyze these data. Logistic regression estimates the probability or likelihood of the occurrence of a specific outcome that is dichotomous in nature (that is, it either has or has not occurred (Menard 1995; Pampel 2000). Although some parts of the book are based on this type of statistical analysis, the findings are presented in a language that is accessible to all.

I supplement this quantitative data with qualitative data gathered across different geographical scales. To obtain a picture of workplace charity at the national level, I conducted interviews with representatives from the United Way of America, national-level Alternative Funds, and advocacy groups that have facilitated the formation of Alternative Funds. I also collected publicity material, research findings, and policy recommendations, past and present, from these different organizations.

These macro-level data are supplemented by a comparative and more detailed assessment of workplace charity in two cities: Chicago and San Francisco.[9] Here, fieldwork was an important source of information. I conducted ethnographic research at the United Ways in Chicago and San Francisco. Among other activities, I attended meetings, participated in the training of staff and volunteers, and visited local workplaces when fundraising campaigns were occurring.[10] During that time, I conducted informal and formal interviews with the United Way's staff, volunteers, and members of the board of directors (past and present).[11] These interviews provided historical background on the United Way and the local field of workplace charity (often in short supply given the traditional lack of "institutional memory" [Alexander 1996] on the part of nonprofit organizations), and they allowed for a comparative analysis of the perceptions of and discourses employed by the two United Ways. Primary documents from the two organizations were also useful. I reviewed current and historical documents generated by these United Ways, including fundraising and publicity material, financial documents, and planning documents. I conducted archival research on both United Ways at public and university libraries in the two regions.

In addition, I gathered data from the local Alternative Funds in the two cities. I conducted interviews with their representatives, asking them to describe the history of their formation and subsequent pattern of growth. From each United Way rival, I collected fundraising and publicity material, financial documents, and planning material, both past and present. Some Alternative Fund representatives allowed me to accompany them to workplace campaigns, giving me important insights into how open, competitive campaigns differ from United Way-only campaigns. Let me note that this data collection took place prior to the events of 9/11, so it is important to note that these two United Ways have changed since the time period that I describe.

I expanded upon this primary data with secondary research on the two cities. Data from government agencies at the national, state, and local levels allowed me to determine the economic and demographic composition of the two cities over the two time periods in question. Secondary documents, including governmental reports, media publications, and scholarly research, served to explicate the relevant political, social, and economic changes that have influenced workplace charity in the two cases under study. The qualitative data generated by these mixed methods were analyzed using the technique of grounded theory, permitting theoretical implications to emerge through the ongoing analysis of findings during the process of data collection (Glaser and Strauss 1967).

Organization

The next chapter sets the stage by introducing the case of workplace charity. It shows how the United Way embodies a traditional model of community based on place. Drawing from primary documents, the chapter emphasizes how the construction of a place-based conception of community has constituted a necessary condition in the formation and survival of the United Way. Located between donors and recipients, the United Way strove to legitimate its intermediary position by highlighting its benefits for the community. Despite a series of challenges, the chapter outlines how the United Way system retained a commitment to a community of place up through the 1960s.

Chapters 3 and 4 provide an introduction to Alternative Funds. Chapter 3 outlines the different types of United Way rivals that have entered the field over the last three decades. It shows how these federated fundraisers represent various communities of purpose. Alternative Funds have expanded the traditional model of community by altering the basis of community, the mode of facilitating community, and the scope of community. Chapter 4 accounts for the emergence of Alternative Funds within workplace charity. I examine the rise of new fundraising participants in workplace charity both in terms of the particular historical moments at which Alternative Funds appeared and where they individually have provided rivalry to the United Way.

Having set the scene, the next chapters focus on the outcome of this contestation over community. Chapter 5 establishes that competition over community takes place at two levels: as struggles over entry to workplace charity and as conflict over employees' donations. I show that, to constitute viable alternatives to the United Way, Alternative Funds must not only be formed as organizational entities but also must gain access to fundraising sites in the workplace. Alternative Funds have faced resistance not only from institutional actors (i.e., from firms) but also from the United Way. Local United Ways have sought to invalidate the appeal and legitimacy of Alternative Funds among gatekeepers through an assortment of tactics.

Chapters 6 and 7 turn to the question of the outcome of competing conceptions of community in the pursuit of charitable contributions. Here, the task is to compare two cities with opposing logics of community and to account for why different models of community have become dominant in different places. In Chapter 6, I begin with the case of Chicago. In Chicago, despite the presence of Alternative Funds, the field is now centered on a place-based logic of community. I argue that the United Way, by adopting the tactics of differentiation and revenue diversification, has capitalized on the local corporate community's commitment to the economic well-being of Chicago. Chapter 7 focuses on San Francisco, where communities of purpose now dominate workplace charity. Here, Alternative Funds have benefited from a decentralized view of philanthropy held by business leaders. Further, the United Way itself has been reorganized around the solicitation of workplace gifts for communities of purpose.

A concluding chapter summarizes the book's findings and elucidates their relevance for scholarship on the nonprofit sector and community. Three themes are highlighted: a view of philanthropy as a social relationship, the implications of competition for the nonprofit sector, and an organizationally mediated perspective on the question of community.

The United Way and a Community of Place

The chest, sometimes called "the budget plan of benevolence," made giving less
an act of personal charity than a form of community citizenship, almost as
essential as the payment of taxes.

— ROBERT BREMNER *(1960:141).*

Workplace charity provides a window into the changing meaning of community in American public life. Within this one key site of the nonprofit sector,
different federated fundraisers have appeared that represent both communities of place and purpose. This chapter and the next one provide an overview
of the different conceptions of community currently present in workplace
charity. This chapter focuses on the United Way, showing how it has relied
upon a traditional notion of community – one based on place. This conception of community was the outcome of the central principles of efficiency
and effectiveness, proposed by both business leaders and social service professionals, which drove the formation of the United Way (then called the
Community Chest) in the 1910s. Despite a series of challenges, this notion
of community has remained central to the United Way system.

The Creation of Workplace Charity

Workplace charity emerged in the early 1900s as one manifestation of the
larger Progressive movement that was dominant in American society at the

time. By the late 1800s, the United States had undergone social disruption caused by large-scale immigration, urbanization, and industrialization. The goal of the Progressive movement was to correct for the deleterious effects of modernity through the application of scientific techniques to various social spheres, including the economic, the political, and the religious (McCarthy 1991). In politics, for example, it was hoped that democracy would be improved by the implementation of institutional reforms, such as direct primaries, the direct election of U.S. senators, and the possibility of electoral recalls. Similarly, in the free market, Progressives believed that government adoption of regulatory and trust-busting laws could help prevent corporate abuses (Buenker 1988; Sklar 1988; Sandel 1996). In all, there was a concern for efficiency and rationality in organizational form and practice.

This same "gospel of efficiency" was extended to the burgeoning non-profit sector through the application of "scientific charity." In response to the nation's new social problems, a proliferation of charities and voluntary associations had emerged in the decades following the Civil War. Until the late 1800s, there had been no systematic method for the provision of social welfare. Instead, the charitable acts of a growing population of organizations resulted in the overlapping, fragmented, and unsystematic provision of assistance and aid to the needy. Philanthropy was mired in the "sloughs of sentimentality and alms-giving" (Lubove 1965:1).

Two different groups – local elites and social service professionals – expressed concern about the organization of charity; one outcome of this concern would be the formation of the Community Chest model. The Community Chest brought together the financial federation and the charity organization society. In the early twentieth century, business leaders developed a new and sudden interest in ensuring the well-being of American society. Although firms and their owners benefited from the free market, there was a growing sense that its societal effects were too harmful to be ignored. Big business felt that its own prosperity, and the prosperity of the larger economy, was not served by allowing capitalism to operate unfettered. To prevent the growth of government, as had happened in Europe, business leaders sought to alter and improve the social conditions of the day by developing a private sector alternative to government welfare (Wenocur, Cook, and Steketee 1984; Katz 1986; Hall 1992); their efforts turned charity into what Lubove (1965:5) calls an "instrument of urban social control for the conservative middle class."

In part, the corporate elite devoted time and resources to welfare capitalism, ensuring the health and well-being of those geographical locales in which their companies were located; doing so by drawing on common understandings of the time. Like the Progressive movement, business leaders employed the principles of rationalization and centralization, believing that amelioration of societal problems could be achieved through cooperation among different social groups (Hall 1992). Businessmen came together with leaders of other sectors to address a range of social ills. They sought to make charitable giving effective and efficient by applying the logic of the market to charity. In the mid-1910s, for instance, one observer noted that, "Charity is a business.... To protect you from the chance beggar and to relieve the worthy person is the object of organized charity.... Organized charity relieves real distress and helps the object to become again self-supporting. But organized charity must have a business management" (American Association for Organizing Charity 1917:185).

One result of such thinking was the formation of financial federations – umbrella organizations that raised funds for affiliated charities. Modeled after the pre-existing Jewish Federation and Welfare Fund, established in 1895, financial federations corrected for an array of existing problems. Before, individuals had been repeatedly solicited for gifts by local charities. Local elites felt that this method of fundraising was disruptive, expensive, and inequitable (Cutlip 1965). Cleveland's Chamber of Commerce concluded that the existing system had "become most unjust to a liberal public and tends through the innumerable appeals which constantly come to them to antagonize a large number of generous contributors" (Norton 1927:71). The existing method of uncoordinated appeals by a number of charities also was not perceived to encourage giving by all residents. In 1909, for example, a survey of charitable giving by the Cleveland Chamber of Commerce revealed that only 5,386 of the city's more than 600,000 residents had made a donation in the last year (Hall 1992). Federated giving was meant to educate a larger pool of donors as to the needs of the community through "continuous educational publicity" (Norton 1923:4). Finally, the federated fundraiser entailed a "new system for protecting the contributor" (United Way of America 1977:25). Ungoverned fundraising did not differentiate between worthy and unworthy recipient organizations. It was left to donors to make uneducated determinations of the worth and ability of different agencies to help. The Cleveland Community

Chest, for one, was formed out of the Chamber of Commerce's Committee on Benevolent Associations and was intended to set standards and monitor charities on behalf of givers.

Another group also embraced the application of scientific efficiency to the nonprofit sector. Social service professionals worried that the provision of resources and services by multiple charities was inefficient and ineffective. "The charities of a given locality, which should for useful result be systematically directed to the accomplishment of their common purposes are usually a chaos, a patchwork of survivals, of products of curious compound, in which a strong ingredient is ignorance perpetuated by heedlessness" (Warner 1894:359). This newly emerging group employed the same principles of coordination and centralization to rationalize the delivery of philanthropy to a locale and to legitimate the profession's role in the process (Abbott 1988). Scientific charity took the principles of the age and extended them to the charitable realm. The following, taken from the 1916 annual report of the Buffalo Charity Organization Society, summarizes this perspective: "Why need we organize so sweet a thing as charity? We organize music which would otherwise be discordant. We organize religion. Without organization, charity would be to a large extent waste and error" (Watson 1922:139).

The charity organization movement, originating in England in the late nineteenth century (Norton 1927), created a new mechanism by which to proffer aid to the needy. In each city, a charity organization society was formed, functioning as a bureaucratic conduit between clients and agencies. Individuals would apply for assistance to the charity organization society and be directed to a specific organization. Typically, the charity organization society had a dual purpose: to maintain a registry or exchange in which a record of care was kept and to systematically measure need through a survey of the community. Underlying this movement was the premise of Social Darwinism, the belief that indiscriminate direct relief to the poor would result in dependency and profligacy (Katz 1986). By 1911, the charity organization movement had become widely diffused across the nation's major metropolitan areas, with 129 charity organization societies in existence (United Way of America 1977).

The Community Chest was proposed as a viable organizational form to bring together the financial federation and the charity organization society. As established in the early 1910s, the Community Chest was intended to rationalize the gathering and distribution of charitable contributions. This new entity would have a board of directors composed of local citizens and representatives from member agencies, a paid administrative staff of social service professionals, and a membership of social and welfare agencies from the local metropolitan area (Procter and Schuck 1926).

With this composition, the Community Chest played two roles: federated fundraiser and fund allocator. First, as a federated fundraiser, it offered benefits to donors by reducing fundraising costs and ensuring quality control of recipient organizations (Rose-Ackerman 1988). The Community Chest replaced a multitude of campaigns by local charities with a single annual consolidated campaign that gathered donations for all member agencies. Fundraising was focused on wealthy individuals and business elites within the community, although employees, homemakers, and others were also solicited (as we will see, it was only after World War II that the Community Chest became explicitly connected with the workplace). The goal of the Community Chest was not only to ease the burden of existing donors. It was also intended to increase giving by the "regimenting" of the charitable appeal, the education of givers through campaign material, and the use of the media to raise awareness of the campaign and charitable need (Norton 1927).

The Community Chest secondly served as a fund allocator, determining the needs of the local city or town and distributing funds accordingly to member agencies (Litwak and Hylton 1962). It typically relied on a survey of the city or town to determine the region's social problems and the relative volume and quality of needed services (Community Chests and Councils, Inc. 1937). The Community Chest then allocated revenue to member agencies through a budget of allocations, which provided the "best possible program of social welfare and health services for a community" (Community Chests and Councils, Inc. 1938:5). According to one city's report on federated financing, the Community Chest could achieve such ends because "in the process of the discussion of budgets, unmet needs are pointed out, duplication of effort is checked up, gaps in services and facilities are filled in, and the work and budgets of the various agencies are planned, as far as is practicable, from the view of the community needs as a whole" (Procter and Schuck 1926:95).

Although local Community Chests often claimed to represent the needs and interests of the local community, they typically did not include all charities operating in that locale. Take the case of the city of Philadelphia, where the idea of a Community Chest was promulgated by the local Chamber of Commerce. A 1921 survey showed about 1,000 nonprofits working in the city, with a total budget of $150 million. However, of that total population of charities, less than a third was subsequently invited to join the Community Chest (United Way of America 1977).

Instead of incorporating all local agencies into its fold, the leaders of the Community Chest movement tended to select charitable organizations that reflected both the conservative interests of the business community and that appealed to the general population (Carter 1961). A 1926 study of Community Chests divided member agencies into only five categories of activity: family welfare and relief, child care, hospitals and health promotion, recreation, and character building (including settlements, the YMCA and YWCA, and the Scouts (Clapp 1926). Notably absent from the list were agencies for cultural improvement, civic agencies, organizations oriented to economic/political reform, and religious groups; these organizations were all excluded from affiliation as they were perceived unsuitable by organizers and/or deemed unable to elicit community-wide support (Norton 1923; Community Chests and Councils, Inc. 1937; Trolander 1973; Wenocur and Reisch 1989). Member organizations were expected to "play it safe, to stress service to the community, to refurbish established practice rather than to encourage social reform and change the existing order" (Trattner 1974:22). An address to the Community Chest movement's national conference in 1924 by one senior executive, C.M. Bookman, articulates the reasoning behind the selection of member organizations. He asserted,

> An element of danger is that a Chest may take the position that it should be all-inclusive and that no social work should go on in the community save under its guidance. Community Chests, in order to be successful, must develop public opinion favorable to their work. There are, however, many social movements instigated by minorities which, though sound in their social point of view, are nevertheless militantly opposed. In their own interest, as well as in the interest of the Community Chest, these minorities should not entrust their programs to public opinion. Such agencies should not be members of the community Chest (as quoted in United Way of America 1977:53–54).

THE IDEA OF COMMUNITY

In embodying the central principles of the Progressive era, the Community Chest entailed much more than the application of rationality and efficiency to the arena of philanthropy. It also involved the construction of a new recipient of charitable giving. To justify its centralized existence between donors and member agencies, proponents of the Community Chest put forward the community of place as the motivation for charitable giving and the beneficiary of those contributions. The necessity of "community" was derived from the two-sided organizational structure of the Community Chest as both a federated fundraiser and as a fund allocator.

The Community Chest departed from existing methods of philanthropy by asking for a single gift from donors. In so doing, it entailed a new relationship between contributors and recipients. As a federated fundraiser, the Community Chest was founded on the idea of eliminating competition for charitable gifts. A single unified campaign reduced the costs of fundraising for social service agencies and minimized the disruption to local elites that was caused by repeated solicitations. A single unified campaign also replaced gifts by donors to individual charities of their own choice with one gift to the Community Chest. As a condition of membership in the Community Chest, agencies could not gather funds from potential givers on their own; donors were immune from additional appeals. As a result, individuals could either make a donation to the Community Chest or not make a donation at all. Rather than deciding which nonprofits should receive their gifts, donors now entrusted the Community Chest to make that decision for them.

A single gift to the Community Chest was necessitated by the guiding principles of rationalization and centralization. It also reflected a larger sea change within philanthropic giving during the Progressive era. Throughout the nineteenth century, donors – consisting of the local elite – had been highly involved in choosing which charity should receive their gift. This model of individual philanthropy espoused a managerial role for contributors. Donors, it was understood, were motivated to give by their personal interest in the recipient organization or cause. Giving, consequently, was intuitive and highly personal (McCarthy 1991; Hall 1992). In his treatise on philanthropy entitled "The Gospel of Wealth," Andrew Carnegie (1962) laid out this perspective. The duty of the man of wealth, he argued, is to "consider all surplus revenues which come to him simply as trust funds, which he is called upon to administer, and strictly bound as a matter of duty to administer in the manner which, in his judgment, is best calculated to produce the most beneficial results for the community" (p. 25).

With the growth of the scientific efficiency movement, in contrast, social service professionals replaced donors as the decision makers in the non-profit sector. Philanthropy, it was claimed, no longer would be driven by the ephemeral and changing desires of donors and administered by volunteers (Katz 1986). Instead, impartial and expert observers who carefully measured the wants and needs of beneficiaries would lead philanthropy (Wenocur and Reisch 1989). This new group asserted authority over the field of philanthropy by employing scientific knowledge, a competency derived from professional training and expertise. The early 1900s witnessed the growth of the profession of social work through the formation of graduate schools and national associations (Persons 1922; Lubove 1965). As a result, donors were generally considered, of all involved actors, the least qualified to make decisions about how charitable contributions should be distributed. In her study of Chicago area philanthropy at the time, McCarthy (1982) summarizes this development: "Donors were increasingly asked to pay for projects they often could neither touch nor comprehend, deferring to the wisdom of reformers and managers of every stripe and hue" (p. 56). Individuals were solicited to make charitable contributions, but without attaching any conditions to their gifts (Lubove 1965; McCarthy 1991; Hall 1992; Clotfelter 1997).

This new philosophy of giving, as represented by the Community Chest, raised concerns among some observers and social service professionals (American Association for Organizing Charity 1917; Devine 1921; Leebron 1924; Andrews 1950; Seeley, Junker, and Buford 1957; Cutlip 1965). The replacement of individual charities and specific causes with a federated fundraiser was deemed one of the major disadvantages of the Community Chest. In his definitive study of philanthropic giving, for instance, Andrews (1950:154) noted that the "preservation of the giver's choice in the destination of his gift is one of the chief stumbling blocks in a federation's path." Criticism of this new structure of giving almost derailed the initial formation of the Community Chest. A 1906 study by the Cleveland Chamber of Commerce, for example, concluded that contributors would be unwilling to relinquish their vested interests in their "pet" institutions and instead substitute an impersonal participation in support of all agencies (United Way of America 1977). A 1917 report on the viability of financial federations sponsored by the Rockefeller Foundation similarly concluded that federated fundraising should not replace independent campaigns by social service agencies, largely because a single gift divorced the donor from the recipient of his or her contribution (American Association for Organizing Charity 1917).

In the early 1920s, moreover, the Chicago Council of Social Agencies stated that "one gift to many agencies removes the giver from first hand contact with the result achieved by his money and dissipates his interest accordingly" (Leebron 1924:184). A report to the Buffalo Chamber of Commerce on Community Chests also noted that "undesignated giving and immunity from specific appeals tend to produce general lack of personal interest and of intelligent participation in social work by givers" (American Association for Organizing Charity 1917:184). Even within the Community Chest movement, professionals took notice of the unfavorable consequences of a single gift by donors. In 1938, the Community Chest and Councils, Inc., the national association for local Community Chests, noted the foremost advantages and disadvantages of the Community Chest model. The list of disadvantages included the following: "Undesignated giving and immunity from specific appeals tend to produce general lack of personal interest and of intelligent participation in social work by the givers, thus weakening the social agencies" (p. 8).

To sell to donors the idea of the Community Chest, contemporary observers urged Community Chests to develop a new recipient of giving to encourage the charitable impulse in donors. A 1926 survey of the fledgling movement, for example, concluded, "Certain devices and safeguards must be developed to overcome it . . . The Chest organization must hold and increase the special interest of the contributor in the work being financed" (Procter and Schuck 1926:99). In response, early Community Chests, individually and through their trade association, promoted a new recipient of giving. They claimed that donors now were contributing to the "community." With the Community Chest, the making of multiple gifts by individuals to their specific and personal interests was replaced with a single charitable gift to the community. So, the president of the trade association for local Community Chests concluded that the "genius" of Community Chests was in the making of a common cause – the community – from the different and various social service organizations of the local town or city (*The Bulletin* 1932:4).

As a federated fundraiser, Community Chests attempted to instill a desire in donors to give to the community. They constructed the expectation that a contribution to the Community Chest was a necessary part of civic duty – of membership in the community. A federation in the mid 1910s told donors that "it is the duty of the citizens in the community in which distress exists to do everything which can be done to relieve this condition" (American Association for Organizing Charity 1917:183). A scholar at the time noted that the Community Chest "promulgates and presses home the doctrine that the welfare of the individual is the concern and responsibility of the entire community" (Leebron 1924:144).

The Community Chest's explication of a discourse of community was also derived from its function as a fund allocator. In this role, local Community Chests sought to legitimize their position, both to the general public and to affiliated charities, as the dispenser of funds for its member agencies. They needed to convince member agencies of the merits of coordination and over-sight by a second party. It did so by emphasizing its role as a "social planner" for the community. In this capacity, the Community Chest determined and addressed the needs of the local town or city and distributed funds to that end. The benefit of the Community Chest as opposed to independent non-profit organizations, according to popular sentiment at the time, was that individual charities "see only the little fields that each is organized in, and that the city-wide problems are neglected – problems, for example, that de-mand legislative or administrative changes, or call for the creation of some new form of social activity in the city" (American Association for Organizing Charity 1917:200). One public leader wrote that participants in the Com-munity Chest "are coming more and more to see that we have a community problem and that no one phase of social work stands by itself, separate and apart, but that it is only by co-operation that we are going to get ahead" (as quoted in American Association for Organizing Charity 1917:188).

By placing a discourse of community at the center of its rhetoric, the Community Chest both reflected and participated in larger trends at the time. In the early twentieth century, the forces of immigration, industrial-ization, and urbanization had resulted in a general concern over the loss of the traditional form of community based around small-town life. At one and the same time, social reformers, such as Jane Addams, Thomas Dewey, and others, believed that the scale of social life in contemporary America both weakened but also held the potential for resuscitating "community" amidst modernity (Quandt 1970). Yet, the revitalization of community would not happen automatically – instead, it needed to be facilitated by the newly emergent class of professionals and experts. The goal of social reformers at this time was both "procedural" and "formative," to follow Sandel (1996). Their goals were procedural in that they sought to employ bureaucratic techniques for the improvement of modern society. As part of that project of reason and order, however, they also worked to instill in citizens a sense of genuine community – "of common citizenship and shared purpose" (Sandel 1996: 209–210). Similarly, Kusmer (1973:662) describes the Charity Organization movement, of which the Community Chest formed a later part, as one in which "the expertise of the professional and the administrative machinery of charity organization was but a means to an end – the restoration of the community ideal."

Such a dual purpose was at the heart of the Community Chest movement. At a procedural level, it applied the logic of efficiency to rationalize the administration of philanthropy. At the formative level, as with the larger Progressive movement, the Community Chest sought to create a common cause among donors and nonprofit organizations. It did so by offering a vision of community that closely resembled the traditional, structural view of community that has dominated much of sociological research, as we saw in Chapter 1. In all, the Community Chest both offered and depended upon a vision of a community of place. It did so by proffering a conception of community that was geographically local, inclusive, and interdependent in its scope and composition (Rudolph 1993).

As an organizational form, the Community Chest drew its purpose and legitimacy from its member agencies, for which it acted as social planner and coordinating agency (Litwak and Hylton 1962). According to the Community Chests and Councils (1937:20), a Community Chest "promotes the social welfare and health of a community by coordinating existing programs of service, preventing duplication, conducting research, promoting group thinking and planning, administering common services, and improving standards." Therefore, the Community Chest's emphasis on the "local" was determined by the geographical scale of its agencies (Seeley et al. 1957). These nonprofits, including the Catholic Charities, the Lutheran Charities, the Salvation Army, and the YMCA, operated only within a particular city or town. Few national charities existed in the first two decades of the twentieth century. Even for those national organizations that did participate in Community Chests, including the YMCA and the Boy Scouts, their member chapters were embedded in the local city or town (United Way of America 1977). It was not until the post-World War II period that national agencies became incorporated into local United Funds (Brilliant 1990).

The Community Chest, secondly, relied on a conception of community that was inclusive. If the Community Chest was to replace successfully all other appeals to donors, it needed to incorporate any and all of the potential interests of contributors (Community Chests and Councils 1937). Moreover, as a geographically bounded entity, the community included all citizens of that region, encompassing persons of different races, ethnicities, economic positions, and genders. An appeal issued by a federation in the 1910s notes that a single gift by the donor will "cover the care of every person in need, from infancy to old age and from the strong man out of a job to the sick child. The work of these organizations of mercy is city-wide, covering persons of every need" (American Association for Organizing Charity 1917:184). A 1926 study of Community Chests in nineteen cities showed that the work of their member agencies was focused on a wide range of issues, including ill health, neglected children, unmarried women, poverty, military veterans, illiteracy, unemployment, delinquency, and character building (Clapp 1926).

The community, finally, was presented by the Community Chest as an interdependent whole, consisting not only of recipients but also of donors, a collectivity in which the well-being of the disadvantaged few affected the well-being of all. The improved condition of some, albeit the poor or down at heel, would make for a better community for all. Through education and publicity, the Community Chest worked toward donor awareness of and responsibility for the needs of the local community. Part of its task, the national trade association claimed, was to "develop better public understanding and support of both private and public social work" (Community Chests and Councils 1937:20). If made aware of the presence of poverty in their midst, citizens of a city or town would not abide other individuals and families being destitute. According to one magazine article, the goal of the Community Chest was to increase the number of "well-informed and well-disposed citizens, doing what they can to secure a good life for themselves and their neighbors" (Devine 1921:496). An academic observer noted that the Community Chest "makes it evident even to the 'man in the street' that the insuring of human welfare is one big problem to be solved in a big community way, rather than a series of unrelated small ones to be solved as separate entities by unconcerted and uncoordinated action" (Leebron 1924:180).

The Growth of the Community Chest Movement

In response to initial concerns about the replacement of a gift to charities with a gift to the Community Chest, the first Community Chests promoted the concept of the local community, of a community of place, as the new recipient of a charitable contribution. They adequately convinced donors and member nonprofits of the merits of this new recipient of giving. The first Community Chest was formed in Cleveland in 1913. As shown in Figure 1, the fiscal success of the Cleveland Community Chest led to the spread of the movement to a limited number of other cities (Leebron 1924). But, it was the War Chests of World War I that served to promulgate the idea of the

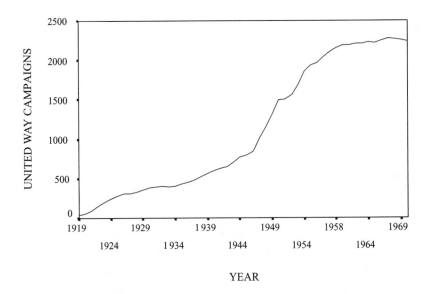

Figure 1 Growth in Local United Way Campaigns
Source: United Way of America 1977

Community Chest. The model of the centralized federated fundraiser was employed to gather funds for the war effort in cities across America. War Chests were extremely popular with Americans and were financially successful, but they were made obsolete once the war was won. Of the about 300 to 400 War Chests in existence during the war, most were converted into Community Chests (Dunham 1958:76; Lubove 1965; Brilliant 1990). Referring to the effect of the War Chests on the Community Chest movement, one observer at the time concluded that "there is no doubt that the federation movement gained a momentum in one year that would have required ten years of peacetime activity" (as quoted in United Way of America 1977:42).

Galvanized by the success of the War Chests, the number of Community Chests quickly increased, encompassing over 245 cities in 1925 and almost 800 cities by 1945 (United Way of America 1977). Although they spread fruitfully as an organizational form across the nation's cities and towns, Community Chests experienced both financial setbacks and gains during the 1930s. Predictably, as shown in Figure 2, the Depression lowered levels of giving to

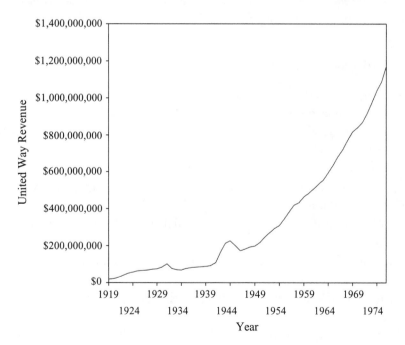

Figure 2   Growth of United Way Revenue
Source: United Way of America 1977

the Community Chest. Total giving continued to increase during the early 1930s (the result of an increase in the number of Community Chests), but actual campaign amounts for local Community Chests were declining, as citizens possessed less inclination and ability to give to those less fortunate than themselves.

However, the Community Chest movement was aided by a significant change in the federal government's regulation of corporations' activities. In 1936, the Internal Revenue Service began permitting companies to deduct up to 5 percent of pretax earnings from taxable income through charitable donations (Brilliant 1990; Muirhead 1999). Expanding beyond financial support from individual citizens, Community Chests now began to receive significant revenue from corporations. Reflecting the long-time commitment of business leaders to the Community Chest, firms now began to direct their own charitable contributions primarily to it. In his comprehensive survey of corporations, for example, Andrews (1950) found that businesses in the 1940s gave two-thirds of their contributions to the health and human services. Moreover, he determined that half of these firms made *all* of their philanthropic contributions through the local Community Chest.

THE FORMATION OF THE UNITED FUND

Community Chests were affected by World War II, but in different ways than by the previous war. Rather than benefiting from the consolidation of the War Chests, the Community Chest movement now faced rivalry from competitors that had gained legitimacy during World War II. Popular health research charities, such as the American Cancer Society and the American Red Cross, had gained a voice and government support during that conflict. These new health agencies were organizationally different from the vast majority of charities that preceded them and that constituted the membership of Community Chests. They existed at the national level, with a central headquarters that raised funds from across the country and then distributed revenue to local research centers, hospitals, and treatment clinics.

After World War II ended, health research charities sought to extend their pattern of success. They entered into rivalry with the Community Chest, running separate and competing fund drives for individuals' contributions. Much public debate took place over the implications of charitable competition. A rash of exposé articles appeared in popular magazines during this time, examining the impact of the "charity wars" on donors and on recipient populations (Meyer 1945; Sontheimer 1952; Sanders 1958; Maas 1960). The general consensus was that too many charitable appeals were occurring, exhausting the philanthropic spirit of donors. Moreover, the success of the health agencies resulted in much scrutiny. These nonprofits were criticized for their high costs and for raising amounts far in excess of their actual needs, according to a widely cited report by the Rockefeller Foundation in the late 1940s (Sontheimer 1952).

In the late 1940s, the increase in charitable competition had resulted in a competitive, exhausting, and disorganized situation – one similar to that found thirty years earlier. By one count, more than a dozen charitable campaigns occurred per year in the workplace ("Detroit Gathers Charity Drives" 1949). As earlier, the sheer number of charities and the multitude of appeals raised concern among local business elites over the disruption caused by repeated solicitation. This time, however, the concern was about disruption within the workplace, hindering productivity, and "proving a headache for management and workers alike" ("Charities: All for One, One for All" 1949:25). The Ford Company, in a well-publicized press release, noted that it lost $40,000 in executive time and production for every plant solicitation (Sanders 1958). A 1959 United Fund "position paper," as quoted in Cutlip (1965:496), recalls the origins of the United Fund as being "an outgrowth of the annoyance of business leaders and labor leaders, essentially, at the number of campaigns they were called upon to conduct in their plants."

In cooperation with business elites, the Community Chest reestablished its monopoly through the creation of the United Fund in 1949 in Detroit. Initially, a single all-purpose campaign drive within the workplace was created in the Detroit area by leaders of the automobile industry, headed by Henry Ford II. The United Fund encompassed the local Community Chest plus local charities and the local office of some national charities. It worked by co-opting its health-oriented competitors into a single fund drive (Cutlip 1965). Its motto was "give once for all" (Sontheimer 1952:36). The first United Fund proved to be extremely successful, raising more money than the previous year's separate campaigns. The single, all-inclusive model of workplace campaign was widely promoted by the national association of the

Community Chest movement and was quickly replicated in other communities. By 1959, over 1,200 United Funds were in existence (Cutlip 1965).

The creation of a single campaign, however, was fiercely resisted by the "big three" national health drives: the American Cancer Society, the National Foundation for Infantile Paralysis, and the American Red Cross (Seeley et al. 1957). These charities initially refused to participate in a single drive within the workplace, being unwilling to hand over control of the fundraising process to the United Funds. Health research charities also believed that the United Fund's emphasis on the local community was inimical to their interests. As the American Red Cross stated, "Joint fund raising, even on the community level, is unsatisfactory from the Red Cross standpoint. Red Cross is a national and international organization with national and international obligations to fulfill. It would be unfair to expect that purely local fund raising agencies, concerned primarily with meeting local needs, should grasp the significance of or feel deep sympathy for operations far beyond their responsibility" (American National Red Cross 1949:17).

Despite these protests and with the support of business, the United Fund continued to exclude national health charities from its campaign. Reiterating its commitment to the local community, it raised money in the name of those generic health issues (cancer, heart disease, polio, etc.) but for nonprofits operating within their own town or city. Eventually, by the late 1960s, the majority of the local chapters of the national health charities either had merged with United Funds or retreated from rivalry with United Funds. The move toward the independent participation of health research agencies within the workplace did not occur again until later. The United Fund had regained control of workplace charity and was now more successful than ever; it had reasserted the equation of workplace charity with the United Fund, which meant a gift to the local community.

The years after World War II set the stage for the United Way as we know it today. The new United Fund focused almost exclusively on workplace fundraising, adopting the technique of payroll deduction from labor unions. Prior to the formation of the United Fund, Community Chests had solicited most residents of the town through door-to-door fundraising, but lacked a systematic mechanism by which to approach donors and to gather their pledged gifts. In 1943, the federal government allowed for the compulsory withholding of income taxes and Social Security taxes from employee wages. This move paved the way for payroll deduction of charitable contributions, thus allowing workers to give more through small but incremental donations. The shift to payroll deduction also furthered the earlier goal of Community Chests to diffuse responsibility for social welfare from business leaders only to a larger population of givers. Up until then, most of the revenue had been gathered from a small group of individuals. In 1937, for example, over 50 percent of gifts were $100 or higher, and 25 percent of gifts were $1,000 or higher (Community Chests and Councils of America 1937).

Two other characteristics of the contemporary United Way system were also put in place in the 1940s and 1950s. The support of labor, central to the growth of the United Way movement, was established during this period. As one observer has noted, the "labor movement is the foundation upon which the United Way movement rests" (Glaser 1994:39). Typically, local United Ways have drawn upon the organizational structure of unions to facilitate and stimulate employee contributions. During World War II, the AFL-CIO and the United Way system entered into a partnership.

In addition, with the creation of the United Fund, the United Way system expanded the geographical scope of its affiliated agencies beyond the local city or town. Through partnerships with selected health agencies, many local United Ways added national charities to their membership of organizations (Brilliant 1990). The United Ways in Cleveland and Chicago, for example, were among the majority of United Ways that included the American Red Cross (United Way of America 1977).

By 1960, over 1,000 United Ways existed in the United States and Canada. Beginning with World War II, the United Way system gathered ever-increasing amounts of charitable gifts. Figure 2 demonstrates that the United Way was an extremely successful fundraiser, experiencing an annual growth rate of approximately 5 to 10 percent, buttressed by an expanding manufacturing-based economy. The United Way system benefited from a burst of financial growth in the post-World War II period and again in the late 1950s. By 1960, gifts made in the workplace totaled just under a half-billion dollars a year (Brilliant 1990).

The United Way in Question

Despite its earlier success, the United Way system faced challenges beginning in the 1960s. The growing salience of new communities of purpose, coupled with the expansion of federal funding for the health and human services, put into question the fundamental assumptions underlying the United Way. No longer could the United Way claim to best represent its local community in an unquestioned and unproblematic manner. Although the newly energized United Way at the national level would implement a sustained strategic response to these challenges, local United Ways continued to operate much as they had in the past.

By the end of the 1960s, the traditional model of American society, based on seeming consensus and shared goals and interests, had been replaced with a new vision of the nation based around pluralism. New social groups, based on race/ethnicity, gender, and sexual orientation, had emerged as important players in American society, as had novel types of political interests (Melucci 1980; Cohen 1985; Berry 1997). The United States witnessed a series of social movements, as different groups sought equal political rights and equal access to political, economic, and social resources and opportunities. For the United Way, the rise of these new collectivities presented a fundamental challenge to the primacy of a community of place: of an interdependent, inclusive, and locally bounded conception of a social collectivity. These groups demanded a fair share of resources gathered by the United Way in the workplace. "As communities became more pluralistic – and as previously unempowered constituencies, especially blacks and women, became more insistent in their demands for community services – United Way found it increasingly difficult to serve their needs" (Hall 1992:304).

At the same time, the United Way faced a challenge to its centrality in the health and well-being of the local community. Beginning with Lyndon Johnson's 1964 declaration of a "war on poverty," the federal government had expanded its involvement in domestic policy. Through a series of acts, including the Economic Opportunity Act (including Head Start, Job Corps, and VISTA) and the Social Security Act (resulting in the provision of Medicare and Medicaid), the federal government increased the scope and scale of its role in the provision of health and human services. The development of the Community Action Programs and Model City Programs also involved federal funding at the city level, as the federal government encouraged local groups and constituencies to participate in decision-making processes (Smith and Lipsky 1993).

The growth and changing mode of federal funding put into question the necessity and centrality of the United Way (Glaser 1994). For one, these changes in resource flows upset the United Way's previously stable relationship with member agencies. Government support, by the mid-1970s, had grown from one-third to one-half of total annual revenue for the nonprofit sector (Salamon 1987). Consequently, nonprofits' reliance on the United Way for funds had declined. In addition, the federal government was empowering a local grassroots approach to social change. These shifts introduced new groups and constituencies to community planning, different from the business leaders and social service representatives that had previously led the provision of aid to the local community through the United Way.

By the mid-1970s, the United Way system had both altered and stayed the same. The most significant response to this array of social changes was occurring at the national level, spearheaded by the newly formed United Way of America. A national association of United Ways (then called Community Chests) had been formed in 1911, under the name of the National Association for Organizing Charity. The organization had served as a "clearinghouse for the exchange of information and experience between cities" and also provided research and advice for local organizations (Heald 1970:118; United Way of America 1977). In the 1970s, the national association expanded its role (Brilliant 1990). The adoption of the name of the "United Way" by all local entities was part of this consolidation of power by the national organization. In 1963, Los Angeles became the first organization to adopt the name of the United Way, when thirty local funds came together into a single entity. By 1970, the title of the United Way was officially adopted by local United Ways and by the national trade association, now known as the United Way of America.

The United Way of America, under the leadership of a newly elected president, William Aramony, implemented a national growth program in the late 1970s entitled the "Program for the Future" (Roberts 1977). It sought to proactively respond to how the United Way system had developed over the course of the century. The United Way (then called the Community Chest) had brought together two distinct groups, business leaders and social service professionals, and merged two organizational models: the federated fundraiser and the fund allocator. Over the course of the twentieth century, tension had repeatedly arisen over which element should dominate the organization's mission and practices. A quote from Seeley, Junker, and Jones (1957:109–110) summarizes the debate, as being between "those who regard the Community Chest primarily as a semi-sacred movement in the realm of 'community organization' [for which money is, incidentally, needed] and those who regard money-raising as the common sense and natural heart of the enterprise." Similarly, one long-time observer of the field of workplace fundraising told me that "the United Way has a split vision, a split mission: to be the fund-raiser for the community, and to be the allocator of resources, and there's always a struggle inside the United Way system over which of those is their primary identity."

For most local United Ways, an emphasis on the function of fundraising had become dominant by the 1960s (Brilliant 1990). Community welfare councils, responsible for determining the needs of the local community, had either been entirely disbanded within the United Way or had lost any real influence in the organization's decision-making processes. The United Way had evolved into a fundraiser and no more, with its primary goal the raising of increasing amounts of funds each year. Although such a focus was acceptable in a time of consensus and hegemony, the United Way's identity as solely a fundraiser paled in light of the changes occurring in the larger society.

To justify its existence as primarily a fundraiser, the United Way of America proposed a a new and more prominent role for the United Way. The United Way of America returned to a discourse of community, but provided itself and the United Way system with the new role of facilitating community. It began to talk of itself as "building community" and as a "catalyst" for solving community problems. However, as Brilliant (1990) shows, it is unclear what substantive changes to the United Way system resulted from that declarative assertion. There is no doubt that substantial and extended disagreement existed among United Way staff and volunteers, at all levels and locales, as to how to implement that vision. Several alternatives were offered, but none was systematically taken up and pushed by the United Way of America (Brilliant 1990).

At the local level, United Ways remained largely intact and unchanged in terms of their distribution of funds. They continued to follow the same dual model of federated fundraiser and fund allocator, with the majority of power held by the fundraising arm. Although some debate occurred among local United Ways and at the national level over the proper role of the United

Way, the United Way system continued to employ a discourse of a community of place to generate resources for a largely set and fixed assortment of charities (Dinerman 1965; Rose-Ackerman 1988). By the end of the 1960s, the majority of local United Ways "provided support for a traditional core of agencies which had over the years received large shares of United Way funding nationwide" (Brilliant 1990: 78); these included the Boy Scouts, Salvation Army, YWCA, YWCA, Red Cross, YMCA, and the Girl Scouts. These core agencies were notable in that they were large and well-established nonprofits largely limited to the provision of health and human services for the middle-class (Wenocur, Cook, and Steketee 1984; Salamon 1987; Polivy 1988). In his survey of the United Way at the time, Smith (1977:1360) concluded that the set of agencies supported by the United Way was "a very limited and specialized fragment of the total voluntary sector."

The United Way's continued commitment to the funding of these particular nonprofits, despite facing larger challenges to their legitimacy, can partly be understood by its organizational structure. The United Way served as a coordinating agency for its member agencies (Litwak and Hylton 1962; Warren 1967; Pfeffer and Leong 1977). Despite the growth of the United Way of America and its attempts to identify the unique role and contribution of United Way in the process of workplace charity, the United Way effectively constituted only a fundraising and fund allocation system for its affiliated charities. Coordinating agencies such as the United Way must operate on the basis of consensus, satisfying the demands of member agencies. Wenocur (1974, 1975), for example, points out that legitimacy for local United Ways comes from the public's financial support of legitimating agencies, and thus, its member organizations cannot be ignored. In her study of the Los Angeles United Way, Dinerman (1965) similarly claims that the avoidance of conflict is the major task of United Ways, particularly in the allocations process, which tends to reflect the status quo and is driven by the strong support of the public for certain member agencies. Because of these financial concerns, local United Ways were largely unable to respond to demands by new social groups and nonprofit organizations to expand patterns of funding beyond their historically core group of affiliated charities.

By the 1960s, the United Way faced both the growth of pluralism and the threat of growing irrelevance in the functioning of the nonprofit sector. Despite these series of challenges, or perhaps in response to them, the United

Way restated its commitment to a traditional model of community, one based on place and propinquity. As we see in the next chapter, the United Way did not completely succeed in its attempt to align workplace charity with the interests of the local community and a condition of monopoly. Excluded groups, both new and old, took on a new organizational form, the federated fundraiser, as they attempted to gain entry to workplace charity.

CHAPTER 3

Alternative Funds and Communities of Purpose

We've always said that the appeal of Alternative Funds derives from their ability to foster community giving and community growth.

— EXECUTIVE VICE-PRESIDENT, ALTERNATIVE FUND.

Despite the United Way's initial consolidation and success, the fundraiser faced a range of challenges beginning in the 1960s. Along with the expanded presence of the federal government in the provision of social services, new social groups sought voice in the governance and decision-making processes of the nonprofit sector. These diverse constituencies, as well as previously vanquished United Way rivals, adopted a new type of organizational form in order to participate in workplace charity. As nonprofits, these groups now gathered together to form federated fundraisers, or Alternative Funds, to compete alongside the United Way. The emergence of Alternative Funds challenged not just the fiscal monopoly of the United Way in workplace charity but also its vision of the public good. Not all of these conceptions of communities are of recent origin, as we will see, but almost all Alternative Funds represent understandings of the public good that differ fundamentally from that of the United Way.

Alternative Funds as Federated Fundraisers

Alternative Funds are coalitions of charities that seek access to local employee campaigns, hoping to compete alongside the United Way for donors' gifts. Like the United Way, Alternative Funds have taken the form of the federated fundraiser to participate most successfully and efficiently in workplace campaigns. Professional staff oversees fundraising and fund distribution for member agencies. Member agencies, which otherwise would independently solicit revenue from other sources (including corporations, foundations, and individuals), join together for the purpose of soliciting gifts in the workplace. Those charities affiliated with Alternative Funds vary in geographic scale, size, and purpose: they range from regional chapters of national associations (such as the ACLU and the Sierra Club) to small, grassroots groups embedded in the local city or town. Member agencies vary in their assorted missions from mass organization for lobbying and/or demonstrations, to participatory service-delivery charities, to expertise-centered educational efforts, and to identity-based cultural work.[1]

Alternative Funds differ from the United Way in that the intermediary fundraising organization itself – located between donors and member agencies – exists solely to gather and distribute funds. Unlike the United Way, which possesses the additional and institutionalized function of ascertaining community need and allotting moneys to charities so as to meet those needs, Alternative Funds are concerned only with fundraising efforts and with dispersing resources based on a mathematical formula that is predetermined by members. Affiliated agencies receive a proportion of total gifts to the Alternative Fund based on the amount of their membership dues, and they also collect any earmarked contributions. In short, Alternative Funds represent the outsourcing or contracting out of workplace fundraising by independent nonprofits to an independent contractor. Hence, as we will see in the following chapters, the identity and discourse of Alternative Funds are affected and constrained by their organizational form and mission in different ways than in the United Way.

Alternative Funds also differ from the United Way in their representations of community. As organizations, Alternative Funds embody and enact communities of purpose in the field of workplace charity. In so doing, they both reflect and form an important part of the transformations occurring in American society over the last four decades. They represent mostly new social groups in our society that do not conceive of the community as being locally based, inclusive, and interdependent. Instead, Alternative Funds represent modes of social collectivity that are distinct from each other and from the United Way. They constitute organizational examples of an interpretive perspective on community by drawing from shared understandings of purpose and belonging among their members.

As I discuss later in this chapter, these new federated fundraisers expand existing understandings of community in workplace charity by altering the proper scope of community, by offering different methods by which to facilitate the public good, and by shifting the geographic scales of collectivity. As a result, the presence of Alternative Funds in workplace charity alongside the United Way has two significant implications: first, they allow donors to make charitable contributions based on a wider range of altruistic affiliations, concerns, and interests, and in addition, they allow a more varied and expansive population of recipients to benefit from workplace donations.

Community as Collective Identity

The first group of Alternative Funds offers a different vision of community, one oriented around a collective identity. We can think of collective identity as consisting of a social group's "agreed upon definition of membership, boundaries, and activities" (Johnston, Larana, and Gusfield 1994:15). Examples of collective identity include gender, race/ethnicity, sexual orientation, mental health, homelessness, and physical disability. Central to the New Social Movements of the 1960s and later, collective identities are understood to be new and distinct forms of orientation in that they are not based around class, place, or the nation. Further, social groups oriented around collective identities transcend traditionally separate political arenas, such as education, health care, criminal justice, economic development, and so forth (Cohen 1985; Touraine 1985).[2]

The premise of collective identity as a basis for social activism is that a particular group has faced systematic forms of inequality – members have been left behind in gaining access to needed social resources, have been excluded from social networks and other types of access to social capital, and, in all, have not been perceived as legitimate members of society. Social movements have combated these injustices on various fronts, typically without a specific concern for the political sphere (Offe 1985; Rimmerman 2002). In the voluntary sector, social movements based on collective identities have taken a range of organizational forms (such as grassroots associations and advocacy-based national groups, among others), all devoted to addressing the position of these groups in American society. Similarly, charitable giving oriented around collective identity has been "organized around a general 'rights' framework emphasizing the need for equal political representation and social protection" (Jenkins 1988: 242–243).

In workplace charity, Alternative Funds exist that represent three different sources of collective identity: race and/or ethnicity, gender, and sexual orientation. Despite serving divergent collectivities, they all share a conception of community that is particularistic, interdependent, and translocal. As we will see, the logic of collective identity has also been employed by Alternative Funds oriented around religiosity, animal rights, and children's rights.

RACE AND ETHNIC FUNDS

One set of Alternative Funds is oriented around the collective identity of race and ethnicity. The first of these Alternative Funds to appear in workplace charity emerged from the African-American community. The African-American community has been shaped by the legacy of a forced diaspora, the institution of slavery, systematic political and economic injustice, and by its members' contemporary struggles to overcome oppression. Over the last half-century, the civil rights movement has sought to obtain equal rights to resources and opportunities for all people regardless of race (Morris 1984; McAdam 1999[1982]).

Although African-American philanthropy, particularly through religious institutions, had always been strong, local and national leaders in the civil rights movement sought to form voluntary associations and nonprofit organizations to promote the group's interests (Fairfax 1995). However, the African-American community soon faced the challenge of acquiring funding from traditional revenue providers (Davis 1975; Ylvisaker 1987; Carson 1999; Jenkins and Halcli 1999). As these scholars have shown, the majority of corporations and foundations were hesitant to provide adequate support for African-American charities.

The paucity of available revenue from these sources resulted in a turn to workplace charity as a new source of support. The Black United Fund movement began as a single, local federated fundraiser in Los Angeles as a response to the Watts riots. Formed in 1972, the Brotherhood Crusade was conceived as a means to help the African-American community in those affected neighborhoods revitalize itself. The goal of the Brotherhood Crusade, and the Black United Fund movement as a whole, was to provide a cost-efficient mechanism by which African-Americans could donate to nonprofits managed by and oriented toward the needs of their own community (Brilliant 1990; Carson 1983). Given the immediate financial success of the Brotherhood Crusade, this model of federated fundraising was later adopted elsewhere by other Black United Funds, currently totaling twenty-one local or state-level funds in all.[3] For many of these otherwise independent local funds, the National Black United Fund exists as a national trade association. In addition, at the national level, the National Black United Federation of Charities and the Human and Civil Rights Organizations of America gather funds in the name of the African-American community. Together, this set of Alternative Funds raised approximately $8.5 million in 2000.[4]

The model of the Black United Fund has been adopted by Alternative Funds oriented around other racial and ethnic identities as well, although in smaller numbers. The Hispanic-American or Latino community comprises individuals who trace their roots to Spanish-speaking nations in Central and South America and the Caribbean. Consequently, the experience of Latinos in the United States is diverse and varied. Nonetheless, in the public sphere, these groups have often come together as a single identity, bounded by a shared language, cultural heritage, and an awareness of injustice over the community's location within and treatment by the larger Anglo-American society. A sense of a common culture and history developed into a concerted social movement in the 1960s, reflecting a growing concern over Hispanic-Americans' unequal access to and exclusion from full political rights, social justice, and economic justice (Padilla 1985; Oboler 1995). Regions of the nation with large Hispanic populations, such as New York, Los Angeles, and San Francisco, witnessed the growth of nonprofits dedicated to serving the specific needs of the community (Camarillo 1991). However, as with other communities of collective identity, mainstream funders provided a disproportionately small percentage of their resources to Hispanic-American recipients. The Hispanic-American community has responded by developing a growing number of funding institutions of their own (Cortes 1991).

In workplace charity, Alternative Funds representing this collective identity have been formed relatively late in the history of the field. The United Latino Fund was formed in 1990 to support the Latino-American community in Los Angeles. Additionally, in the federal government's workplace campaign, the Hispanic United Fund consists of "high-quality national charities working with the Hispanic/Latino community in the U.S. and around the world" (Hispanic United Fund 2006). Together, these two Alternative Funds gathered around $650,000 in 2000.

Similarly, the Asian Pacific Community Fund was founded as an alternative workplace-giving mechanism to the United Way in the greater Los Angeles area. Following the loosening of the federal government's immigration laws in the mid-1960s, there was a growing awareness of the particular needs of this quickly growing population. Although composed of members from diverse national origins, a single and homogeneous identity of Asian-Americans has emerged, both imposed by the dominant society but also wielded by insiders, which incorporates and spans these national groups. Commencing in the late 1960s, Asian-Americans strove for equal access to education, health and human services, and political participation and fought against racism, discrimination, and violence (Espiritu 1992).

Yet, although new community-based institutions and nonprofits were formed to address the challenges specific to Asian-Americans, they found only minimal financial support from the philanthropic community (Shao 1995). This disjuncture between community need, charitable activity, and funding was apparent to the Asian Pacific Community Fund (APCF), an Alternative Fund formed in Los Angeles in 1990. At the time, according to the organization, the United Way in Los Angeles funded only six Asian Pacific service organizations. The APCF was formed to try and correct for this disparity between needs and resources in that community. Gathering over $2 million from various sources in 2000, the APCF through its agencies provides services to diverse Asian and Pacific Islander populations.

WOMEN'S FUNDS

A second group of Alternative Funds is oriented around the collective identity of gender. The "second-wave" women's movement emerged out of the historical period of social change and upheaval that produced the civil rights and anti-war movements, reflecting women's distinct experiences and perceptions at the time (Evans 1979).[5] The principles underlying the goal of women's emancipation are not new (Buechler 1990), but the women's movement of the 1960s represented the first organized movement over which women possessed full control. The women's movement is multifaceted (including both the women's rights and women's liberation movements), but is fundamentally based on the premise that women in Western societies share a common oppression and experience because of their gender (Freeman 1975; Ferree and Martin 1995).

The women's movement has been expressed in the nonprofit sector through the formation of charities oriented around the support and empowerment of women (Minkoff 1995; Bordt 1997). This group of nonprofits has emerged both at the national level with formal, hierarchical organizations (examples include the National Organization for Women [NOW] and NARAL) and, at the local level, with associations that are more porous and decentralized. But, as with minority-ethnic nonprofits, funding for women's groups has been particularly difficult to obtain; few resource providers have been perceived as willing to give to "women's issues" (Capek 1998).

The result has been a long-term and sustained effort to generate revenue for women's issues through targeted philanthropic entities, beginning with the creation of the Ms. Foundation in 1972. The Women's Funding Network, a national umbrella association of Women's funds that gather donations both inside and outside the workplace, currently has over 100 members, both nationally and internationally. In workplace charity, women-oriented nonprofits have formed Alternative Funds to gain access to donations (Brilliant 2000b). The first was the Women's Way, founded in 1977 in Philadelphia. Currently, six Women's funds exist at the local and state level, and one federated fundraiser, Women, Children, and Family Service Charities of America, gathers contributions at the national level. In all, women's funds gathered $2.2 million in 2000.

GAY AND LESBIAN FUNDS

Finally, Alternative Funds have appeared that represent a community based on sexual orientation, what John D'Emilio (1992) has called a "sexual community." The gay liberation movement in the United States is generally understood to have begun with the Stonewall riot in 1969 (Armstrong 2002). Inspired by the success of the earlier social movements of the decade, the gay community mobilized in the pursuit of civil rights for its own members. Like other New Social Movements, it also directed its attention to personal expression for its members: the movement "sought to build a new gay culture where gay people could be free" (Karl 1987:74).

Although initially associated with homosexual men, the movement has expanded to include lesbian and transgender identities. This sense of community exists despite debate and disagreement over the viability of constructing a single collectivity based on divergent sexual orientations. Armstrong (2002:3), for example, claims the GLBT community can exist because it defines itself based on an opposition to heterosexuality: "what we share is that we are all different from straight people." Similarly, the Pride Foundation (2004), an AF in the Pacific Northwest, stresses both commonality and difference in its vision of community: "Working with diverse communities, Pride Foundation is able to promote philanthropy and provide leadership in the gay, lesbian, bisexual and transgender (GLBT) community" (Pride Foundation 2004).

Over the last two decades, a myriad of social groups, voluntary associations, and community organizations have been formed to pursue the interests of the GLBT community (Rimmerman 2002). Within workplace charity, Alternative Funds oriented around the gay and lesbian community are present, but are limited in number. In all, two charitable entities gather workplace donations for this social collectivity: the Pride Foundation (located in Philadelphia) and the AIDS Fund (located in the Pacific Northwest). Both Alternative Funds direct contributions to GLBT organizations in their particular locale. In 2000, they raised just over $200,000.

SOCIAL MOVEMENT COMMUNITIES

Despite serving distinct sets of populations, Alternative Funds based on the collective identities of race/ethnicity, gender, and sexual orientation proffer a similar vision of community, one that differs sharply from that provided by the United Way. Steven Buechler (1990) has labeled this conception of collectivity a "social movement community." It is particularistic, interdependent, and translocal. First, these Alternative Funds alter the scope or reach of the collectivity. Unlike the United Way, this version of community is not inclusive: it does not seek to encompass a divergent and mixed assortment of members. Instead, the scope of community and the means of membership extend only to those possessing a specific characteristic or trait. So, for example, Women's funds are organized around helping the community of women only. For example, the Women's Fund of New Jersey claims that it is "dedicated to improving the lives of women."

The issues and needs of the particular population are specific, derived from the challenges and disadvantages stemming from the group's structural position within the larger society. Members of the particular community face a unique set of challenges. The Women's Funding Alliance, an Alternative Fund in the greater Seattle area, states, "Women and girls still face critical issues. Issues include violence (both domestic violence and rape), equal access and rewards in the workplace, and support for women in the private sphere (both in terms of reproductive freedom and as primary caregivers)." James Joseph, the former head of the National Black United Fund, explained that Black United Funds emerged because "the Black community knows it must deal with the inequitable distribution of power and resources in society. We know that it is going to be difficult to find outside resources to direct at that problem" (National Committee for Responsive Philanthropy 1986:38).

As a result, a charitable gift to one of these Alternative Funds is a gift toward ending the challenges faced by that community. Collective identity funds provide resources for nonprofits that address only those specific difficulties; what other scholars have called the "alternative institutions" of the larger social movement community (Taylor and Whittier 1992). The majority of affiliated nonprofits engage in a limited and comparable set of activities; these include the arts, education, health, and youth and family services, among others. However, each group of charities is distinctive from others in that each is tailored to and serves only members of its particular community.

Like the United Way, a community based on a collective identity also constitutes an interdependent whole, comprising both donors and recipients. Donors are solicited for gifts based on their membership in that social group.

Alternative Funds appeal to workplace givers based on their affiliation with and responsibility to the well-being of that particular collectivity.[6] These Alternative Funds constitute a case of "indigenous philanthropy" whereby a "culture-specific group pools their financial and volunteer resources to address group concerns" (Carson 1999:249). For example, the Black United Fund's official motto is a play on the United Way's historical motto of "the helping hand"; in contrast, it adopted the motto of the "helping hand that is your own." Similarly, the Pride Foundation, a gay and lesbian fund, presents itself as facilitating a process of "giving together – building community."

Finally, funds oriented around collective identity offer a conception of community that is not determined by place and propinquity. The determinants of space do not determine the boundaries or the criteria for membership of these communities. Although many of these Alternative Funds exist at the city or state level, their vision of community exists both within a community of place and across multiple communities of place to only include those members who share a particular characteristic. The Black United Fund of Illinois, for example, supports those in need within Illinois' African-American community. It does so by helping "thousands through grants to over 450 grassroots organizations statewide that address critical needs of the African American community" (Black United Fund of Illinois 1998).

Although these are three major types of Alternative Funds oriented around collective identity, the discourse of collective identity is employed by two other sets of United Way rivals as well. The first set of Alternative Funds here consists of religious organizations involved in the provision of health and human services.[7] Like other Collective identity funds, these federated fundraisers draw upon a notion of a distinct but shared identity among donors and recipients. A religious community is based on individuals who share faith, rituals, and practices oriented around a belief system concerning a transcendent reality (Durkheim 1964[1893]; Geertz 1973; Orsi 1985). At the national level, for instance, two different United Way rivals, Christian Services Charities of America and Christian Charities USA, gather contributions for their membership of Christian charities. In 2000, these two Alternative Funds raised about $12 million.

A second set of Alternative Funds is derived from the extension of the logic of collective identity to groups that are not able to protect their own interests. For both the animal and children's rights movements, an insistence on inalienable rights has been applied to collectivities beyond human adults (Hawes 1991; Jasper and Nelkin 1992). These Alternative Funds differ from other collective identity funds because donors are not members of the community, but instead are sympathetic to its challenges. At the national level, Animal Charities of America is oriented around the goal of "animal welfare," and additional charities are participants in social action funds. Another group of Alternative Funds, three at the local level and one national fund, solicit contributions in the name of children: that is, member nonprofits that serve only children and/or children with particular needs. In 2000, these nonprofits gathered around $1 million in total revenue.

New Ways to Facilitate Community

A second group of Alternative Funds provides a different, novel model of community. They do so by maintaining a definition of community based on place, as with the United Way, but they proffer different mechanisms by which to facilitate community. Carl Milosky (1979) has argued that the nonprofit sector is characterized by different "traditions of participation" or understandings of the proper means by which to pursue the public good. The United Way, by most accounts, funds and hence promotes the rationalized provision of social services as the optimal means to benefit the community. In contrast, this specific set of Alternative Funds focuses either on social change philanthropy or the proffering of health research and services as the optimal means to improve community.

As I discussed in the last chapter, the United Way has relied on a particular strategy for facilitating the community, one that is bureaucratic and ameliorative in nature. The majority of United Way resources have been directed to a small and fixed assortment of agencies that are overwhelmingly large, hierarchical, and professionalized in nature. These charities also draw on an ameliorative mode of assistance that focuses primarily on addressing the symptoms rather than causes of social problems. Member agencies, by and large, provide programs oriented around the social services: social welfare, health, and recreation (Polivy 1988). As we see, with the growth of rival federated fundraisers, two additional strategies for facilitating community have emerged, incorporated in Social action funds and Health funds.

SOCIAL ACTION FUNDS

Unlike Alternative Funds based on collective identity, Social action funds are not oriented around the rights of a particular social group. Instead, these non-profits span a wide array of issues and interests. Table 1 lists the types of member agencies of Social action funds.[8] Almost a third of member nonprofits are oriented around a wide array of collective identity groups, including such populations as African-Americans, Hispanic-Americans, Asian-Americans, Native Americans, women, children, the gay/lesbian community, the disabled, and senior citizens. Another 15 percent of the charities are concerned with the environment or animal rights. A third group of these agencies reflects another change in the composition of the nonprofit sector: the rise of citizens' rights (Skocpol 1999). Just under one-quarter of member agencies are focused around such issues as community and economic development, legal justice, and peace issues. A fourth and final group of member agencies of social action funds, over one-quarter in all, are surprisingly focused around more traditional causes, such as the needs of families and children.

Despite this variation in mission, the members of a Social action fund enter workplace charity as a single entity. They are joined by their commitment to the vitality of the local geographic entity, be it a town, city, or state. Like the United Way, a gift to a social action fund is a gift to that local community. However, Social action funds differ from the United Way in their fundamental assumptions and beliefs about how to improve the well-being of that community. They are characterized by a distinct organizational form and by a unique vision of social change.

Table 1 Missions of Member Agencies of Community Funds

Mission	Percent of All Member Agencies
Arts and education	7
Citizens' rights	23
Collective identity	29
Environment and animals	15
Health and human services	26
International	<1
TOTAL	**100**

First, member organizations have based their organizational form on their values, what Calhoun (1995:191) has called the principle of "self-exemplication." Implementing their belief in equality and egalitarianism, members of social action funds overwhelmingly employ the technique or mode of community organizing or community action. In her analysis of social change activism, Polletta (2002:1) concludes that "activists have sought to live the better community as they built it, to enact in their own operation the values of equality, community, and democracy that they wanted on a larger scale." The tradition of community organizing arose out of the success of the civil rights and anti-war movements and government support for citizen participation. By the mid-1980s, according to one estimate, there were over 8,000 community organizations in existence across the United States (Delgado 1986). Community organizing is grassroots, mass-based, and multi-issue in nature (Boyte 2004). Similarly, member agencies of social action funds are typically small, local, and volunteer-run entities, with only a minimal presence of local chapters of large, national organizations.

Social action funds also share a belief in social change rather than amelioration as the optimal means by which to facilitate community. Like "social movement" philanthropy as a whole, social problems are seen to result from large-scale structural inequalities derived from political and economic oppression (Perlmutter 1988; Rabinowitz 1990; Ostrander 1995). The slogan of Bread and Roses Community Fund, a social action fund in Philadelphia, is "42 Reasons to help effect 'change,' not charity" (National Committee for Responsive Philanthropy 1986:43). Thus, Social action funds aim to alter social structures to ensure economic and social justice for underrepresented or disadvantaged groups. Through advocacy rather than the provision of services, these United Way rivals seek to obtain equal opportunities for political and civic participation for all individuals (Reid 1999). The Public Interest Fund of Illinois, for example, claims its goal is "working to build a community whose citizens are part of the system, not alienated by it" (Public Interest Fund of Illinois 2000).

In workplace charity, thirty-three Social action funds are in existence at the city and state level, totaling around one-third of all Alternative Funds.[9] Otherwise independent, many Social action funds have recently begun to adopt a shared brand – "Community Shares of _____" (add the name of the particular city or town for which fundraising occurs) – and to affiliate with a national trade association, Community Shares USA. Perhaps reflecting their commitment to the local community, there is only one Social action fund at the national level – the Human and Civil Rights Organizations of America. In 2000, Social action funds gathered just under $10 million.

HEALTH FUNDS

A second type of Alternative Funds–Health funds – also challenges the United Way's espoused method of facilitating community, although its conception of community is not particularly new. As discussed in the last chapter, health-related fundraisers are the oldest group of rivals to the United Way. At present, forty Health funds exist at the state level, providing research, patient service, and outreach in the local community. All are members of Community Health Charities of America, a national association. Community Health Charities was created by the merger in the 1990s of two different types of Health funds: national voluntary health agencies, and combined health appeals. In addition, Medical Research Charities of America and Health and Medical Research Charities of America gather contributions in the Combined Federal Campaign. In 2000, Health funds reported total revenue of over $42 million (National Committee for Responsive Philanthropy 2003:49).

Like the United Way, Health funds share a conception of community as geographically bounded and local. Health funds direct contributions only to member agencies that operate in that particular region of the nation. Overall, local or state affiliates of a relatively set assortment of national health organizations, such as the March of Dimes, the Arthritis Foundation, and Muscular Dystrophy Association, constitute the membership of most Health funds, although local health-oriented nonprofits may also join.

Unlike the United Way, Health funds believe that community well-being is gained not solely through the provision of social services. Instead, the health of the community is determined, in part, by the physical health of its members. For Health funds, to improve the health of citizens is to improve the health of the community; the two are indistinguishable. So, Community Health Charities of Florida emphasizes that "Without our Health, our Quality of Life is diminished" (Health Charities of Florida 2003). The goal of Community Health Charities of California is a "healthy California." Or, in the words of the CHC of Illinois – "money can't buy good health, but it can buy research, education and life-saving medical intervention. Eradicate devastating illnesses. Help teach a child to walk. *In short, build safer, healthier communities through medical research*" [italics mine] (Community Health Charities of Illinois n.d.). As a result, unlike Social action funds that seek to replace the United Way, Health funds aim to supplement the work of the United Way in facilitating the well-being of the local community by improving the health of residents.

Community Beyond the Local

The third group of Alternative Funds is characterized by a reconfiguration of the geographic scope of community. Like the United Way's traditional conception of community, these Alternative Funds retain the premises of a community of place and that members of a community share a common and inclusive interest, despite their diversity. However, both Environmental funds and International development funds change the geographic scale of community. Environmental funds alter the criteria of community from the social to the ecological. In contrast, International development funds extend the scope of community from the local to the global.

ENVIRONMENTAL FUNDS

The first set of Alternative Funds has emerged out of the environmental movement. The environmental movement as a whole traces its history to the nineteenth century, when proponents emphasized the preservation of nature. It reemerged in the 1960s with a focus on society's increasingly perilous consequences for the environment, leading to the formation of environmental organizations in the following two decades (McLaughlin and Khawaja 2000). Today, the environmental movement encompasses a variety of different strands: conservation, preservation, the deep ecology movement, environmental justice, and ecofeminism, among others (Brulle 2000).

In workplace charity, Environmental funds constitute an important rival to local United Ways. Nineteen Environmental funds exist at the state level. The first one, EarthShare of California, was created in 1982. Although first formed as autonomous entities, grounded in the local community, by 2002 all but five Environmental funds were members of a national trade association: EarthShare of America. Earth Share of America was founded in 1988 by eighteen national environmental charities seeking to coordinate workplace fundraising. Additionally, at the national level through the federal government's Combined Federal Campaign, Conservation & Preservation Charities of America raises resources for eighty-eight local, state, and national charities. In all, Environmental funds gathered just under $20 million in 2000.

Environmental funds are based on a conception of community that replaces socially defined territories derived from clusters of residents – the neighborhood, city, state, or nation – with ecologically defined spaces. Ecology refers to the relationship between living things and their environment. By locating individuals within a larger ecology, human health and well-being are intrinsically linked to that of the ecosystem. From an environmental perspective, "the needs and interests of animals, plants, and natural resources are equated with human needs and interests" (Spangle and Knapp 1996:7). Environmental funds place donors in this "community of Public Crisis" (Fowler 1995) by emphasizing the relationship between individuals and the environment: the health of both is in question. So, Earth Share of America claims that "Earth Share's member organizations work hard every day to safeguard *your* health and the environment, by combating global warming, protecting ancient forests, protecting our water from toxic contaminants, and saving endangered species" (Earth Share of America 2004).

Further, environmentalism not only changes the criteria of community but also often extends the geographical scale of community. When an emphasis is placed on ecology, environmental discourse tends to extend beyond the local by linking and making inseparable the multiple scales of community. The mission of Earth Share of Washington reflects this vision of community: it is an "alliance of 65 leading environmental organizations that helps to protect our environment and quality of life-locally, nationally and internationally." Or, consider the motto of EarthShare – "One Environment. One Simple Way to Care for It."

International Development Funds

The geographical scale of community has also been rearticulated by Alternative Funds concerned with international development. Although the concept of foreign aid began in the late nineteenth century, the current form of the international relief movement was established between World War I and World War II. Starting with the formation of Save the Children in

1919, other nongovernmental organizations (NGOs) have formed to provide assistance to individuals abroad. Between 1960 and 1996, the number of international NGOs grew from 1,000 to 5,500.[10] The discourse and activities surrounding international development vary widely and include the provision of economic assistance and emergency aid relief, the development and protection of human rights, educational provision, and environmental protection (Salamon and Anheier 1996). Although NGOs concerned with international aid have historically been located in the West, the forces of globalization and changing resource flows have resulted in the growth of indigenous, locally grounded organizations (Edwards 1999).

The first International development fund was International Service Agencies (now called Global Impact). It was formed by the federal government as part of its rationalization of the federal government's Combined Federal Campaign in 1959. Global Impact's main competitors are Do Unto Others: America's Emergency Relief, Development and Humanitarian Outreach Charities and America's Charities, a national Alternative Fund of which some member agencies are involved in overseas relief and development work. Together, International Service Agencies and Do Unto Others raised over $18 million in 2000.

As with Environmental funds, Alternative Funds concerned with international development expand the scale of community proposed by the United Way. But they do so in ways similar to the United Way. As with the United Way, International development funds draw upon a discourse of collective interdependence. This conception of community relies on and attempts to inculcate feelings in donors of awareness of and responsibility for the disadvantaged in the community. It stresses both difference and similarity between donors and recipients. One federated fundraiser, for example, frames international issues in terms of their saliency at the local level. In its publicity material, Global Impact stresses that "global concerns are important to Americans. Worldwide issues and challenges do affect us daily" (Global Impact 2005a).

However, the geographical scale of assistance provided by these funds' member agencies goes beyond the local emphasis of the United Way on a particular town or city. Instead, International development funds extend the scope of community from the local to the nonlocal: expanding beyond the local town or city and even the nation to the entire globe. In so doing, these funds reflect the growing conceptualization of a world polity as a "unitary social system" (Boli and Thomas 1999). Akira Iriye (2002:8) labels this conception of collectivity a "global community" or a "global consciousness." Accordingly, a past head of International Service Agencies noted that "our focus is international and United Way is local."[11] Do Unto Others stresses in its publicity material that its charities "work in every corner of the world" to ease suffering (Do Unto Others 2004). Similarly, Global Impact claims that it is committed to helping the "poorest people on earth" and tells contributors that their support "makes a world of difference" (Global Impact 2005b).

Human Services Funds

A final type of Alternative Funds deserves discussion here, those concerned with health and human services.[12] Like the United Way, these Alternative Funds represent a place-based vision of community, one that can be facilitated through the ameliorative provision of social services. At the national level, two Alternative Funds have formed out of this population of charities. America's Charities and the Human Service Charities of America gather funds for health and welfare agencies. These workplace fundraisers gather contributions in the name of the same community of place as that offered by the United Way. Their appearance in workplace charity reflects not only the expansion of the nonprofit sector in the 1960s and since but also the inherent inability of the United Way to incorporate newer charities into its federation (Polivy 1988; Rose-Ackerman 1988). Constrained by its commitment to existing affiliated agencies, the United Way could not offer membership to the growing pool of health and welfare organizations formed after World War II. As a result, some of these newer charities have formed Alternative Funds as a mechanism to gain access to workplace revenue, whereas others have joined Social action funds. In 2000, these United Way rivals gathered $22 million.

Conclusion

For workplace charity, the appearance of Alternative Funds marks a radical expansion and multiplication of the conceptions of community present in the field. Although the United Way represents a traditional vision of community, the presence of these rival organizations entails strikingly different understandings of what kind of community should motivate charitable giving. Alternative Funds complicate community by offering not only new criteria for and scales of community but also by providing different mechanisms by which community may be realized. In this chapter, I have shown how Alternative Funds represent many of the communities of purpose present in the larger American society. In the next chapter, I examine how and why these visions of community came to be institutionalized in the organizational form of the federated fundraiser within workplace charity.

CHAPTER 4

The Emergence of Alternative Funds

Alternative Funds are just a very logical outgrowth of the charity movement as a whole ... I think it's just a natural outgrowth of charities looking for new revenue sources and to diversify their income base.

— SENIOR EXECUTIVE, ALTERNATIVE FUND

This chapter focuses on how communities of purpose came to assume organizational form and appear as Alternative Funds in workplace charity. The analysis occurs at two distinct levels, not only accounting for when Alternative Funds were created but also for where they have appeared as individual participants in workplace charity. It begins with an investigation of the growth of Alternative Funds in workplace charity at a particular historical moment. I ask why much of the varying and contested nature of community that appeared in the larger American society did not materialize in workplace charity until the 1960s and 1970s in the form of Alternative Funds. The chapter then turns to an examination of the appearance of specific Alternative Funds across locales. For, although Alternative Funds have grown in number, they are not present in all cities and towns across the nation. The chapter outlines why Alternative Funds have arisen in some locales but not in others.

The Determinants of Alternative Funds

The study of the rise of Alternative Funds in workplace charity speaks to the larger issue of how conceptions of community are translated into organizational form. Research on communities of purpose has proliferated in recent years, including analyses of the environmental, women's rights, civil rights, gay/lesbian rights, and children's rights movements (Hawes 1991; Freudenberg and Steinsapir 1992; Ferree and Martin 1995). Although much has been learned about these novel forms of collective participation, little is known about the conditions of their formation. A substantial body of literature examines the determinants of nonprofit organizations in general (Wolpert 1993; Bielefeld and Corbin 1996; Gronbjerg and Paarlberg 2002). But, lessresearch has been conducted on the emergence of these more recent organizational forms of community (Chambre 1995; Minkoff 1995).

Current scholarship on communities of purpose has indicated the need for this type of comparative analysis. In his study of new forms of voluntary association, for example, Wuthnow (1998) asserts that different sorts of connections will emerge based on the particular conditions of their location, with a specific focus on variation across the inner city, the suburb, and the small town. However, he fails to provide a systematic analysis of the specific determinants that result in disparity across locales. Other scholars have offered case studies of voluntary associations in individual cities (Fiorina 1999; Hall 1999; Renz 1999). They have sought to identify the specific economic, demographic, and cultural characteristics of a community that result in the appearance of different types of collective activity over time. To date, no comparative research has taken place along these same lines. Two prominent participants in the debate over civic vitality have attempted to specify the sources of traditional forms of voluntary association. Both Robert Putnam (Gamm and Putnam 1999) and Theda Skocpol (Skocpol et al. 2000) have analyzed the regional, political, and institutional origins of organizations derived from communities of place, but they have yet to ask if these same forces or others explain the rise of identity and interest-based modes of participation. This chapter constitutes a first step toward filling that theoretical and empirical gap in the literature on community. It employs the case of workplace charity to specify where, when, and why communities of purpose become institutionalized as organizations. I begin by outlining those broad historical processes that allowed for the growth of the Alternative Fund movement in workplace charity.

THE GROWTH OF ALTERNATIVE FUNDS

Although workplace charity arose during the Progressive era, rivals to the United Way have only emerged in workplace charity at particular points over the twentieth century. As we will see, two distinct patterns of entry are present, based on the type of Alternative Fund seeking to gain access to workplace funds. The first type of Alternative Fund, Health funds, appeared in workplace charity after their exclusion as independent, stand-alone nonprofits from workplace campaigns within the private sector after World War II. The second group of Alternative Funds is primarily oriented around collective identity, social change, and environmentalism, the central concerns of the social movements of the 1960s and 1970s. These participants formed in workplace charity as the result not only of shifting understandings of identity but also of changes in the availability in resources, coupled with a new awareness of the structure of workplace charity. Together, these two groups of Alternative Funds legitimated the notion of competition within workplace charity, and other types of United Way rivals were then quick to appear.

Health Funds

Health funds were the first rival federated fundraisers to form alongside the United Way in workplace charity, and their history is distinct from that of other types of Alternative Funds. Health funds trace their emergence to earlier efforts by their member agencies to gather resources in the workplace. As I discussed in Chapter 2, many of those affiliated organizations had first appeared as competitors to the United Way during and after World War II; these agencies included the American Cancer Society, the National Association for Infantile Paralysis, and the American Red Cross. Each charity engaged in its own annual fundraising campaign (Cutlip 1965), entering into competition with each other and the local Community Chest. Business leaders in Detroit responded to this multiplicity of appeals by forming the United Fund in 1949. The United Fund was a single federated fundraiser designed to combine the Community Chest with national agencies representing health causes. The "Torch Drive" or United Fund superseded the local Community Chest by combining it with all national, one-cause charities. The first United Fund proved to be extremely successful, raising more money than the previous year's separate campaigns. The single, all-inclusive

model of workplace campaign was widely promoted by the national association of the Community Chest movement and quickly replicated in other
communities.

The creation of a single campaign, however, was fiercely resisted by the
"big three" national health drives: the American Cancer Society, the National
Foundation for Infantile Paralysis, and the American Red Cross (Seeley,
Junker, and Jones 1989[1957]). These charities initially refused to participate
in a single drive within the workplace. Instead, in published reports and press
releases, the health charities made strong case for the need for competition,
employing many of the arguments to be found again in the 1990s (American
National Red Cross 1949; Seeley, Sim, and Loosley, 1956). Throughout the
1950s and 1960s, the big three health agencies largely persisted in their
pursuit of independent fundraising campaigns. Although some local United
Ways successfully created partnerships with local branches of popular national health agencies (these included the American Cancer Society and the
American Heart Association), other health-related nonprofits reemerged in
the field in the form of federated fundraisers. They did so because corporate and government gatekeepers employed the same logic of efficiency and
centralization that had resulted in the Community Chest. In 1959, local businesses in Baltimore formed the Combined Health Appeal, a single fund drive
for health agencies that had previously campaigned as stand-alone charities,
to eliminate the confusion of multiple workplace drives. The Combined
Health Appeal participated in workplace charity alongside the United Way.
Given the ease with which the Combined Health Appeal gained access to
campaigns in the private sector, that model soon spread to other cities, including Hartford and San Diego. In these cities, however, the local health
funds did not always secure the explicit permission of private firms to solicit
funds in the workplace. Instead, as I discuss in the next chapter, they have
had to struggle to gain access to employee drives.

The second strand of Health funds, national voluntary health agencies,
was created by the federal government in the 1950s when it regularized the
solicitation of federal employees. The Combined Federal Campaign (CFC) is
the federal government's annual workplace charity drive. It is the largest single workplace campaign in the country, comprising 387 regional campaigns
and gathering $206.4 million in 1999 (Combined Federal Campaign 2004b).
The CFC emerged out of the efforts of President Dwight Eisenhower

to systematize multiple appeals to federal employees. In 1956, he created the precursor to the CFC, the Federal Service Fund Raising Policy and Program. In 1961, President Kennedy recognized four organizations as legitimate participants in the federal workplace campaign: alongside the United Way and the American Red Cross, two other federated fundraisers were granted entry, a coalition of international service agencies and the National Voluntary Health Association. Local versions of the national voluntary health agencies were soon formed in each state to participate in the federal government's CFC (Brilliant 1990). The coalition of international service agencies and the National Voluntary Health Association would later merge to form a single Health fund at the national and local levels: Community Health Charities.

Social Movement Funds

A second set of Alternative Funds emerged out of the social upheavals of the 1960s and 1970s. The successive waves of social movements during this time involved the appearance and increasing salience of many new constituencies, derived from a collective identity (race/ethnicity, gender, sexual orientation, among others) or a shared interest (environment, anti-war, consumer rights, and so forth). For our purposes, these social movements radically altered the composition of the nonprofit sector. The nonprofit sector became not only much larger in size but also much more varied in scope. The total population of voluntary sector organizations increased from a mere 50,000 in 1950 to over 300,000 by 1967 (Weisbrod 1997). By the mid-1980s, in other words, just over two-thirds of all charitable service agencies had been formed since the 1960s (National Committee for Responsive Philanthropy 1986). The nature of the nonprofit sector also underwent considerable change, shifting from a concentration of agencies oriented around health and human services to a wide assortment of charities focused on the environment, health, international affairs, arts, and other issues. With many of these new charities, the scope of viable organizational models expanded from an insistence on professionalized, hierarchical bureaucracies to the emergence of locally grounded, grassroots associations (Boyte 1980; Delgado 1986; Smith 1999).

Although the changing cultural climate of the 1960s and 1970s resulted in the formation of a sizable population of new and varied nonprofits, these charities did not immediately seek access to workplace gifts. Instead, their entry into workplace charity was facilitated by changes in resource flows at the government level and a heightened awareness of existing practices within workplace charity. Shifting patterns of federal funding help account for the necessary prerequisites of Alternative Funds – a sizable population of nonprofit organizations and a need for additional revenue – whereas the changing culture of philanthropy explains why Alternative Funds turned to workplace charity as a site to gain access to new resources.

Resource mobilization theory helps explain the enormous growth of the nonprofit sector during this period (McCarthy and Zald 1977). This theoretical framework posits that the formation of social movement organizations (as well as their structure and activities) is determined by the availability and type of external funds. Literature has shown that charities are more likely to emerge in locales where funds are already present, whether from public or private sources (Booth, Higgins, and Cornelius 1983; Wolch and Geiger 1983; Gronbjerg and Paarlberg 2001).

Similarly, the formation of nonprofits in the 1960s and 1970s was accelerated by the growth of a new kind of revenue. Craig Jenkins (1988) has shown how changes in government policy at the federal level, coupled with an increase in foundation money, served to spur on the proliferation of charities. Particularly important at this time was the institutionalization of federal funding to nonprofit organizations through the development of contracted services in the 1960s, including such programs as Medicare, Medicaid, and Head Start. For the first time, the federal government was supporting social change and community development through organizations in the nonprofit sector (Smith and Lipsky 1993). A similar explanation for the growth of nonprofit agencies was also offered by long-time participants in workplace charity. When asked to account for the origins of United Way rivals, one executive began by noting the centrality of federal funding for the nonprofit sector: "So, the proliferation of charities – a huge number, an increased number of charities, especially in the social/human service arena, was thanks entirely to the availability of government money."

The proffering of federal support helps explain the growth of a more vast and varied assortment of nonprofits – the necessary prerequisite for the emergence of Alternative Funds. However, the subsequent decrease in federal funding accounts for their actual formation. Under President Ronald Reagan during the 1980s, the federal government began the process of dismantling the welfare state. Federal support of social and health services was slashed, and many states followed by cutting their own budgets. This diminishment of resources drastically affected existing nonprofits, many of whom depended on the federal government for the majority of their revenue (Hall 1992). The decline in government funds led nonprofits to diversify their revenue stream by seeking new sources of funding. Among of the many strategies aimed at expanding their sources of support, individual nonprofits turned to workplace giving.

Workplace giving, by its very nature, holds appeal for nonprofit organizations. It is, in the words of one senior executive at an Alternative Fund, the "most effective fund-raising mechanism ever devised."[1] Workplace fundraising is extremely cost effective because most of the expenses are borne by the workplaces themselves. In addition, unlike other forms of private donations, workplace contributions are typically unrestricted; that is, donors do not attach conditions on how the nonprofit must distribute those funds. According to one Alternative Fund representative, "Payroll deduction provides exactly the kind of money you need for general support – dependable and no strings attached."[2] Workplace gifts also do not require "upkeep," unlike government and foundation funding, in that contributions are not accompanied by requests for outcomes measurement. One consultant to environmental funds explained that "trying to help groups to diversify their funding base enable[s] them to reduce their dependency on those kinds of sources, including foundation grants, individual memberships, special events, government grants [that] come with strings attached and/or lots of maintenance."

The turn to workplace charity also arose from a changing culture of philanthropy, again generated from governmental activity. After the Tax Reform Act of 1969, the Commission on Private Philanthropy and Public Needs (usually referred to as the Filer Commission) was formed and privately funded by John D. Rockefeller III. From 1973 to 1975, the panel conducted a study of the source, scope, and impact of charitable giving in the United States. However, vocal criticism was soon expressed that the Filer Commission had no minorities on its board nor did it have representation from recipient groups. In response, the Donee Group was formed (later to become the National Committee for Responsive Philanthropy). In 1975, along with the Filer Commission, the Donee Group produced a highly publicized report that disparaged the narrow and conservative organizations and causes supported by the United Way (Brilliant 1990; 2000a). This report raised awareness and a sense of outrage among the social justice movement community about the exclusion from workplace charity of various causes and constituencies, including ethnic and racial minorities, women, the environment, and others.

Struggling to find new resources and with attention drawn to workplace charity, many new and emerging nonprofits worked to gain access to funds within the workplace. They did so by adopting two successive strategies. At first, they sought to enter workplace charity by following existing models of action. In the past, individual nonprofits had gained access to workplace contributions by joining the United Way. Similarly, in the late 1960s and 1970s, some new charities fought to become member agencies of the local United Way (Brilliant 1990).[3] In a number of cities, including San Francisco and Chicago (as I discuss later), newly formed nonprofits placed public pressure on the local United Way to expand their pool of funding to include additional organizations (Davis 1975).

This method of access to workplace giving was, to an overwhelming degree, not a success. Most local United Ways failed to incorporate any substantive presence of these new charities into their system of resource distribution (Seeley, Sim and Loosley 1956; Brilliant 1990). In her study of six United Ways, for example, Polivy (1988) concludes that the United Ways had allowed in only 1.5 new charities a year on average. When a United Way did alter its patterns of funding by adding new members, these changes were largely minimal and often seen as little more than ceremonial or cosmetic in nature. Clearly, United Ways either could not or would not adapt to the changing composition and expectations of the nonprofit sector.

In consequence, although some charities gave up on workplace charity, others employed a second strategy. Following the model of Health funds, these nonprofits formed Alternative Funds as a mechanism by which to gather workplace revenue. Rather than joining the United Way, they came together with other nonprofit organizations sharing a similar mission and sought to compete alongside the United Way for contributions (Brilliant 1990). The growth of these newly emerging Alternative Funds was facilitated by another outcome of the changing culture of philanthropy in the United States. The report of the Filer Commission galvanized a range of actors to strive to break the United Way's monopoly of workplace charity. As a result, several national-level organizations were formed to assist local attempts by nonprofit organizations to obtain workplace funds. In his study of changes in community organizing, Delgado (1997:2) identifies "organizer training intermediaries" as one of the primary forces shaping the emergence and structure of voluntary and grassroots associations. Organizer training intermediaries consist of nonlocal centers providing expertise to local leaders and charities.

On of these organizer training intermediaries, the National Committee for Responsive Philanthropy, had emerged out of the Filer Commission. It was soon joined by several other national organizations that encouraged the formation of local Alternative Funds: these include the Environmental Support Center and the National Alliance for Choice in Giving. All are Washington, DC-based organizations that are committed to the creation and continuing success of Alternative Funds at the local, state, and national levels. They work to disseminate the concept of the Alternative Fund to charities within a specific community and to identify and facilitate local nonprofit executives to lead the formation of Alternative Funds. Bob Parkinson, the head of one of these groups, described to me the process of starting up a United Way rival at the local or state level.

> The typical scenario would be identifying some [local] person, or persons who are interested in exploring this idea and then asking them to convene a meeting of the broadest representation of [that nonprofit] community as possible. . . . Then it involves sitting down with that group of folks and explaining workplace solicitation generically, talking to them about how it has been useful to other groups in other places, talking to them about what needs to happen in order to form and nurture a federation.

The Environmental Fund of Illinois is an example of this route to organizational formation. Formed in 1992, its emergence can be traced to this interaction between local nonprofit leaders and nonlocal organizer training intermediaries. Although local environmental agencies had often collaborated on various projects, the Environmental Fund of Illinois was formed in response to the efforts of a representative from the Environmental Support Center, a national organization whose mission is to provide support for environmental groups. As had happened elsewhere, the Environmental Support Center brought together and presented the case of workplace charity to an assortment of local activists and nonprofits, highlighting the benefits of workplace gifts and the opportunity for entry into workplace charity as an Alternative Fund. As a result, after some discussion and effort, the Environmental Fund of Illinois was created by local environmental organizations in Illinois in order to obtain revenue from local workplace campaigns.

In all, a range of Alternative Funds, emerging out of two different historical moments, fought to participate alongside the United Way. For these federated fundraisers, one final and central force in their emergence lies in the realm of the public sector. Existing scholarship has emphasized the importance of the public sector for understanding the scope and dimensions of the nonprofit sector. Using the concept of "coercive isomorphism," Paul DiMaggio and Walter Powell (1991) delineate how governmental regulation often affects organizational forms and practices. In related research, Theda Skocpol and others (2002) have demonstrated the centrality of the federal government for the formation and success of various charitable organizations, including the American Red Cross. This latter research illustrates how American involvement in wars, both domestic and abroad, fostered the formation and success of various voluntary associations, accompanied by a subsequent rise in levels of civic engagement. More broadly, in his comparative history of the United States, Britain, and France, Dobbin (1994) documents how a nation's political culture – those shared understandings of the proper relationship of the state and the market – affected the development of the railroad industry in each nation.

Similarly, the growth of competition in workplace charity cannot be understood without attention to changes in policy at the level of the federal government, specifically at the level of its workplace campaign, during the 1970s and 1980s. From 1956 and until the 1970s, only four charitable organizations could raise funds in the Combined Federal Campaign. The United Way was the major fundraiser and typically managed the workplace campaign. In addition, the National Voluntary Health Association, a federation of international service agencies and the American Red Cross were also granted permission by the federal government to solicit gifts from federal employees (Brilliant 1990). These United Way rivals were illustrative of the formal criteria of inclusion: they needed to be national in scale, possess a low overhead, and have member agencies that were involved only in the provision of health and welfare services.

However, as the result of both wider social changes and the Filer Commission, awareness and indignation developed among outsiders over the limited and conservative nature of causes and issues present in the Combined Federal Campaign. In the late 1970s, as Brilliant (1990) discusses, a combination of acts on the part of other governmental bodies and litigation by independent groups led to the opening of the federal government's campaign to other charities. A series of hearings held by Congresswoman Patricia Schroeder resulted in a loosening of restrictions and the formation of the National Service Agencies as a new participant in the CFC. The inclusion of the National Service Agencies was particularly notable given that its membership included several minority-based groups. Additionally, through the late 1970s and into the next decade, several political advocacy groups, including the NAACP Legal Defense and Education Fund, the Puerto Rican Legal Defense and Education Fund, and the NAACP Special Contribution Fund among others, mounted a series of legal challenges in lower courts to the CFC's exclusion of nonhealth and welfare organizations. This highly combative process of litigation, involving resistance by federal government and appeals to and action by the U.S. Congress, ended in 1988 when new legislation was passed that widened the criteria for participation in the CFC. Since passage of that law, almost any Alternative Fund or nonprofit organization has access to the revenue available through the CFC's annual campaign, as long as it meets the campaign's guidelines.

The opening of the Combined Federal Campaign spurred the formation of Alternative Funds in two ways. First, United Way rivals had successfully challenged the monopoly of the United Way in the single largest workplace campaign in the nation. Their victory appeared symptomatic of similar changes to come. It encouraged nonprofit organizations to form local funds that might also gain access to other types of workplace campaigns. While the United Way had previously enjoyed largely unchallenged control over workplace funds, now its rule seemed fragile and precarious.

Second, the Combined Federal Campaign provided an easy and inexpensive source of revenue for Alternative Funds. The long-time leader of one organizer training intermediary noted that, "if the change at the federal government hadn't started, it's the largest employer in the United States, opening up gradually, that... it gave these alternatives some resources that they otherwise they wouldn't have been able to get." In 1984, for example, United Way rivals gathered $53 million of the total $122 million donated by federal employees (National Committee for Responsive Philanthropy 1986).

Not surprisingly, some nonprofits quickly organized into federated fundraisers in order to take advantage of this new and lucrative supply of revenue. The opening of the CFC served to spur on the formation of Alternative Funds oriented around a wider range of causes and issues. Alternative Funds appeared that represented the GLBT community, the Christian community, animal rights, children's rights, and veterans' rights. As the president of one Alternative Fund noted, "Without the opening of the Combined Federal Campaign in the first place, there never would have been a venue for [this organization]."

Taken together, these shifts in the availability of resources and in shared understandings of the nonprofit sector helps account for both why Alternative Funds emerged at a particular historical moment and also their subsequent pattern of growth. Figure 3 traces the historical growth of Alternative Funds

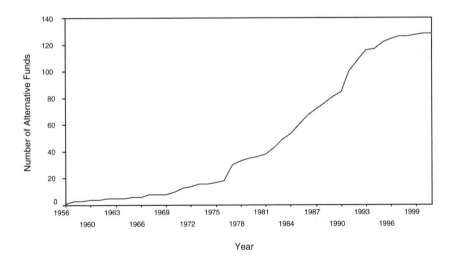

Figure 3   Growth of Alternative Funds, 1956–2001

over the last five decades. Several distinct waves of formation are present. The first Alternative Funds formed at a slow but steady rate from the mid-1950s – in the form of Health Funds – through to the mid-1970s, as Social Movement funds began to appear. A period of explosive growth occurred in the late 1970s, spurred on by access to funding from the federal government, and it continued through the 1980s. The total population of Alternative Funds continued to grow at a slow rate through the early 1990s, leveling off to their current population of almost 150 in all by 2001.

The Formation of Individual Alternative Funds

Yet, an assessment of these broad, underlying social conditions does not provide a full explanation for the rise of Alternative Funds. For, although they account for the particular historical moment at which the Alternative Fund movement emerged (and their subsequent pattern of growth), they cannot elucidate where and why individual Alternative Funds have formed. Although Alternative Funds have indeed emerged over the last three decades to challenge the United Way system, this challenge is uneven. That is, rather than operating in all cities across the country, competing with all 2,000 United Ways, Alternative Funds are only present in one-third of all metropolitan areas. This disparity means that only in some cities of the United States do donors have the option to give their money to different and emergent notions of community. And it poses an important question, both empirically and theoretically: why this variation? What explains where Alternative Funds have emerged and, therefore, where and why individual donors possess significant charitable choices in the workplace?

The most common framework for understanding the emergence of Alternative Funds, offered by both participants in the field and academic observers, links their emergence to the increasing embrace of new identities and interests over the last three decades. These United Way competitors constitute the organizational outcome of individuals' changing beliefs and values. One senior executive at an Alternative Fund traced the growth of United Way rivals to a change in donors' expectations – "the wave of the future is increasing choice. People like that" (Walter 1992:102). This viewpoint embodies a theoretical framework that explains the scope of philanthropic activity in terms of the demands and desires of donors (Weisbrod 1988).

However, as I show below, a systematic analysis finds that donors' demands do not predict the presence of Alternative Funds. Instead, although Alternative Funds represent new identities and interests and, as a result, provide employees with the ability to make gifts based on these concerns, the presence of those identities and interests among local residents does not explain where Alternative Funds have appeared. That is, donor demand for new funding opportunities is not a necessary condition for the emergence of United Way rivals. Rather than being driven from changes occurring below – that is, at the level of donors – Alternative Funds are instead determined from the top – by the configuration and dynamics of the organizational field and by the work of nonprofit entrepreneurs.

To demonstrate these results, I employ the findings of a survey of Alternative Funds that I conducted in 2000. I asked respondents to identify those cities in which they formed a local presence (that is, where they participated in workplace campaigns). The dependent variable of interest is whether the city possessed one or more Alternative Funds.[4] Table 2 contains the findings of my statistical analysis.[5] Using the technique of logistic regression analysis, the table conveys whether the variable is significant (when other variables are present) and the influence of the independent variable on the outcome. A variable is denoted as significant by the presence of a * (representing a

Table 2 Determinants of Cities' Likelihood of Having Alternative Funds

	Significance	Odds Ratio
Demand-Side Characteristics		
% Ethnic/Racial Minority of Population		.207
% New Residents of Population		136.153
Supply-Side Characteristics		
Government Funding	*	1.945
Donative Support		.997
Nonprofit Organizations	*	1.399
Community Characteristics		
City Size	*	15.819
Government Employment		1.065
Philanthropic Culture		2.441

significance level of equal to or smaller than .05). The last column of the table states the odds ratio or the influence for the variable. The odds ratio can be interpreted as the change in the odds of a city having an Alternative Fund when the independent variable changes by one unit, all other factors being controlled.

Demand Side Characteristics

The central hypothesis proposed by past research is that donors shape the composition of the nonprofit sector. Drawing from existing literature, two demand-side factors have been employed to explain variation in the size of the local nonprofit sector. Population heterogeneity suggests that the presence of diversity among residents results in more nonprofits, as the result of more varied demand (Corbin 1999; Bielefeld 2000). Empirical research on workplace charity suggests that the presence of racial diversity might result in the formation of Alternative Funds. Since the late 1960s, minority-based community groups have continually criticized the United Way for failing to adequately support their cause (Carson 1983; Brilliant 1990). In her study of workplace campaigns in the Bay Area, Witty (1989) found that ethnic and racial minorities were the least likely to make donations to the United Way. In all, we expect to find that a more diverse population results in the presence of rivals in workplace charity.

A second proposition that tests a demand-side theory of the nonprofit sector is that of residential mobility. Duration of individuals' residence is positively associated with the size of the nonprofit sector (Lincoln 1977; Gamm and Putnam 1999). To account for this relationship, Putnam (2000) proposes that residential instability leads to a lower level of civic engagement and, hence, fewer voluntary associations – what he calls the "re-potting hypothesis." This hypothesis appears relevant for the case of workplace charity. The United Way represents a local, geographically bounded conception of community. Recently settled residents to a city, however, tend not to be committed to the local community (Fink 1990; Wellman 1999). This proposition results in the expectation that communities with a more transient population will be more likely to possess Alternative Funds.

However, as shown in Table 2, none of the two measures of donor demand significantly influences the likelihood that cities will possess a United

Way rival once other variables are introduced. Neither the amount of racial heterogeneity nor the degree of residential mobility significantly influences the likelihood that metropolitan areas will possess a United Way rival once other variables are introduced. In all, the multivariate analysis suggests that Alternative Funds are not formed on the basis of individual demands and desires.

Supply-Side Characteristics

A second possible theoretical framework emphasizes the importance of the composition of the organizational field in which donors make contributions, with particular focus on funding opportunities and the density of participants. In general, nonprofit activity is seen to be spurred by the level of available resources (Smith and Lipsky 1993). Nonprofit formation has been shown to be positively related to the presence of public, governmental funding (Bielefeld 2000; Gronbjerg and Paarlberg 2002). As predicted, the amount of federal funding does significantly affect the presence of United Way rivals. The higher the level of federal funds to a community, the more likely they are to possess Alternative Funds. This finding confirms that public generosity is associated with a larger and more secure nonprofit sector (Salamon 1987; Bielefeld 2000).

In addition to government funding, nonprofits also rely on support in the form of charitable donations. Nonprofits, it has been argued, will be present in a community in direct proportion to the amount of charitable donations received (Booth, Higgins, and Cornelius 1989; Wolch and Geiger 1983). Contrary to this research, however, the availability of private funds is not a significant predictor of the formation of Alternative Funds. The amount of workplace giving does not function as a "pull" for Alternative Funds; it does not encourage competition in workplace charity.

This study also includes a consideration of the density of nonprofits for the formation of Alternative Funds. In existing literature, the presence of non-profits within an environment is understood to facilitate the genesis of new organizations (Lincoln 1977; Wiewel and Hunter 1985). As discussed above, United Way competitors represent coalitions of nonprofits with shared missions. As expected, Alternative Funds are more likely to appear in cities that already possess a greater presence of nonprofits.

Community Characteristics

A final theory to account for geographical variation in the presence of Alternative Funds examined here has to do with community characteristics. Regardless of the particular demands and behaviors of their residents, metropolitan areas are seen to possess certain structural qualities that are irreducible to individual-level traits: these include the city's economy, its culture of philanthropy, and its size (Lincoln 1977; Wolch and Geiger 1983; Booth, Higgins, and Cornelius 1989).

One significant dimension of the economy is the presence of the government as an employer. Due to litigation on the part of United Way critics, the majority of government workplace campaigns now allow for some form of open competition between the United Way and rival federated fundraisers (Brilliant 1990). Although individual workplaces in the private sector are able to decide if Alternative Funds should be allowed to participate alongside the United Way, most public sector workplaces are legally mandated to permit other fundraisers. However, despite these expectations, the composition of a metropolitan area's economy is not relevant. The presence of government employment is not a significant factor in a multivariate analysis. Alternative Funds are just as likely to be present in a city where the private sector dominates the local economy as a city where government agencies are a significant presence as employers.

For some scholars, a region's charitable behavior can be explained by another community characteristic – a distinctive and shared local culture of philanthropy (Hall 1992; Schneider 1996). Philanthropic culture typically has been conceptualized through use of Daniel Elazar's (1984) typology of political cultures. Given its specific religious, economic, and political history, a region possesses one of three political cultures: traditionalistic, moralistic, or individualistic. Each type of political culture holds a different degree of affinity with the idea of Alternative Funds. Traditional cultures, characterized by paternalism and a commitment to existing institutions, would hold little support for Alternative Funds. In contrast, moralistic cultures, oriented toward collective well-being, would tend to support multiple participants in workplace charity in order to meet the needs of all citizens. Similarly, individualistic cultures will be likely to support forms of charitable activity that express the particularistic concerns of citizens. In both of the latter cases, we would expect to find Alternative Funds.

But, as shown in Table 2, the variable of philanthropic culture does not predict the presence of Alternative Funds. However, although the philanthropic culture of a city does not affect the formation of Alternative Funds, its size does. A city's size possesses a positive influence on the outcome of interest: Alternative Funds are overwhelmingly located in large metropolitan areas. As Hawley (1971) predicts, urban areas entail diversity and scale, creating a critical mass of interested and like-minded professionals and organizations, the necessary preconditions for the formation of Alternative Funds.

In all, these findings provide a particular account of why Alternative Funds appear in some communities across the nation but not in others. These Alternative Funds matter because they not only allow certain nonprofits to gain access to workplace resources for the first time but they also provide donors with a new and wider range of altruistic choices. However, my research shows that donors' identities and interests do not account for the emergence of these Alternative Funds. Rather, United Way competitors are formed out of the configuration and dynamics of the local nonprofit field. Alternative Funds appear in large cities, where a thriving nonprofit sector receiving ample funding already exists.

An attention to nonprofit entrepreneurs helps to specify the causal mechanism by which community and supply-side conditions result in the formation of Alternative Funds, as confirmed by interviews with Alternative Fund representatives in Chicago and San Francisco. In these interviews, I asked respondents to specify the history of their organization's formation. On multiple occasions, I was told that the founder of the Alternative Fund had been a long-time leader of locally-based nonprofits. These individuals had single-handedly led the process of joining together previously independent nonprofits to form an Alternative Fund. Like many other nonprofits, Alternative Funds "trace their lineage back to the enterprise and vision of a founder" (Cordes, Steuerle, and Twombly 2004, p. 115). Hence, Alternative Funds are created when these nonprofit entrepreneurs act within a specific social context so as to obtain new funding in the field of workplace charity. In large metropolitan areas, the prior presence of multiple charities with a shared mission, combined with a high level of government funding, serve to provide a pool of experienced nonprofit professionals who are familiar with and seek access to resource opportunities in that city, doing so through the formation of Alternative Funds.

Conclusion

In this chapter, I have argued that the appearance of Alternative Funds in workplace charity represents the organizational expression of large-scale cultural transformations in American life, as mediated by the availability of funding and shifting understandings of philanthropy. The next set of chapters examines the implications of Alternative Funds for workplace charity. The emphasis is on how the participation of Alternative Funds has not been straightforward, but instead has been characterized by contestation and negotiation between concrete forms of community. As we will see, these struggles have led to different logics of community being dominant across different locales.

CHAPTER 5

Contestations over Entry

We can explain the history of our growth in the workplace charity by looking at employers – when they have opened up their campaigns to more choice, then we raise more money. It's not really about the employees, because we know that most of them want the choice of choosing a specific charity. It all comes down to the employers, really, and that's all.

— PRESIDENT, NATIONAL ALTERNATIVE FUND

Representing a range of distinct and divergent communities of purpose, Alternative Funds challenge not only the financial monopoly of the United Way but also its conception of community. The central question to be explored is how this competition between the United Way and Alternative Funds unfolds within and across different sites of workplace charity. Once formed, Alternative Funds face two distinct and sequential challenges: they must gain entry to workplace campaigns, and once in, they must persuade donors to give to them. This chapter examines the challenges and opportunities faced by Alternative Funds as they seek to convince institutional gatekeepers to permit them access to employees' gifts. Their efforts have been complicated by the varying response of United Ways to the growth of rival organizations.

The Challenge of Access

Headquartered in Stamford, CT, Pitney Bowes™ is a mail and document management company with 35,000 employees worldwide and over $4.9 billion in revenue in 2004 (Pitney Bowes 2004). For many years, Pitney Bowes had an employee drive with the United Way as the only participant. However, beginning in the mid-1990s, in response to a run of mediocre annual drives, senior management expanded the firm's workplace campaign beyond United Way to include other choices for employees. For these Alternative Funds, including EarthShare, Community Health Charities, International Service Agencies, and America's Charities, participation in the Pitney Bowes campaign has resulted in a substantive flow of resources. In the first year alone, employees donated an additional $300,000 to the Pitney Bowes Employees' Giving Program (Consulting Network 2000).

This overhaul of workplace giving at Pitney Bowes – from a United Way monopoly to an open and fair competition among multiple fundraisers – constitutes the ideal for Alternative Funds. It is how they envision their place in workplace charity when they initially form out of an existing population of charities. Yet, a fundamental divide exists between accounting for the appearance of Alternative Funds and understanding the extent of their participation in workplace campaigns. The problem or, rather, the challenge for Alternative Funds is that their entry into the field of workplace charity does not guarantee their participation in workplace drives. Alternative Funds can only enter into contestations with the United Way over community once they have gained entry to one or more employee campaigns.

The question of access to fundraising sites constitutes the second and central issue in understanding the presence of new conceptions of community in workplace charity. This challenge of access to funding sites constitutes an overlooked in the literature on nonprofit activity. In general, scholars have sought either to account for the formation of charities (Wolch and Geiger 1983; Ben-Ner and Van Hoomissen 1989; Galaskiewicz and Bielefeld 1998; Gronbjerg and Paarlberg 2002) or, alternatively, to document their struggle to acquire resources from donors (Rabinowitz 1990; Ostrander 1995; Alexander 1996). However, systematic and sustained attention also needs to be directed to a second and intermediary step between organizational founding and organizational fundraising – that of organizational entry to fundraising sites. Nonprofits often must struggle to acquire the right or ability to solicit contributions from potential donors.

Gaining access to donors constitutes a particular difficulty for those non-profits who participate in charitable arenas that have gatekeepers. The concept of a gatekeeper has traditionally been employed by sociologists of culture (Hirsch 1972). Rather than see cultural objects, such as art, music, and movies, as the direct expression of producers' creative visions or as produced to satisfy audiences' demands, scholars instead view cultural consumption as mediated by the work of gatekeepers: those actors situated between producers and consumers. Thus, gatekeepers act to selectively filter the objects available to audiences; examples of gatekeeping activities include the influence of British publishers in African literature (Griswold 1992) and the role of talent agents in the careers of screenwriters (Bielby and Bielby 1999).

But the concept of gatekeeper can be readily applied to other spheres, including the nonprofit sector. Here, gatekeepers have served to filter the multitude of nonprofits, causes, and issues otherwise faced by donors when they decide to make a contribution. Given the proliferation of charities, for example, many consumer watchdog organizations have formed over the last two decades to assess the relative effectiveness of potential recipients for donors. These organizations, including the American Institute of Philanthropy, Better Business Bureau, Evangelical Council for Financial Accountability, and the National Charities Information Bureau, publish standards of operation by which donors can judge nonprofits on their relative fitness (Silvergleid 2003). Gatekeepers are also found in foundations; their professional staff often provides advice and guidance to the board of directors and/or elite givers as to how the foundations' grants should be distributed (Ylvisaker 1987). As Lenkowsky (2002:359) notes, foundations "enable donors to be more confident that their gifts are going to high-priority uses (whether in a community or in a treatment of a disease), because a trustworthy organization can weigh them against the alternatives."

In workplace charity, fundraisers must gain legitimacy from two distinct actors – employees, whom they petition for their contributions, and employers, whom they must first solicit to gain entry to their charitable campaigns. Workplace managers, therefore, act as gatekeepers in that they filter the appeals of federated fundraisers to employees. The owners and/or senior management of a workplace, as other research also has shown (Paprocki

1988; Polivy 1988; Brilliant 1990; Otto 1994), determine the specific scope of donative choices offered in its workplace campaign; that is, they decide whether competition from Alternative Funds will exist for the local United Way.

In this chapter, I examine the means by which Alternative Funds have gained access to fundraising sites through gatekeepers. I find a shared and overarching trajectory, one in which Alternative Funds, both as a whole and individually, have moved from the easiest workplaces to open to the most difficult ones to enter. In all, United Way rivals have achieved a bipartite degree of access to workplace charity: although they have obtained entry to workplace campaigns in much of the public sector, they have faced severe difficulty in gaining access to those within the private sector. The mechanisms of entry have also differed based on the particular fundraising site. In the public sector, workplace access has been largely governed by government regulation. In the private sector, these coercive processes have not proved viable, and instead, the means of entry has been mediated by social networks and by the local institutional environment.

ENTERING THE PUBLIC SECTOR

Both as a whole and at the individual level, Alternative Funds have begun their quest for workplace funds by targeting gatekeepers in the public sector. Employing both appeals to the legal system and to the public interest, Alternative Funds have benefited from the processes of what the New Institutionalist approach calls "coercive" isomorphism and "mimetic" isomorphism (DiMaggio and Powell 1991). However, this process has been hard fought, and based on the type of Alternative Fund seeking permission and the geographical location of the campaign, the outcome has varied.

Alternative Funds, as discussed in the last chapter, began the process of altering the composition of workplace charity by gaining access to the federal government's employee campaign – the Combined Federal Campaign. Subsequently, Alternative Funds across the nation have taken advantage of coercive isomorphism, that process by which organizations are forced to implement certain structures to be deemed legitimate, regardless of their own preferences, interests, and goals. Coercive isomorphism results from formal and informal pressures from a variety of external actors – resource providers, state agencies, and successful competitors – as well as from shared under-standings and expectations in the larger society (DiMaggio and Powell 1991).

The Combined Federal Campaign is not a single entity, but rather com-prises 300 separate campaigns across the country and internationally. Con-ducted by the federal government through the Office of Personnel Manage-ment, each individual campaign gathers donations from federal employees (both civilian and military) within a particular geographical region. Although each campaign is conducted by its own Local Federal Coordinating Com-mittee – made up of an assortment of federal officials and workers – all of the CFC campaigns are governed by the same set of rules and regulations. As a result, despite the inclinations of the local committee to either permit or reject the appeals of Alternative Funds, they are forced by law to allow in United Way rivals.

Most federated fundraisers, once formed, first gather money through en-tering the local Combined Federal Campaign operating in their region. Said one long-time leader of a Chicago area Alternative Fund, "The first thing that you usually do when you are a workplace payroll fundraising organization is you try to qualify for the Combined Federal Campaign." The Combined Federal Campaign provides a dependable and cost-effective source of rev-enue for United Way rivals. By 2002, United Way rivals (including both Al-ternative Funds and independent nonprofits) gathered approximately three-quarters of all contributions made by employees of the federal government (Combined Federal Campaign 2004a).

However, the federal government constitutes just one small arena of all potential revenue available through the workplace. According to the CEO of one national fund, "Of approximately the \$2 billion raised from employees, only about 10 percent or so is coming from federal employees of the CFC." As a result, Alternative Funds have also sought to gain entry to other types of public sector workplace campaigns at the state, county, and local levels. Take, for example, the case of America's Charities, a national fund that includes a variety of member agencies. In 1987, it was completely dependent on the Combined Federal Campaign, gathering "one hundred percent" of its rev-enue from federal employees. By 2001, it had managed to diversify its sources of funding and gathered over a third of its revenue in other types of sites.

After gaining access to the federal workplace, Alternative Funds then turned to government campaigns at the state and local levels, hoping to apply the same strategies of legal coercion, lobbying, and media pressure that worked in the case of the CFC. In Rhode Island, for example, the Fund for Community Progress, a social action fund, successfully litigated for access to the state's workplace campaign. In Maryland, as a result of extensive and public lobbying by two Alternative Funds, local government officials allowed in United Way rivals. By 1979, 23 states had opened up their charity drives to competition, and more than 100 city and county governments allowed rivals to participate in their workplace campaigns (National Committee for Responsive Philanthropy 1986).

Alternative Funds have also benefited from the process of mimetic isomorphism. Mimetic isomorphism occurs when organizations, either intentionally or unintentionally, imitate or mimic other members of the field to appear legitimate (DiMaggio and Powell 1991). With workplace charity, many government offices at the city and county level have followed the lead of the state and federal government. Rather than expend the time and energy needed to reach their own decision regarding the question of workplace competition, some government agencies have simply adopted or mimicked the actions of other governmental entities. The presence of Alternative Funds in the CFC conveyed legitimacy to other gatekeepers in the public sector. In the words of John McConnelly, the head of a trade association for Alternative Funds, "The change at the federal government was a huge precedent, not just in terms of funds, but also for other governmental employers at the state and local level. It made it seem viable for us to participate alongside the United Way."

This process of mimetic isomorphism has also been actively fostered by Alternative Funds. They frequently bring their participation in the CFC to the attention of local government agencies, hoping to use it as proof of the legitimacy of their participation alongside the United Way. Barbara Erickson, the head of an Alternative Fund, explained that "they have strict standards to participate in the CFC and so what you do is you use that as leverage to get into other public sector campaigns." As a result, the majority of state sites and many local public sector campaigns have now opened up to competition.

However, the presence of United Way competitors in government campaigns varies based on the criteria for participation. Most public sector campaigns limit the percentage of revenue that can be used for overhead and require 501(c)(3) status with the Internal Revenue Service. Other governmental requirements preclude the participation of certain United Way rivals altogether. The majority of national-level Alternative Funds are only in about half of all state campaigns, for example, because the other 50 percent of state campaigns limit workplace participants to local nonprofits, requiring both the member agency "beneficiaries" and the members of the Alternative Fund's board of directors to be located in the state itself. Some public sector offices make the process of qualifying particularly labor and time intensive. In sum, beyond the Combined Federal Campaign, Alternative Funds have been highly effective in gaining access to other sites in the public sector, but their success has not been universal.

ENTERING THE PRIVATE SECTOR

To achieve equal and full access to workplace donations, the ultimate goal of Alternative Funds has been to gain access to the employee campaigns of businesses. The private sector constitutes the largest source of revenue for workplace fundraisers – about 75 to 80 percent of all potential resources, according to most participants in the field. At the same time, companies have also been the most difficult to enter. In contrast to the public sector, the private sector lacks the mechanism of coercive isomorphism by which to facilitate access for Alternative Funds.[1] Without recourse to the law, Alternative Funds must approach and must be accepted by businesses on a case-by-case basis. Their success has depended on the composition of social networks and the characteristics of the local institutional environment.

Social networks matter in the private sector because Alternative Funds need a sponsor internal to each firm to successfully gain entry to the workplace campaign. Alternative Funds must first make contact with and then gain the support of a company gatekeeper, called "targets" or "prospects" by members of the Alternative Fund community. Gatekeepers can take a variety of roles: according to representatives of Alternative Funds, they could be a member of the human resource department, one of the senior management staff, or someone on the board of directors. When asked to explain how his Alternative Fund achieved access to local corporations in Chicago, for example, John Wycliffe responded, "It's . . . a question of who you talk to and that's really it. Basically, after all the efforts that you make, you do catch somebody's interest. They decide that they want to do this. That's basically how it comes about." Similarly, at one annual conference of Alternative Funds that I attended, participants were advised on "getting in the door": key steps included identifying "key targets" in local firms.

To that end, Alternative Funds employ a variety of strategies to contact and identify firms' gatekeepers, ranging from the formal to the informal.[2] Representatives reported that they attend events like annual conferences of human resource managers where they can have the opportunity to speak with company staff. They also rely on another method of contact: they "cold call" the human resources offices of local businesses. But the results of the cold-calling approach are minimal. One state-level Alternative Fund in California, for example, approached over 1,700 targets in 1999, but only eight new campaigns were opened as a result. Some have followed the model of the United Way, by seeking to have local business elites join their board of directors, in the hopes that those individuals will then use their personal networks to assist the AF (National Committee for Responsive Philanthropy 1986).

Alternative Funds also draw upon informal social networks between themselves and gatekeepers within the private sector. The world of nonprofit professionals in cities and towns is relatively small (Himmelstein 1997), and individuals often move between raising money and distributing resources – working at individual nonprofits, the United Way, and corporate and private foundations through the course of their careers. Hence, the staff of Alternative Funds and their member agencies may know individuals who are responsible for or can influence a firm's decision to allow in workplace competition. When seeking to account for the "democratization" of local campaigns in the private sector, one long-time head of an Alternative Fund in Chicago stressed the importance of personal networks. She noted that "corporations only open up when we know someone at that worksite." In the case of a high-profile open campaign in the Chicago area private sector, for instance, I was told that the decision was made to allow in United Way rivals by an executive in the firm's department of human resources who had previously worked for a social change agency.

These struggles for entry take place within a larger context. Although an Alternative Fund may gain the ear and support of a gatekeeper at a local company, its inclusion must be approved by the firm itself. Ultimately, the responses that Alternative Funds receive from corporations are shaped by two opposing tendencies within the institutional environment. The institutional environment consists of those "rules and requirements to which individual organizations must confirm if they are to receive support and legitimacy" (Scott and Meyer 1991:123). On the one hand, corporations face isomorphic and efficiency-based pressures that preclude or make difficult the inclusion of United Way rivals in their workplace campaigns. On the other hand, recent changes in the ways in which firms perceive their managerial ideology and operate their philanthropic programs have put in question the monopoly of the United Way.

In their quest for entry, Alternative Funds face the institutional environment of local corporate gatekeepers. As discussed in Chapter 1, different communities possess "distinct climates of giving" (Useem 1988:83). With some exceptions, corporate elites in a city or town tend to hold a shared understanding of what the charitable process should be like – what I call a "cultural model of philanthropy" (McElroy and Siegfried 1986; Galaskiewicz 1985, 1991; Himmelstein 1997). A model, in a general sense, refers to a shared conceptualization of a set of goals and the legitimate means by which to achieve them (Bourdieu 1990; Lamont 1992). A model of philanthropy contains an understanding of or a prescription for the proper management, governance, and trusteeship of charitable activities (Elazar 1972; McCarthy 1987; Hall 1992; Abzug 1996).

Different cultural models of philanthropy hold different degrees of affiliation with Alternative Funds. In general, two competing visions of charity can be found in the institutional environment of workplace charity, driven by the assumption of whether philanthropy should be centralized or decentralized. A centralized model of philanthropy is premised on the principles of rationalization and efficiency, suggesting that knowledgeable and objective actors (i.e., social service professionals) should organize charitable activity (and hence giving). When this cultural model of philanthropy is dominant, firms tend not only to distribute their own contributions through the United Way but also to extend this logic to their employees' workplace campaign as well. As one long-time participant in workplace charity explained, large firms "have a very in loco parentis kind of attitude about what kind of charities their company will be affiliated with, and that includes what charities they'll allow their employees to support in payroll deduction."

This particular conception of philanthropy is diffused and intensified across a city's firms through social networks. Although personal relationships with gatekeepers often provide Alternative Funds with a foot in the corporate door, they also serve to block their entry to the company's employee campaign itself. As firmly established by extant research, ties between companies' staff, in the form of membership in firms' and nonprofits' boards of directors, as well as participation in civic groups, create linkages among them, resulting in the spread of local understandings and norms among members of the local corporate elite (Ratcliff, Gallagher, and Ratcliff 1979; Useem 1984; Galaskiewicz 1985; Domhoff 1998). In the case of workplace charity, firms' executives tend to be members of the United Way's board of directors (Middleton 1987). What is commonly noted by United Way rivals is the importance of social connections between senior executives at local firms and United Way members (either members of the board of directors or senior volunteers). The presence of these linkages among local corporate elites results in the spread of a particular model of philanthropy. These shared understandings may, in the case of a centralized model of philanthropy, be favorable toward the United Way and may lead firms to reject appeals from rival federated fundraisers. Moreover, this process of isomorphism does not always occur as the result of informal and unintended processes, as predicted by New Institutionalism. Instead, it is suggested by members of Alternative Funds that the United Way draws on these connections to place pressure on corporate executives to "toe the party line," to quote from one member of an Alternative Fund in Chicago. Consider the following scenario offered by the head of a national Alternative Fund to describe the challenges faced by United Way rivals.

> When you approach an organization to participate in their workplace campaign, that is not, the CEO is not on the United Way board, once the United Way hears about, let's say, my federation, going in to run a workplace campaign, or to be added to their workplace campaign, then the United Way CPO will get his board together and somebody or not most of the people on that board will approach that CEO of that organization and say, hey, you're undermining the United Way system and all that we've worked for our community... [they exert] peer pressure on the CEO to back away from the commitment.

Finally, regardless of their understandings of philanthropy or the networks in which they are embedded, gatekeepers in the private sector may be hesitant to involve Alternative Funds for reasons of pragmatic efficiency. The inclusion of rivals results in additional administrative effort and financial cost for gatekeepers. As discussed in Chapter 2, firms have historically viewed workplace charity, as managed by the United Way, as a relatively simple and cheap method by which to allow employees to donate as well as to be a good "community citizen" (Rose-Ackerman 1988). Reggie Ross is a long-time advocate for Alternative Fund participation in workplace campaigns. When asked to list the central obstacles faced by United Way rivals, he stressed the importance of simplicity and ease for corporate gatekeepers: "What most workplaces care about is that the whole process interrupts the workplace to the absolute bare minimum necessary." By seeking inclusion, Alternative Funds are asking firms to commit time and labor in ways that may not appear worth the effort for gatekeepers. As a result, corporate managers are hesitant to expend energy on changing a seemingly successful institution.

The presence of these efficiency-based concerns, coupled with isomorphic constraints within the institutional environment, has historically led private sector workplaces to maintain a United Way-only employee drive. However, Alternative Funds have benefited from recent changes in the institutional environment of the field. One important development in the private sector has been the emergence of new managerial ideologies. Many firms have emphasized employee participation as a new mode of relating to their workers (Barley and Kunda 1992). Starting in the 1970s, firms have encouraged employee engagement as a means to improve corporate performance. For example, corporations have tried to facilitate workers' involvement in decision making through the implementation of quality circles, employee ownership, and representative participation in the work process itself (Walton 1985). The principle of employee ownership has been extended beyond the production process itself to the sphere of workers' benefits, resulting in many companies offering a selection of health insurance and 401(k) investment plans (Lawler 1994). In some instances, facilitated by new technology, corporations similarly have provided workers with a choice in the distribution of their charitable gifts, creating "open" campaigns that introduced competition for the United Way (Levy 1999).

Recent scholarship, as well as anecdotal evidence from the field, has demonstrated the influence of this changing managerial ideology on the success of Alternative Funds. In her study of workplace charity, Deborah K. Polivy (1985) found that the reason most commonly mentioned by firm leaders for expanding payroll deduction options was to improve employee relations. Similarly, John Sabo, the head of a national rival fund, told me that his organization's success in entering private sector campaigns "follows the culture of the employers, where they value giving employees the added option of choice in their campaign. And they tend to give employees added choice in other areas of employee benefits as well."

The case of Foote, Cone & Belding,™ an advertising firm in Chicago, exemplifies these processes. Although it was affiliated only with the United Way for many years, the corporation's management decided to add Alternative Funds in the early 1990s to increase employee satisfaction with and participation in their workplace fund drive. To select additional federated fundraisers, moreover, the company surveyed small groups of employees about their philanthropic interests, adding Earth Share, Volunteers of America, and the Off the Street Club, a Chicago community center, to best allow their workforce to donate to their own specific concerns (Walter 1997).

Additionally, firms have increasingly employed diversity management in their relationship with employees. Beginning with the Civil Rights Act of 1964 and continuing as the nation's workforce has become increasingly heterogeneous, diversity management has become increasingly widespread across the private sector. Many companies have sought to provide a working environment that formally and informally, through hiring, training, and support, recognizes difference based on race, ethnicity, gender, and physical ability. By 1998, for example, three-quarters of Fortune 500 companies possessed some form of diversity program (Ryan, Hawdon, and Branick 2002). Despite some concern that diversity management is largely symbolic in nature, the central principles of diversity management have often been extended by firms to workplace charity. Alternative Funds have been allowed to participate in companies' employee drives on the principle that workers should be able to donate based on their membership in communities of purpose. Those corporations often are responding to employees' requests for donative choices that reflect their own particular interests and identities. Most notably, in the 1980s, Bell Labs™ and a local office of IBM™ gave local Black

United Funds access to their workplace campaigns as the result of African-American employees' demands for choice (Wenocur, Cook, and Steketee 1984; Polivy 1985; National Committee for Responsive Philanthropy 1986).

Alongside these new managerial ideologies, another major transformation in the institutional environment has also benefited Alternative Funds. In the 1980s, a new model of philanthropy emerged in the nonprofit sector. A decentralized model of philanthropy is premised on the needs of donors. The purpose of philanthropy here is to realize the varied and diverse philanthropic goals of resource providers. Consequently, donors accord less status to intermediaries between themselves and beneficiaries. Over the last two decades, this cultural model has become increasingly viable with the growth of strategic philanthropy in the corporate sector. Strategic philanthropy entails a shift in corporate giving from a narrow and predictable set of community-oriented causes, like the United Way, to a notion of enlightened self-interest, in which firms' contributions are targeted to meet both their business objectives and recipients' needs (Himmelstein 1997; Marx 1997; Saiia, Carroll, and Buchholtz 2003). Firms tie their philanthropic activity to issues of profits and productivity (Alperson 1995). In general, companies focus on philanthropic areas especially close to their own mission and products, resulting in contributions to a narrow range of causes (Hall 1989).[3]

The rise of strategic philanthropy has implications for workplace charity. For one, it has negatively affected the revenue stream of the United Way system. The United Way, with its focus on the community and the provision of health and human services to all, offers relatively little return or benefits to corporations interested in aligning themselves with specific causes. Consequently, firms with strategic philanthropy programs have decreased or halted their own financial support of local United Ways. In his study of 226 large firms, Marx (1997) found that the vast majority of companies possessed a strategic giving plan. Further, firms with a strategic giving plan were far less likely to give to the United Way than to other recipients. Similarly, firms' donations to the health and human services have declined as strategic philanthropy has taken hold, declining from 66 percent of all gifts in 1947 to less than 30 percent by the mid-1990s (Himmelstein 1997).

Accordingly, as the equation of corporate philanthropy with the United Way has disintegrated with the rise of strategic philanthropy, so too has the equation of employee giving with the United Way. Having embraced a principle of strategic philanthropy, firms are often likely to extend the principle of decentralized philanthropy to their employees as well. Take the case of Sears™, a company headquartered in Chicago. Sears is the single largest company headquartered in the Chicago area, with gross revenue of $41 billion and a workforce of 200,000 employees across the nation and over 10,000 in the Chicago area alone in 2003 (Sears, Roebuck, and Co. 2004). Over the course of the 1990s, Sears shifted its philanthropic programs from a concern with the health of the local community to a focus on the health of the company itself. The transformation reflected Sears' larger attempt to reposition itself within the market. It adopted a new brand, complete with a new slogan – "Come see the softer side of Sears." Sears sought to expand beyond its traditional appeal to men (through hardware, appliances, and automotive parts) to also reach out to women by offering a wide range of affordable but fashionable apparel and house ware goods (Murphy 2001).

Sears followed through on its rebranding by implementing a complementary philanthropic program. Beginning in 1995 in Chicago, and adopted nationwide in 1999, Sears expanded beyond the United Way to include other federated fundraisers and nonprofits in its employee campaign. They allowed in Alternative Funds that reflected their new emphasis on both women and on choice (although here for employees rather than consumers). Now, an environmental fund, an African-American federation, and Gilda's Club – a nonprofit devoted to women's causes – compete alongside the United Way for contributions (Consulting Network 2000).

The Role of the United Way

In part, the effort of Alternative Funds to gain entry to workplace sites has been constrained by the response of the United Way to their formation. Almost universally, United Ways believe that the addition of Alternative Funds will result in a decline in their own receipts (Polivy 1985), despite some evidence that suggests donors' levels of giving actually increase with added choice (Millar 1991). Not surprisingly, local United Ways have not been content to simply observe Alternative Funds as they sought to challenge their monopoly of workplace funds. As I noted above, representatives of Alternative Funds frequently reported that United Ways would try to intercede in gatekeepers' decisions concerning their rivals' entry. Local United Ways have understandably also adopted a range of other tactics by which to try and prevent Alternative Funds from gaining access to workplace campaigns. These strategies are more formal in nature, with varying implications for the local field of workplace charity.

Some United Ways have responded to competition by forming relationships with members of the local nonprofit sector. United Ways have done so in two ways: through expanding their pool of member agencies or by establishing partnerships of various sorts with unaffiliated nonprofits. Facing rivalry, some United Ways have accepted new charities that serve the same causes and communities represented by Alternative Funds (National Committee for Responsive Philanthropy 1986; Polivy 1982). The director of one Alternative Fund in Chicago, for instance, wryly noted, "Since we've been around, the United Way in Chicago has funded many more organizations like ours," including several nonprofits that were founding members of the Alternative Fund itself.

Other United Ways have created their own versions of Alternative Funds. They have formed affinity groups out of the pool of local nonprofits with shared missions that parallel those of their rivals. In the city of San Francisco, for example, the United Way engaged in a program called "Strategic Partners" in the 1990s. The United Way contracted with nonprofits representing different identity-based groups, including African-Americans, Asian-Americans, Hispanic-Americans, Filipino-Americans, women, and the GLBT community. These strategic partners received grant payments from the United Way in return for withdrawing as independent rivals and for being listed as a federation on its pledge card. These new federations were presented to the public as United Way-based initiatives (United Way of the Bay Area 1996).

In other cities, United Ways have formed connections with Alternative Funds. In a small number of cities, including Baltimore, San Diego, and Hartford, the local United Ways have created a single combined drive with the local health fund. While the United Way manages the workplace campaign, the health fund is listed as an equal partner in fundraising material (Hatfield 1970; Bothwell 1998). Other United Ways have established partnerships only with the largest and most popular member charities of Alternative Funds. The United Way of America, for example, recommended that local United Ways enter into partnerships with the most successful members of Community Health Charities (Bothwell 1998). By 1986, over 100 United Ways had formed partnerships with the American Cancer Society (National Committee for Responsive Philanthropy 1986). Other United Ways affiliated with local branches of the American Red Cross and the American Heart Association. Typically, these nonprofits withdraw as a separate competitor in exchange for a listing in the United Way's fundraising material and a set annual allocation.

Other United Ways have been charged with altering their relationships with donors in response to the presence of Alternative Funds through the adoption of donor choice. Traditionally, donors have made a gift to the United Way, entrusting it to disperse their contribution. But with a policy of donor choice, the United Way gives donors the opportunity to earmark or designate their gifts to a cause or nonprofit of their own selection. The United Way, however, retains its monopoly of workplace fundraising. By 1990, almost 90% of local United Ways allowed for some type of donor choice (United Way of America 1999). Although no systematic research has been conducted on this topic, representatives and supporters of Alternative Funds view the United Way's adoption of donor choice as an attempt to limit the appeal of its competitors with gatekeepers (Wenocur, Cook, and Steketee 1984). Take the response of Justin Hall, a long-time advocate of workplace competition. When asked to discuss donor choice, he traced its growth to Alternative Funds, noting that "United Ways are forming and developing donor choice policies in the wake of the development of Alternative Funds. They're strictly responding to competition. They're not responding to anything else." In the words of one long-time organizer of Alternative Funds, "If somebody in a company brings up the idea of donors having choices, the United Ways often will say 'you have that already, because we offer donor choice. Choice is not an issue here when we run the show.'"

Patterns of Access

Certainly, although some local United Ways have adopted one or more these tactics, it is not necessarily the case that they have done so as a concerted response to the presence of Alternative Funds. However, whether intentional in nature or not, Alternative Funds perceive the consequence of these

United Way strategies as being one of impeding their access to workplace campaigns in the private sector. In all, as a result of the composition of the institutional environment and of these United Way actions, Alternative Funds have achieved only a bipartite pattern of access to workplace campaigns. By 1997, only 30 percent of all companies that ran on-the-job drives included federated fundraisers other than the United Way (Dickey 1998b). In that same year, access by Alternative Funds to firms' employee campaigns was negatively associated with firm size. Larger firms were less likely to allow for competition: just 12 percent of Fortune 500 companies included non-United Way funds in their on-the-job drives (Dickey 1998a).

Not surprisingly, Alternative Funds receive the majority of their revenue from the public sector. In 1997, for example, the Combined Federal Campaign provided just under half of all contributions to United Way rivals. However, the precise percentage of funding from the public sector varies across the total population of Alternative Funds. The geographic scale of United Way rivals appears to matter here. In 1997, national funds received 84 percent of their revenue from the federal government's Combined Federal Campaign, with the remaining funds generated from public campaigns at the state and local level as well as some private campaigns. In contrast, Alternative Funds at the local and state level received only about half of total revenue from government campaigns, with 20 percent coming from the private sector and a substantive portion of all revenue (28%) generated by the United Way's donor choice program. The dependence of Alternative Funds on the public sector also varies by mission. Although Black United Funds report that almost half (41%) of their funding is generated from businesses, Women's funds and Environmental funds receive less than a third of all donations from the private sector (National Committee for Responsive Philanthropy 1998). Clearly, to speak of a single pattern of Alternative Funds' entry into workplace charity is to miss variation across different types of these federated fundraisers.

Conclusion

As Alternative Funds have sought to enter workplace charity, they have faced not only the constraints of the institutional environment but also the tactical responses of the United Way as well. To gather workplace gifts, Alternative

Funds must be permitted access by gatekeepers. As a result, their participation in workplace campaigns has been uneven, depending on what types of workplaces are in question. Even when permitted to participate, Alternative Funds have also faced attempts by the United Way to minimize their appeal to gatekeepers. As we will see in the next chapters, these contestations over workplace charity between United Ways and Alternative Funds are not limited to the issue of access. Moreover, these conflicts over community play out in different ways across different locales.

CHAPTER 6

Chicago: The Persistence of a Community of Place

Be a part of the community solution; when you give to the United Way, you are giving to your family, neighbors and community.

— FUNDRAISING BROCHURE, UNITED WAY/CRUSADE OF MERCY

Although our understanding of community has broadened in recent years, we know little about how the debate about community unfolds across different areas of contemporary society. In the case of workplace charity, two different sets of federated fundraisers – the United Way and Alternative Funds – represent changing visions of collectivity and the public good. In the next two chapters, I examine the implications of this competition for different sites of workplace charity. I do so by comparing two cities where workplace charity is dominated by two different understandings of community. In Chicago, despite the emergence of Alternative Funds, workplace charity has largely remained oriented around a place-based understanding of community. In San Francisco, the formation of Alternative Funds has been followed by a reorganization of workplace charity around communities of purpose. The task here is not only to trace variation in dominant models of community but also to show why different outcomes are found in different locales.

The Cases of Chicago and San Francisco

The cities of Chicago and San Francisco provide two contrasting cases for understanding how the logic of community affects workplace charity. Each field of workplace charity is organized around a distinct conception of community: Chicago is oriented around a community of place, whereas San Francisco is structured around communities of purpose. This difference in the logic and meaning of community is evident when looking at several characteristics of workplace charity in San Francisco and Chicago. To begin, consider the number and scope of nonprofit organizations that are able to participate in workplace charity in the two cities. In the Bay Area, a large and disparate assortment of United Way rivals participates in local workplace campaigns. In all, five local and state Alternative Funds, all of the national funds, and over 3,500 nonprofits participate in the majority of all workplace campaigns – both in the public and private sectors. In contrast, in Chicago, Alternative Funds – although present in equal numbers to the Bay Area – participate in fewer workplace campaigns. They, accompanied by national funds and only a handful of independent nonprofits, participate in a limited number of workplace campaigns, mostly concentrated in the public and nonprofit sectors.

Not surprisingly, workplace competitors in San Francisco raise more money than in Chicago. In the Bay Area, local and state Alternative Funds alone gathered over $6 million as participants in open workplace campaigns in 1997.[1] Additionally, those funds and other independent charities received just under 75 percent of all earmarked gifts made in United Way-run campaigns in 1999–2000 (United Way of the Bay Area 2000c). In contrast, in Chicago, local and state Alternative Funds gathered just over $1.5 million in open workplace campaigns in that same year. These rivals, along with independent nonprofits, also receive designated gifts. In Chicago, those earmarked contributions constituted less than 20 percent of all donations made through the United Way in 2001 (United Way of Chicago 2002).

The two cities also differ in terms of where workplace funds go in the nonprofit sector. Historically, as I discussed in Chapter 2, only United Way member agencies received workplace donations: these charities typically have been older and larger than member agencies of Alternative Funds and provided health and human services to clients. Accordingly, San Francisco's United Way, the United Way of the Bay Area (UWBA), had traditionally distributed its annual revenue to about 200 member agencies. In contrast, over 7,000 Bay Area nonprofits and federated fundraisers, representing a wide range of causes and issues, received revenue from workplace charity in 1999 (United Way of the Bay Area 2000c). In the case of Chicago, however, the traditional mode of distributing workplace revenue is still firmly in place. About 400 United Way charities, most affiliated with the United Way/Crusade of Mercy (UW/CM), now called the United Way of Metropolitan Chicago since its formation in 1934, received the majority of funds in 2002.[2]

Even the two United Ways look very different in terms of both their organizational structures and their discursive practices. In Chicago, the United Way still maintains its traditional form of organization. It allocates its revenue based on a time-honored method (Brilliant 1990). Although volunteer-run committees determine the community's priority of needs and disperse funds accordingly to member agencies, a large portion of the United Way's revenue is according to fixed formulas, with little change from year to year. As we see later in the chapter, the United Way is also oriented around a traditional conception of community – promising to provide a safety net of health and human services to residents of the greater Chicago area.

In the Bay Area, the United Way looks fundamentally different. Divided into two separate entities, it has devolved its responsibility as a fundraiser to a separate organization and now acts solely as a fund allocator. Even in fulfilling its allocation responsibility, the UWBA no longer functions according to the traditional model of the United Way. The United Way in San Francisco historically had distributed its annual revenue to about 200 member agencies. In contrast, today over 7,000 different Bay Area nonprofits and federated fundraisers, representing a wide range of causes and issues, receive revenue from workplace charity (United Way of the Bay Area 2000c). In its public discourse, the United Way of the Bay Area employs a particularistic model of community to justify its system of fund distribution. It seeks to partner with contributors to facilitate their own varied and specific conceptions of community (United Way of the Bay Area 2000b).

The existence of such differences in the two fields of workplace charity raises the question of why – that is, how and why has one city's field of workplace charity been reorganized around a new and expanded conception of communities of purpose while another city's field of workplace charity has remained oriented around a community of place? Several explanations, drawn from both participants' accounts and scholarly literature, seem potentially useful here for accounting for these two outcomes.

First, differences in community might be explained by the ecological composition of the local field of workplace charity: that is, variation in the presence of Alternative Funds might explain the outcome of interest. An ecological framework draws attention to the population density of a field: that is, the number of organizations competing for similar resources (Steinberg 1987; Tuckman 1998; Barman 2002; Young and Salamon 2003). In our case, the greater the number of Alternative Funds, the more likely that the traditional model of community, as represented by the United Way, will lose its legitimacy. However, the local United Ways in the two cities have a comparable level of competition. In Chicago, the United Way faced five local Alternative Funds oriented around the issues of health research, minority concerns, the environment, social change, and women's concerns. In the Bay Area, the United Way faced four locally based Alternative Funds oriented around the issues of health research and treatment, minority concerns, the environment, and social change. Yet, only in San Francisco have these United Way rivals succeeded in restructuring the field of workplace charity around communities of purpose. Therefore, we cannot look to differences in the extent of competition to account for our outcome of interest.

Similarly, differences in the two cities might be explained by the availability and scope of resources in the local field of workplace charity. A micro-level approach to philanthropy explains the composition of the nonprofit sector in terms of the desires and demands of donors (Jencks 1988; Piliavin and Charng 1990; Mount 1996; Musick, Wilson, and Bynum 2000). These studies have examined how social characteristics, such as race, class, and gender, affect the probability and rate of donations (White 1989; Jencks 1988; Conley 2000; Steinberg and Wilhelm 2005). The basic assumption underlying this demographic explanation is that "belonging to a particular section of the population will predispose one towards altruism" (Monroe 1996:8).

Here, differences between the characteristics of residents in San Francisco and Chicago might satisfactorily account for why community means different things in the two cities. After all, San Francisco is considered the home of identity and interest politics (Castells 1983; Armstrong 2002; Boyd 2003), whereas Chicago is often perceived as a staid Midwestern town, one heavily working class and Catholic (Mayer, Wade, and Holt 1969; Duis 1976). It would be easy, therefore, to view difference in the meaning of community across the two cities as reflecting differences in donors' demands. Individuals in San Francisco would direct their gifts to nonprofits concerned with particularistic communities of purpose. In contrast, those in Chicago would

Table 3   The Field of Workplace Charity in San Francisco and Chicago

	San Francisco	Chicago
Donors		
% White	69.4	71.6
% 35 years of age or under	52.7	54.6
% with BA+	39.0	29.1
% born in State	53.2	72.3
Median income	$35,918	$45,099
Economy (As Percentage of Total Firms)		
% Manufacturing	10.8	9.3
% High-income service	38.6	39.2
% Low-income service	50.4	51.4
% Employed by federal government	5.6	3.1

Source: United States Census Bureau 1992

be content to entrust their contributions to a centralized nonprofit – the United Way – that disperses their gifts to the local community. However, an examination of the demographic characteristics of the cities confirms that donors' characteristics are strikingly parallel in the two cases. Table 3 provides a picture of San Francisco and Chicago, showing that the demographic profiles of the two locales are far more similar than dissimilar. In both cases, the pool of donors is racially and ethnically diverse, young, and well educated – all demographic characteristics expected to predict a more open and competitive workplace charity (Carson 1983; White 1989; Witty 1989; Hoge et al. 1996). Clearly, then, it is not solely variation in donors' expectations that explains differences across workplace charity.

These two findings, taken together, suggest that neither the ecological nor the resource composition of the local field alone can explain differences in the dominant models of community. An alternative theoretical approach, one that looks beyond the presence of competition and the demands and desires of donors, is necessary. In this chapter and the next, I show that contestations over community, and their ultimate resolutions, must be understood as involving two distinct but sequential battles: first, the quest of Alternative Funds to gain access to workplace campaigns, and, once permitted entry, the struggle between the local United Way and Alternative Funds to obtain donors' contributions. These two struggles are determined by organizational contestations within institutional constraints.

First, the challenge of entry to fundraising sites for federated fundraisers highlights the importance of the institutional environment. Local corporate leaders hold particular models of philanthropy that determine the extent and ease with which Alternative Funds, representing new identities and interests, can gain access to workplace campaigns. However, the institutional environment does not directly determine the outcome of interest. Instead, it constitutes the setting within which both Alternative Funds and the United Way struggle to assert their competing models of community and to influence donors. They seek to gather resources and legitimacy within these external constraints. Only by understanding both of these two processes, as they have interacted and altered over time, can we account for differences in workplace charity between Chicago and San Francisco.

Chicago and a Community of Place

Workplace charity in Chicago traces its history to the Depression, when social service agencies acquiesced to long-standing and ongoing demands by business leaders to coalesce into a single fundraising entity. Formed in 1934, the United Way/Crusade of Mercy began with sixty-five member agencies representing the major nonprofit providers of health and human services in the city (United Way of Chicago 1990).[3] The growth of the United Way in Chicago has paralleled that of the city as a whole. As Chicago developed into a world-class city by the 1990s, the United Way experienced a staggering rate of revenue growth (United Way/Crusade of Mercy 1997b) and it now constitutes the largest United Way in the nation.[4] The United Way operates in five counties – Cook, Lake, Will, Kane, and DuPage counties – with the potential to gather funds from around 300,000 businesses and over 7.5 million employees. In 2001, it raised $91 million and distributed its undesignated resources to about 400 partner agencies (United Way of Chicago 2002).

Despite its success, the United Way in Chicago has not been without external criticism. During the 1960s and 1970s, it began facing pressure from new constituencies and newly vocal communities who questioned the federated fundraiser's practices, along with those of the larger power structures of Chicago. Like San Francisco, Chicago has an ethnically and racially diverse population. The largest minority groups are African-Americans and Hispanic-Americans (U.S. Bureau of the Census 2000). This diversity is reflected in the city's rich history of political and social activism. The African-American community in Chicago became organized in the 1960s, seeking to influence the distribution of resources in the city as a whole (Ferman 1991). Similarly, with the growing presence of immigrants from Central America and Puerto Rico to Chicago, Hispanic-Americans organized for social justice, confronted issues of poverty and health care, and sought to increase their voice in the local political system (Padilla 1985). Chicago also possesses a rich history of grassroots community organizing. Saul Alinsky's model of the mobilization of neighborhood groups was largely developed in Chicago. As a result, the city possesses a strong assortment of local associations, with examples including the Back of the Yards Neighborhood Council and the Woodlawn Organization (Boyte 1980).

As nonprofit organizations were formed that represented these new conceptions of community, they faced the challenge of resource acquisition. Like new nonprofits in other cities across the nation, the first strategy of some Chicago area charities was to obtain workplace funds. They initially sought to do so through by seeking membership in the United Way. They expressed criticisms of the United Way's pattern of resource distribution, claiming that it had been limited to a small number of large and mainstream nonprofit organizations. Despite the changing face of Chicago, these nonprofits argued that the United Way had not altered the ways in which it operated (Gronbjerg et al. 1996). One long-time member of the United Way summarized this perspective, noting that "some people have seen the United Way as sort of a white, male, corporate dominated bastion that could not possibly be sensitive to issues in the [other] communities of Chicago." By the 1970s, for example, African-American agencies threatened to picket campaign kick-offs at local companies unless "they were awarded a more equitable share of campaign proceeds" (*United Way Historical Summary* n.d., p. 3).

Yet, although the United Way in Chicago responded to these criticisms by expanding both its pool of affiliated agencies and its funding of new nonprofits, these changes were considered inadequate.[5] By 1980, for example, although 25 percent of United Way's member agencies were minority controlled, only 10 percent of the United Way's total allocations went to these nonprofits (United Way of Chicago 1990). In all, there was a growing awareness that the United Way/Crusade of Mercy could not meet the needs of nonprofit organizations representing the growth of new communities while maintaining its allegiance to existing member agencies.

By the early 1980s, these charities adopted a new strategy to gain access to workplace funds. Mimicking earlier developments in other cities, many independent nonprofits now coalesced together, taking the form of the Alternative Fund. In the process, their formation served to expand the conception of community present in workplace charity beyond that proffered by the United Way, with its emphasis on a local community. Instead, Alternative Funds represented a wider range of interests and identities, including the African-American community, women's rights, the environment, and social justice issues.

The most substantive rivalry to the United Way was provided by the five Alternative Funds formed at the state level. The earliest United Way rival to appear was Community Health Charities of Illinois (CHCIL), formed in 1982. Although several health research agencies had on-and-off again relationships with the United Way, CHCIL constituted the first coalition of a variety of health research causes. Representing a federation of thirty-six Illinois agencies, it distributed a half-million dollars in 2002 for the purposes of health research, patient services, and education. In its fundraising discourse, CHCIL presents itself as the health research equivalent of the United Way. Like the United Way, it provides companies and employees with the convenience of a "one-stop" opportunity for helping the community, but through the funding of health causes, rather than that those of health and human services (Community Health Charities of Illinois n.d.).

In 1986, the Black United Fund of Illinois (BUFI) was formed. Unlike the other Alternative Funds in Illinois, BUFI does not function as an umbrella organization for member agencies, but rather as an autonomous, foundation-like entity that raises funds and distributes grants to applicant charities. BUFI gathers contributions in the name of self-help by and for the African-American community of Illinois, specifically oriented around the issues of arts, education, economic development, health and social welfare, and social justice. The long-time president has emphasized that BUFI serves as a "vehicle that could be used very effectively in improving the quality of life in the Black Community" in that it allows for "Black people contributing their money, time and skills to help each other" (Drake 1998:4–5). In 1997, according to a representative, BUFI distributed almost $750,000 to thirty-one agencies.

The Illinois Women's Funding Federation (IWFF) came into being in 1987. Its sixteen member organizations provide a broad range of services in more than 100 sites across Illinois. With a motto of "Working to Improve the Lives of Illinois Women and their Families," IWFF raises awareness of and provides funding for issues specific to women as a distinct community, including domestic violence, sexual discrimination, and single parenthood, among others. IWFF began as an attempt at resource diversification by women's nonprofits in the Chicago area. Through the 1970s and 1980s, they largely had relied on support from four different foundations, both private and corporate, but these foundations had all folded by the late 1980s, resulting in a search for new sources of income. Consequently, these agencies created a United Way rival to represent agencies addressing women's concerns.

The Public Interest Fund of Illinois (PIFI) represents the fourth Alternative Fund to be formed in the state. In 2000,[6] PIFI gathered $180,000 for its membership of agencies. Started in 1990, this Alternative Fund was an expression of frustration on the part of social justice agencies with the United Way. Restricted from entering into a partnership with the United Way (as elsewhere across the nation), a health advocacy organization attempted unsuccessfully to obtain earmarked gifts through a United Way in central Illinois. Unhappy with the outcome, organizational leaders started PIFI as a way for social justice agencies to gain more systematic access to workplace charity.

Although PIFI members address a wide array of causes, including AIDS care, community development agencies, and disability rights, they share an emphasis on social advocacy. In workplace campaigns, PIFI positions itself as not only distinct from but also superior to the United Way by emphasizing the different set of methods that it employs to assist those in need. It portrays the United Way as soliciting charitable gifts for an old-fashioned version of philanthropy, one with "patronizing donors and helpless victims" (Public Interest Fund of Illinois 2000). PIFI and its member agencies embrace social change and constituency-controlled organizations as the means by which to eliminate the "social, economic, cultural, and political barriers" that prevent equal participation for all.

The final Alternative Fund to be formed was that of the Environmental Fund of Illinois (EFI), now called EarthShare of Illinois. Created in 1992, EFI distributed over a half-million dollars to twenty-six environmental and conservation member organizations in 2000. Like other Environmental funds, the EFI embodies and promotes the notion of a community of ecology. In its fundraising material, it advances the cause of the environment (and, consequently, that of its member agencies) by emphasizing the connection between the health of the local environment and that of potential donors. One flyer intended for employees notes, "By contributing to EFI, you can help to conserve natural land and wildlife, reduce pollution of our air and water, and improve the quality of life for you and your family" (Environmental Fund of Illinois n.d.).

These five local Alternative Funds constitute the major rivals for the United Way in Chicago. However, they are not the only competitors to the United Way. National fundraisers, including America's Charities, Earthshare of America, Independent Charities of America, and International Service Agencies, also participate in regional workplace campaigns. Some of these national funds are direct competitors with local Alternative Funds (and the United Way in Chicago) by gathering contributions for the same causes but on a different geographical scale, whereas others represent distinct and additional communities of purpose. In addition, a small number of independent, stand-alone charities participate in open workplace campaigns; these include the United Negro College Fund, Special Olympics, and the American Cancer Society.

Alternative Funds, then, represent a diverse set of causes and issues. As we saw in Chapter 3, they go beyond the United Way's conception of community by offering different criteria for membership in community, by employing different modes of facilitating community, and by relying on different scales of community. By seeking to compete alongside the United Way for employees' donations, they allow donors to contribute to a wide range of interests and identities, and they permit a more varied assortment of nonprofits, with an expanded sense of the public good, to gather once prohibited but highly valued resources. The question is why, despite the formation of these Alternative Funds, is workplace charity in Chicago still dominated by a traditional conception of community. As I show below, a place-based conception of community has remained central as the result of both the institutional environment and the United Way's successful response to any challenges to its own vision of community.

ACCESSING WORKPLACE CAMPAIGNS: THE ROLE OF GATEKEEPERS

We have seen that contestations over community between the United Way and Alternative Funds involve two different and successive sites of struggle. To compete for donors' contributions, an Alternative Fund, representing a particular conception of community, must first be granted access to campaigns by gatekeepers. Gatekeepers are those actors within workplaces who filter the fundraising appeals of nonprofit organizations to employees. They decide which charities will be allowed to participate in their workplace campaigns. Once permitted entry, organizations may then compete for donors' contributions with other fundraisers.

Similarly, once formed out of the local population of nonprofits, Alternative Funds in Chicago first faced the challenge of gaining access to workplace campaigns. These Alternative Funds followed the typical trajectory of entry for United Way rivals. They began their quest for entry in workplace charity by initially focusing on the public sector. Their first target was the largest workplace campaign in Illinois (within both the private and public sectors), that of the state of Illinois. The state's workplace campaign provides access to charitable contributions from over 350,000 employees. Although ultimately successful, Alternative Funds initially were unable to participate alongside the United Way in the Illinois state campaign. As has occurred so commonly elsewhere, these rivals gained access only with litigation. In the early 1980s, the ACLU successfully sued the state on behalf of several community organizations that had previously sought and failed to gain access to the state campaign (National Committee for Responsive Philanthropy 1986). In 1983, the state began to allow United Way rivals to participate.

These Alternative Funds have been granted access to other public sector workplace on a case-by-case basis, the result of a mixture of employee pressure, rallying by Alternative Funds, and/or the threat of litigation. By 2000, one or more Alternative Funds were participating in many city and county, school districts, and community college and university campaigns not only in the city of Chicago but also in Springfield (the state capital) and in Urbana-Champaign, the location of the flagship university of Illinois.

To expand on their gradual success in gaining access to public sector campaigns, Alternative Funds in Illinois sought to participate in workplace campaigns in the private sector. It was here, as representatives told me, that the majority of workplace revenue was to be collected. But they discovered that they faced a brick wall. Most Alternative Funds, with the exception of CHCIL, were unable to convince many local businesses of the merits of an open and competitive campaign. Diana Jacob, the head of one rival federated fundraiser, emphasized that by the early 1990s, "Chicago was way, way, way behind." Similarly, the long-time manager of one fund described the situation in Chicago as being one where "a lot of companies keep their doors closed, and limit access to one organization"; another representative of an Alternative Fund stated, "I know that it seems that it's been more difficult than in some other places."

The relative lack of success of Alternative Funds resulted from the particular nature of the institutional environment in Chicago, which consists of those shared understandings held by gatekeepers. To be granted access, Alternative Funds must fit gatekeepers' prior understandings of the legitimate scope of philanthropy. The institutional environment matters in workplace charity because gatekeepers tend to extend their existing understandings of philanthropy, derived from their own firms' charitable practices, to that of their employees' campaign.

In Chicago, the institutional environment had a particular understanding of philanthropy that undermined the legitimacy of Alternative Funds as viable workplace participants. By all accounts, local corporate gatekeepers held a centralized model of corporate philanthropy. In this view, the purpose of corporate philanthropy is to assist the local community, one based on place and propinquity. As explicated in Chapter 5, this is the model of philanthropy that has dominated corporate charity for much of the twentieth century. Here, philanthropy is premised on the needs of the local community and the principles of rationalization and efficiency, necessitating that professionals organize charitable activity.

A variety of scholarship corroborates this picture of corporate philanthropy in Chicago (Cmiel and Levy 1980). Peter Dobkin Hall (1992), for example, has argued that different regions possess different "technologies of collective action," entailing shared understandings of how philanthropy should be organized. In his comparative analysis of the United States, Hall concludes that Chicago's business leaders have historically demonstrated a technology of "federationism," in that they pursue the common good through a commitment to centralized entities, such as charity federations and community foundations.

A more systematic measure of the institutional environment can be found in an analysis of the corporate giving programs of Fortune 500 firms headquartered in a city.[7] Corporate giving programs constitute perhaps the best indicator of how firms conceive of and engage in philanthropy. Consider the stated charitable goals of a randomly sampled number of Fortune 500 corporations headquartered in Chicago in 1994.[8] Most noticeable in these findings is the level of support for a centralized view of philanthropy. Although some firms give to targeted and specific recipients, the majority of these firms demonstrated their commitment to a centralized model of philanthropy: a full two-thirds listed either the community or the United Way as a recipient area (Public Management Institute 1990). It is probable that other firms in the city follow suit: the charitable practices of companies headquartered in a locale tend to be adopted by other firms in the local community as well (Hughes 1994).

The extent of the local elite's commitment to a centralized model of philanthropy is also expressed in the composition of the United Way's board of directors in Chicago. Research has shown that the composition of a nonprofit's board of directors reflects its level of prestige in the community (Gronbjerg 1993; Bradshaw, Murray, and Wolpin 1996). In her seminal study of board composition for nonprofit organizations, Abzug (1996) analyzed the elite status of boards of directors in six major cities across the United States. In those six cities the mean percentage of board members listed in *Who's Who in America* was just over 15 percent. In Chicago, in marked contrast, more than one-third of the UW/CM's board members were listed in *Who's Who* in 1997, demonstrating a high level of support in Chicago on the part of the corporate community for a centralized model of philanthropy, as represented by the United Way.

This centralized model of philanthropy has been extended from corporations' own giving practices to their employees' giving programs. Given their commitment to the local community, firms have tended to equate workplace charity with the United Way. This view of Chicago businesses and their understandings of charity were articulated by members of the United Way. When asked to explain the relationship of the United Way in Chicago to local firms, Jocelyn Harris, a decade-long employee at the UW/CM, explains, "We've been really lucky. Big companies here have always tended to be large supporters of United Way." Similarly, a senior executive at a Chicago-based firm and a long-time volunteer at both the local United Way and at the United Way of America noted, "I have been told for years by people outside Chicago that the corporate leadership and the involvement cooperatively of the corporations is stronger here than elsewhere."

As a result of this understanding of philanthropy, gatekeepers in the private sector in Chicago failed to see the legitimacy of or the need for additional federated fundraisers. By the early 1990s, the field of workplace charity in Chicago had fundamentally altered, with the emergence of Alternative Funds as viable alternatives to the United Way. However, the particular nature of the institutional environment, with its emphasis on a local conception of community and a centralized model of philanthropy, prohibited Alternative Funds' access to donors within the private sector. Thus, the United Way retained its monopoly in most Chicago area workplace campaigns, the majority of donors remained limited in their giving to the United Way, and a traditional conception of community retained its place as the dominant logic of the field.

Trouble for the United Way

But the history of workplace charity in Chicago has not been quite so straightforward. Despite the initial support garnered from gatekeepers, the monopoly of the United Way has been disputed at particular moments by challenges from both inside and outside the local field of workplace charity. Since the early 1990s, the United Way has faced a fundamental threat to its legitimacy as the federated fundraiser in workplace charity, and it has confronted a restructuring of the region's economy. In addition, local Alternative Funds have adopted a new strategy of gaining access to workplace charity. This series of events have served not only to alter the nature of the institutional environment but also to minimize its salience for gatekeepers' decisions. At each historical moment, however, the United Way has implemented strategic responses that have served to mitigate the potential appeal of rival fundraisers.

Scandal at the United Way of America

The first event to affect the composition of the institutional environment was generated from outside the local field of workplace charity. In 1992, a scandal at the United Way of America unfolded. Extensive and ongoing media reports revealed that the president of the United Way of America, William Aramony, had received a salary of almost $500,000 and had extravagant and questionable spending habits (Haider 1995). As a result of the scandal and subsequent prosecution of Aramony, individual donors and corporations across the United States halted or decreased their contributions to most United Ways. In 1993, the total revenue for all United Ways precipitously dropped by $130 million (Millar 1994).

The scandal had similar implications for the United Way in Chicago, despite its being an entity separate from the United Way of America. The incident raised public questions about the legitimacy of the financial practices of the United Way/Crusade of Mercy (Smith 1992). Donors, according to surveys conducted by the UW/CM, displayed a startlingly high level of distrust of the organization (United Way/Crusade of Mercy 1997a). Not surprisingly, the incident at the United Way of America resulted in a severe decline in giving to the UW/CM. After the Aramony scandal, as shown in Figure 4, the United Way's revenue for the next annual campaign dropped from around $105 million to $95 million, a decline of 10 percent in one year.

More troubling for the United Way/Crusade of Mercy were many firms' responses to the Aramony scandal. A substantial number of corporations, either alone or in response to pressure from their employees, felt that the local United Way had lost its legitimacy. Although their commitment to a centralized model of philanthropy had not changed, the United Way was no longer perceived as the best mechanism by which to assist the local community. Firm leaders questioned whether the United Way now deserved the privilege of a monopoly. The Aramony scandal threatened to undo the United Way's successful control over workplace charity and to permit Alternative Fund in as rival fundraisers.

Yet, the United Way prevented such an outcome by its adoption of a policy of donor choice in 1993. Rather than face competitors, it sought to maintain

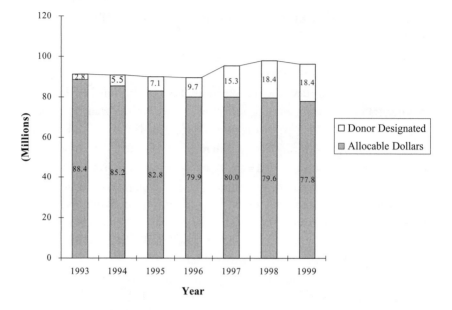

Figure 4 Pattern of Giving to the United Way/Crusade of Mercy

its monopoly by allowing donors to designate their charitable gifts to other United Ways, specific causes and issues, and other unaffiliated charities. As I noted in the last chapter, a United Way policy of donor choice permits donors to give to a wider and more varied conception of community. It allows giving to communities of purpose without allowing in the workplace campaign their institutionalized counterparts in the form of Alternative Funds.

The United Way/Crusade of Mercy gambled that its implementation of donor choice would appease local firms by surrendering its previous control over fund distribution. It chose the potential risks inherent to donor choice over the certain and unpleasant consequences of having gatekeepers allow in Alternative Funds. And, as it turns out, the United Way's adoption of a policy of donor choice did convince the majority of corporations to maintain a United Way monopoly. However, as we see later in the chapter, although the policy of donor choice did "fix" the problem of the Aramony scandal, it also possessed ramifications for the United Way. But, after the scandal, the United Way maintained its monopoly, despite its loss of legitimacy with local business leaders.

Alternative Funds as Workplace Campaign Managers

At the same time, although the United Way had successfully avoided the potentially negative ramifications of the Aramony scandal, other changes were occurring within the local field of workplace charity. In different ways, two events served to undermine the institutional environment's support for the United Way and for a traditional conception of community. In so doing, Alternative Funds gained access to a larger, albeit still limited, number of workplace campaigns within the private sector.

First, Alternative Funds sought to change the decision-making process of gatekeepers, both in the private and public sectors. Previously, as discussed above, they had faced an organizational field where the institutional environment did not grant them legitimacy. Corporate gatekeepers largely refused their requests for participation in their employee campaigns. Alternative Funds responded by turning to another route by which to facilitate their inclusion in workplace charity. Some of these fundraisers no longer seek to gather funds alongside the United Way as a charitable entity. Instead, they have garnered access to workplace funds through the financial management of the workplace campaign.

Corporations rarely manage their employees' annual fund drive. Although firms could supervise the process on their own through a process commonly known as an in-plant federation (Polivy 1985), the vast majority have historically allowed the United Way to oversee the process. The United Way has served as the "fiscal agent," which involves not only distributing donations as specified by donors but also the production and processing of pledge forms, the development of reports on employees' giving for employers, and the compilation of donor acknowledgment cards. In exchange for such work, the United Way has taken a set percentage of total contributions as overhead and retained all nondistributable gifts.

In Chicago, following the lead of United Way rivals in other states, some Alternative Funds have sought to manage these workplace campaigns. In doing so, they have turned the challenge of entry from a philanthropic process into a market-based, competitive one. Here, one or more Alternative Funds make a bid to a local firm, offering to manage its campaign for a set percentage of all donations. Senior management chooses the organization that promises the most services for the lowest cost. In Chicago, the Public Interest Fund of Illinois and the Black United Fund of Illinois have begun competing alongside the United Way to manage public and private sector campaigns. In several cases, gatekeepers have chosen an Alternative Fund over the United Way to serve as fiscal agent.

Acting as a fiscal agent for a workplace campaign has one key benefit for United Way rivals. By successfully bidding to manage the campaign, the Alternative Fund (and its member agencies) has then also gained access to compete alongside the United Way for donors' gifts. It allows them and often other Alternative Funds as well to participate where before management typically did not allow them to do so. The head of one Alternative Fund in Chicago explained to me why his organization began bidding to manage workplace campaigns:

> One benefit is that as we've gotten in the last two or three years into managing campaigns, it's helped us to open new campaigns. . . . So, when we've opened up workplace campaigns in the last couple of years, at least larger ones, it is because we're managing the campaign and that gives us a reason for the employer to have us in, because they want us running their workplace campaign for them.

By acting as campaign managers, Alternative Funds have minimized the importance of the institutional environment. They have altered the criteria by which gatekeepers allow in competitors to the United Way. They have, in the words of a CEO of an Alternative Fund, "leapfrogged" over the gatekeepers. Now, rather than considering the inclusion of Alternative Funds from a philanthropic perspective, these actors now view this decision from an economic perspective. The outcome has been that, in a small but growing number of workplaces, Alternative Funds have gained access to employees' donations.

The Restructuring of the Local Economy

A second event that altered the composition of the field of workplace charity in Chicago was the restructuring of the region's economy in the 1990s. Historically dominated by manufacturing, the Chicago area economy experienced a diversification of its economic base. In a related development, the growth of a global economy resulted in a decline in firms located in Chicago, a city once characterized by the strong presence of corporate headquarters,

These two developments served to alter corporations' commitment to the local community and to facilitate the quest of Alternative Funds to seek entry to Chicago area workplace campaigns.

The growth of the city of Chicago has been intrinsically tied to the strength of its manufacturing sector. Manufacturing is central to its identity: the city of Chicago evokes images of smokestacks, steel mills, and a "city of strong shoulders." In 1990, for example, manufacturing surpassed all other categories of employment except for trade, transportation, and utilities (Carpenter 2003). Through the 1960s to the late 1980s, however, the region underwent deindustrialization and experienced a slow decline in manufacturing employment. Although manufacturing has continued to shrink in importance, over the last decade, the region's economy has been restructured and diversified, and other sectors have emerged as viable alternatives. The service sector, particular in the form of financial services, such as consulting and accounting, has grown in importance. Between 1993 and 1999, for example, jobs in manufacturing declined by 17 percent, whereas jobs in the service sector increased by 21 percent. By 1999, the service sector constituted almost half (43%) of all employment in Chicago (Reinhold 2000).

As part and parcel of this reorganization, Chicago's economy has been geographically rescaled. Local firms are increasingly embedded within the global marketplace (Podgorski and Stuenkel 1994). This shift affected the United Way in that the number of companies with headquarters in the city area decreased. In 1974, the greater Chicago area included 48 Fortune 500 corporations (*Fortune* 1975). The presence of corporate headquarters in Chicago had constituted a boon for the city as a whole and the United Way. Corporations possess a higher degree of civic commitment to those regions where their headquarters are located (Galaskiewicz 1985; Blum and Gray 1998). Locally headquartered companies possess the "largest corporate contributions to the United Way . . . , the largest average contributions by individual employees to the United Way, and the most active involvement by their leaders in prominent local civic and cultural organizations" (Hughes 1994, as cited in Kanter 2000).

Like elsewhere, the Chicago economy was influenced by the rise of a global economy. Starting in the 1990s, mergers, acquisitions, and closures stripped the city of numerous corporate headquarters, including Ameritech, Amoco, Continental Bank, Illinois Central, Inland Steel, Marshall Field's,

Morton International, and Montgomery Ward, to name just a few. By 1999, about half of Chicago's largest public companies that were headquartered there in 1979 were no longer in existence or were located elsewhere (Crown and Hinz 1999). The result of these economic changes has been a shake-up in the model and practices of corporate philanthropy in the city's private sector. One member of the UW/CM's board of directors highlighted the impact of recent changes in the local economy for the United Way. Asked to identify the major challenges recently faced by the United Way, he began by noting that one key obstacle was the "changing nature of corporations. The big companies tended to be large supporters of United Way and, you know, you started to see more competition; with companies leaving Chicago – that has an impact."

However, the implications for workplace charity of this new economy have not been straightforward. On the one hand, the changing economic structure of the Chicago area resulted in a diminished commitment on the part of corporations to the well-being of the local community (Gronbjerg et al. 1996). As Chicago area firms were taken over or moved elsewhere, their centralized model of philanthropy was disappearing. Over the last two decades, for example, the Chicago area has lost nearly two dozen company foundation and related donation programs, costing the area's philanthropic community about $15 to $20 million a year (Crown and Hinz 1999; Podgorski and Stuenkel 1994). In addition, some firms have implemented a new, decentralized model of philanthropy based on their own needs, rather than those of the local community. Strategic philanthropy has become increasingly commonplace in Chicago. It serves the interests of the company, linking the company's charitable activity to their bottom line (Saiia, Carroll, and Buchholtz 2003). As these local firms implemented a policy of strategic philanthropy, their relationship to workplace charity also changed.

In Chicago, Kraft Foods™ serves as an example of strategic philanthropy in workplace charity. Kraft Foods is now a subsidiary of Altria,™ a large multi-conglomerate firm formerly known as Philip Morris, Inc.™ Kraft Foods had a long history in the Midwest area of providing corporate support to the local community. However, as part of the change in brand name to that of Altria, Kraft Foods began a new plan of strategic philanthropy in the 1990s oriented around fighting hunger and promoting healthy lifestyles (Kraft Foods 2005b). The goal of the new program was to extend the image of Altria beyond simply that of a tobacco company (Branch 2001).

This turn to strategic philanthropy affected the company's organization of its employees' workplace drive. Historically, beginning in the 1940s, Kraft Foods had encouraged its employees to give to the United Way. In 1996, Altria (then still known as Philip Morris Companies, Inc.) created its own employee fund as an alternative to a United Way-only campaign. Workers' donations were to be distributed to their local community based on employees' interests and community needs, but also to "complement the company's contributions programs, reinforcing the company's position and social impact in the community" (Munemitsu and Knowlton 2004, p. 9). In 2004, the Kraft Employee Fund gathered $4 million from employees and the company itself in 2004 (Kraft Foods 2005a).

Although some firms have ended or shifted their philanthropic practices, a number of firms that remained headquartered in Chicago sought to counter these economic trends. Beginning in the early 1990s, locally engaged members of the corporate community developed a plan of civic revivification, seeking to address the consequences of the changing economy for the city of Chicago (Haider 1999).[9] The city's Commercial Club embarked on a civic renewal plan, called "Metropolis 2020," that attempted to counter the negative repercussions of the local economy's transition from manufacturing to financial services. The goal of Metropolis 2020 was the formulation of policy guidelines for the optimal organization of the private, public, and the nonprofit sectors in the region (Johnson 1999).

In part, Metropolis 2020 reflected a larger sea change in attitudes toward public policy that had begun to occur in the late 1970s. The Reagan administration had enacted drastic cuts in the federal government's provision of social service, either devolving funding to the state and local level or contracting out to nonprofit organizations. Its actions were premised on the widespread conservative belief that the public good should be met by the nonprofit sector, rather than by big government (Berger and Neuhaus 1977; Hall 1992). As government support of social services declined, community leaders across the nation turned to new actors and mechanisms by which to address local needs. As Smith (1999) points out, many turned to the United Way as a long-standing and centralized means by which to generate resources and coordinate the delivery of services.

Similarly, given the increasing precariousness of corporate philanthropy in Chicago and the decline in government assistance, the Commercial Club turned to the United Way as the intermediary system by which to ensure the health and well-being of the city (United Way/Crusade of Mercy 1998). Overall, Metropolis 2020 led to a renewed commitment by the elite to a centralized model of philanthropy, most clearly expressed in changes in the trusteeship of the United Way. Corporate interests took over many senior positions, including that of the president. As one senior volunteer at the UW/CM notes, "The United Way in Chicago had been on the back burner for some local CEOs, but now a greater amount of attention is being given to us by the executive community."

Soliciting for Charitable Contributions

By the mid-1990s, there was a growing awareness among many participants in workplace charity that the United Way was no longer the only game in town. The United Way faced growing competition from organizational representatives of new communities. The United Way could not rely on local firms as gatekeepers to ensure its position as a monopoly, as the result of economic changes and a new tactic by rivals. It faced near universal rivalry from Alternative Funds in the public sector, and in the private sector, a small number of firms were permitting Alternative Funds to compete. By 2000, local funds participated in anywhere from four to fifty private campaigns. According to their representatives, about 10 to 25 percent of all revenue for Alternative Funds was generated from the private sector in Chicago.

Additionally, the United Way faced a different kind of competition as the result of its earlier implementation of donor choice. Even in those campaigns in which the United Way enjoyed a monopoly, donors were now able to earmark their gifts to specific recipients. By 1997, over 70 percent of local companies with workplace campaigns had some form of donor designation in their campaign – either through the United Way or an open campaign (Haider 1997). Donors were increasingly directing their gifts away from the United Way. Figure 3 tracks the growth of earmarked gifts in nominal dollars. Gifts designated by donors increased from 3 percent of all revenue in 1993 to almost 19 percent in 1998. In real dollar terms, contributors' earmarked dollars grew from $2.8 million to $18.4 million over that same period. Although this amount may still appear minimal, continued growth at the same rate appeared probable, given the existence of other United Ways that had as much as 80 percent of all funds earmarked by donors (Cordes et al. 1999).

It was at this stage in the trajectory of workplace charity in Chicago that contestation between opposing conceptions of community began to take on a new form and content. No longer was it solely centered on the question of whether Alternative Funds could obtain access to employee campaigns. Now, in the form of both federated fundraisers and earmarked nonprofits, the struggle over community expanded to include competition for donors' contributions. Yet, as we saw at the beginning of the chapter, a traditional conception of community has remained the central and defining model of community in Chicago. To account for this outcome, it becomes necessary to turn to the proactive maneuvers employed by the United Way to defend the traditional conception of community on which it relied.

THE UNITED WAY RESPONDS

Given the growing threat of competition, the United Way sought to minimize the appeal of rivals to donors. It did so by implementing two distinct but simultaneous strategies: differentiation and resource diversification. The United Way began by adopting a strategy of differentiation in 1998 (Barman 2002). In general, the strategic response of differentiation involves two distinct steps on the part of nonprofit organizations (Han 1994; Moore 1996). First, in a situation of competition, nonprofits contend with rivals over a finite amount of external support. In response, they seek to maintain or increase their share of a crowded market (Gronbjerg 1993). Nonprofits work to convince environmental actors that they, rather than their competitors, deserve resources. To that end, organizations present a claim of uniqueness or difference from rivals within their field. Second, to differentiate themselves, nonprofit organizations must assert uniqueness based on a particular measure. Differentiation entails the construction of a hierarchical relationship between nonprofits and their rivals according to a certain scale.

In the case of Chicago, the United Way engaged in differentiation by seeking to convince donors of the benefits of a contribution to the United Way over that of rivals. The United Way offered donors a new narrative of giving based around the concept of community. The United Way asserted that a gift to itself was a gift to a local, place-based conception of community.

Previously, with a United Way policy of donor choice, individuals had a number of options: they could make an undesignated gift to the United Way, designate within the United Way (to particular issues such as health or children), or earmark their gift to an unaffiliated charity. Now, with a strategy of differentiation, the United Way changed the beneficiary of an undesignated gift from being the United Way to being the "Community Fund." On the pledge card given to donors, the Community Fund was defined as the distribution of the gift to "organizations that local United Way volunteers have determined to be most effective and most efficient in meeting our community's critical needs" (United Way/Crusade of Mercy 1999). In its public discourse, the UW/CM repeatedly emphasized that the Community Fund targeted the community as a whole, helping "family, friends, and neighbors" and "people of need in all segments of society."

In its new strategy of solicitation, the United Way/Crusade of Mercy attempted to rhetorically persuade donors of the merits of an undesignated gift to the community (or the United Way) over that of an earmarked gift to a specific nonprofit, cause, or issue. For United Way staff and volunteers, this new strategy of solicitation was designed to dissuade donors from sending their contributions to other nonprofits in two ways. First, most competitors – either individual charities or federated fundraisers – gather resources for a single community of purpose. The United Way in Chicago was certainly cognizant of the narrowness of its competitors' missions. One 1993 report noted that "the number and variety of fundraising federations seeking access to the workplace has grown to a point where there are now funds for virtually every category of need (e.g., specialized medical needs, women's issues, minority needs)" (United Way/Crusade of Mercy 1993). The United Way thus made donors aware of the nature of its competitors. An earmarked gift to a rival, the fundraiser asserted in its solicitation material, would only assist a few individuals or groups in the local Chicago community.

In contrast, an undesignated gift to the Community Fund would help many people in Chicago. One United Way pamphlet, addressed to corporate executives, concludes, "Unlike most charitable organizations that raise funds for a single cause, United Way addresses a wide variety of community needs" (*United Way Historical Summary* n.d.). To demonstrate this point, the United Way/Crusade of Mercy, in its solicitation material, bombarded the donor with the sheer range, frequency, and volume of services and resources provided by the Community Fund to the local Chicago-area community. A handout to employees notes that contributions to the UW/CM last year "touched" 862,000 children, 246,000 people with basic needs (including food and shelter), 211,000 individuals with disabilities, 274,000 seniors, 330,000 individuals needing counseling, and 100,000 individuals with health needs (United Way/Crusade of Mercy 1998c).

Second, the appeal of the Community Fund was premised on the United Way's understanding of the concerns of donors. In this view, donors are sympathetic to a local model of community, but do not believe that they possess a clear sense of how to best facilitate the public good. They are overwhelmed and confused by the number and variety of charities now present in the non-profit sector and to which they could designate their gift. In one pamphlet, potential givers are told, "It's everybody's job to ensure that we have strong, safe and nurturing communities. But sometimes we just don't know how to help. That's why United Way is here" (United Way/Crusade of Mercy 1998c). The Community Fund solved this problem for donors by allowing them to give one gift that would assist the whole of the community. A long-time staff member expressed this same understanding of donors. She stated that "our donors are interested in designation, but they don't have time to make the decision, so if you can convince them that the Community Fund is a good thing, that's what they're going to give to."

The United Way's strategy of differentiation was aimed at convincing donors of the merit of a gift to the local community over an earmarked gift to a single community of purpose. The United Way sought to show that a gift to the local community, through the United Way, would prove to be the optimal investment for donors, providing greater results (in terms of numbers of individuals served) than a gift to a single nonprofit representing a specific community of purpose. Donors, it was hoped, would choose "quantity over quality," in the words of one United Way staff, when choosing the recipient of their gift.

At the same time, and also in response to competition for donors' contributions, the UW/CM adopted a second and parallel strategy. It diversified its resources, going beyond mass fundraising among employees within the workplace. An organization engages in resource diversification when it alters its revenue stream to reduce its dependence on funds gathered in a particular setting and/or to obtain additional resources (Gronbjerg 1993; Froelich

1999). In a situation of competition, an organization diversifies so as to increase the proportion of total revenue gathered in other fundraising arenas with no or less rivalry. Consequently, a charity changes the composition of resources derived from different types of donors, earned income/fee-for-service, donations, or government contracts.

The United Way/Crusade of Mercy adopted a strategy of resource diversification to minimize its dependence on donors who had charitable choices. It sought to enter a resource environment where it did not need to compete for donors' contributions and where Alternative Funds lacked legitimacy. Beginning in 1995, the United Way in Chicago turned to "leadership giving" – contributions of over $1,000 by individuals – as its new and optimal source of revenue.[10] A focused leadership giving campaign commenced, with public recognition of donors and the creation of named levels of gifts. Those individuals who gave $10,000 or more, for example, were listed in UW/CM publicity material as members of the Alexis de Tocqueville Club.

For the United Way, leadership giving was a means to prevent donations to other organizations. Leadership gifts held appeal for the United Way because donors overwhelmingly chose the United Way as the recipient of their gift. Thus, the United Way pursued leadership giving as a responsive strategy to the growing rivalry of Alternative Funds representing new communities. A senior executive at the UW/CM, for example, summarized this understanding of the nature of leadership giving. Speaking at a training meeting for loaned executives, he augmented the formal presentation by confiding to audience members, "We do well with leadership givers, who really have low rates of donor choice. What we need to, what we would like to do is extend this pattern of giving to all of our donors. That would be really nice." During staff training, individuals were told to encourage leadership giving by individual employees, in part because there is "very little designation with leadership gifts."

The United Way's two strategic responses of differentiation and resource diversification were intended to minimize the presence of competition by discouraging donors in Chicago from directing their gift to other federated fundraisers or nonprofits. Taken together, these two strategies have been largely successful. Although systematic figures on giving to Alternative Funds are not available, the rate of designation through the United Way does display a marked decline in the wake of the United Way's tactics.

Previously, designation had steadily increased from 1994 through 1999. In the year before the adoption of a strategy of differentiation, for example, contributors in Chicago earmarked almost 20 percent of the total revenue. After the tactics of differentiation and resource diversification were implemented, the percentage designated by donors did not increase from the previous year. To the contrary, as shown in Figure 4, it actually declined to 17.5 percent of total revenue in that year's campaign and remained at about that level in the next two years as well (United Way Metro Chicago 2003). Or, as a senior executive at UW/CM concluded, "The strategic maneuver to see if the United Way can convince donors to give to the United Way has...been successful." Clearly, the United Way in Chicago was successful in its attempt to direct charitable gifts away from Alternative Funds and other nonprofits representing communities of purpose and to a communities of place.

Conclusion

In Chicago, despite the formation of Alternative Funds, workplace charity has remained oriented around the United Way and its vision of community. I have claimed that the persistence of "place" results from organizational contestations within institutional constraints. Workplace charity in Chicago has been shaped by the decisions of gatekeepers in the private sector. Continuing a long-standing commitment to community, local business leaders were committed to a centralized model of philanthropy as a means to ensure the vitality of the city. At moments and in sites in which a place-based conception of community was challenged, the United Way responded in ways that cemented its intermediary position between donors and recipients.

CHAPTER 7

San Francisco: The Ascendancy of Communities of Purpose

Thank you for supporting your community through United Way of the Bay Area. Your gift is being distributed according to your wishes – ensuring that your contribution achieves the results you want.

— DONORS' CARD, UNITED WAY OF THE BAY AREA

The field of workplace charity in San Francisco looks very different from that in Chicago. In all, it is characterized by the decline of the traditional, place-based conception of community. More than anywhere else, workplace charity in San Francisco has been reconfigured around a new model of community. Individual donors can and do give to a variety of interests and identities. A wide range of nonprofit organizations representing multiple causes and constituencies – in the form of both Alternative Funds and independent nonprofits – compete for donations. The United Way itself has abandoned the discourse of a traditional community and ceded the field to multiple communities of purpose. In order to prosper, the United Way has reoriented itself so as to facilitate new and particularistic conceptions of the public good.

The question here is how and why workplace charity in the Bay Area went from being organized around a community of place to being organized around multiple communities of purpose. As in the case of Chicago, I argue that the particular configuration of the field in San Francisco was not determined by the ecological or resource composition of the field. Instead, the centrality of a particularistic community in the Bay Area can be understood

as the result of organizational contestations over community within a particular institutional setting.

San Francisco: Communities of Purpose

Like many other United Ways, the United Way of the Bay Area (UWBA)
emerged out of the Progressive movement. In 1922, a number of local Community Chests were formed by civic leaders and social service professionals
to rationalize the provision of charity. In the post-World War II period, these
Community Chests faced competition from health research agencies. Like
others elsewhere, these federations had stopped campaigning during World
War II and were replaced by a War Chest for national war relief. Consequently, after the war, Community Chests had lost their established right to
a monopoly, and the field of workplace charity was open to rival federated
fundraisers. By 1952, in response to the competitive environment, many Bay
Area workplaces had implemented a single fund drive, the San Francisco
Federated Fund, which combined the campaigns of Community Chest and
some national health agencies.

The basis for the current United Way was established in 1965 when a
single fundraising and fund allocation organization was formed for five Bay
Area counties. In 1997, the UWBA broadened its arena of activity to operate in seven Bay Area counties: Alameda, Contra Costa, Marin, Napa,
San Francisco, San Mateo, and Solano. In 2002, nearly 700 workplaces and
around 400,000 employees participated in United Way-sponsored workplace
campaigns. In all, the United Way gathered $52 million in that year (United
Way of the Bay Area 2002).

Earlier than in other cities, the United Way in San Francisco faced criticism from external actors. More than elsewhere in the United States, San
Francisco has been home to alternative communities of identities and interests. The city has witnessed a "plethora of causes, cultural phenomena
and social movements" since its formation in the mid-nineteenth century
(Matthews 1997:211). Its origins in the Gold Rush, its status as a port city, and
its decentralized political structure have created what some have called "hyper
pluralism" and what other observers see as a vibrant assortment of coalitions
and groups (Wolf 1979; Castells 1983; Browning, Marshall, and Tabb 1984;

DeLeon 1992). San Francisco has been home to communities based around race, ethnicity, gender and sexual orientation, as well as the anti-war, consumer rights, and environmental movements. These movements quickly took organizational form, resulting in a proliferation of nonprofit organizations in the 1960s and 1970s (U.S. Census of Service Industries 1982; Harder, Kimmich, and Salamon 1985). As in other cities, these organizations sought to obtain revenue and quickly turned to workplace charity as one potential funding arena.

These nonprofit organizations first attempted to gain access to workplace contributions through the UWBA. As in Chicago, they made similar criticisms of United Way's traditional mode of fund distribution. Beginning in the late 1960s, various racial and ethnic groups in the Bay Area, including African-Americans, Latinos, and Asians (Brilliant 1990), charged the United Way, then called the United Bay Area Crusade (UBAC), with institution- alized racism. They claimed that United Way resources were directed primarily to white and middle-class agencies and clients, that the UBAC was run by people with "embedded, middle-class interests," and that it needed to include more minority groups in its power structure (Shepherd 1977:1020). These interest groups formed a campaign called "Boycott the UBAC," which raised awareness about the issue and encouraged companies to prohibit the UBAC from raising funds in their workplaces (United Bay Area Crusade 1969).

These charges were exacerbated by criticisms leveled at the United Way by other community groups as well. A local organization, Concerned Citizens for Charity, waged a widely publicized attack on the UBAC (Roberts 1977). As newspaper reports of the time attest, Concerned Citizens for Charity re- ceived much attention from the press for its criticism of the UWBA (Waugh 1977). Recalling the group's efforts, a retired United Way executive noted that it is "hard now to believe how much power the group had in the me- dia." Another group, the Bay Area Committee for Responsive Philanthropy, published a report that severely criticized the United Way for failing to in- corporate newer and more progressive nonprofits into their membership of agencies (Bay Area Committee for Responsive Philanthropy 1979).

The United Way of the Bay Area's response to these criticisms was more substantive than that of the United Way in Chicago, but still remained largely ceremonial in nature. In 1969, the UWBA announced its "New Direction"

program, which allocated $200,000 in funding to "poverty and popula-
tion growth areas" and incorporated a more representative cross-sample of
donors, clients, and agencies onto its board of directors. In 1976, the UWBA
again altered its funding pattern, giving away more than $18 million to an ex-
panded pool of 189 agencies (Brilliant 1990). But, as with the case of Chicago,
these changes in membership and revenue distribution were seen as less than
satisfactory by external critics, according to past executives of the UWBA.
Many nonprofit organizations turned to Alternative Funds as an alternative
mechanism to gather workplace donations.

The first Alternative Fund emerged from the long-standing competition
between the United Way and health agencies. Begun in 1971, the Combined
Health Agencies Drive's (CHAD) emphasis is on the well-being of the local
community. Unlike the United Way, however, which stresses the social welfare of residents, the CHCC argues that the health of the local community is
determined by the physical health of its individual members. In 2000, CHCC
comprised more than fifty independent agencies, as well as local and state
affiliates of national health research charities. It raised $6 million toward
patient services, community education, and medical research (Community
Health Charities 2001).

Three more competing federated fundraisers were formed in the 1980s.
The first Environmental fund in the nation, the Environmental Fund of
California, was formed in 1982. Organized by leaders of local environmental organizations, the EFC sought to counter declining federal government
support for environment regulation and to diversify sources of revenue for
its members. As with a number of other Alternative Funds, it was initially
formed to gain access to write-in gifts through the United Way's policy
of donor choice. Initially, the EFC advertised widely and was quite successful in gathering funds. However, the United Way then forbade it to
advertise. In response, the EFC reorganized as an independent Alternative
Fund (Bothwell 1998). The Environmental Fund of California represents
eighty-seven organizations across the state, divided into seven local regions.
In 2000, it raised a total of $1,750,000.

In 1986, an assortment of progressively oriented social action groups
formed an Alternative Fund to gather revenue independently in the workplace. Led by two activist sisters with the support of the National Committee of Responsive Philanthropy, the Progressive Way represented a shared

frustration on the part of its members that the UWBA was not adequately funding social justice issues. In 1999, the Progressive Way merged with a similar fund, the Common Counsel Foundation in Oakland. In 2000, the newly renamed Social and Economic Justice Fund gathered almost $100,000, which was distributed through an open, competitive granting process to Bay Area nonprofit organizations fighting poverty, injustice, and discrimination (Social and Economic Justice Fund 2001).

The fourth of the United Way rivals in San Francisco is the Bay Area Black United Fund (BABUF). As with other Black United Funds, its mission is to facilitate philanthropy, leadership, and self-empowerment within the local African-American community. The origins of BABUF are quite different from that of other local United Way rivals in San Francisco. BABUF was originally formed by the local United Way in 1979 as an "affinity group," with the support of a coalition of local African-American leaders and nonprofits. By 1986, however, it had broken off its partnership with the UWBA and sought access as an independent fundraiser (Brilliant 1990). In 2000, BABUF raised over a quarter-million dollars in fund development support for its federation of thirty-eight member nonprofits (typically small organizations with annual budgets of under $350,000).

As with Chicago, these four local Alternative Funds constituted the main source of rivalry for the United Way, but they were not the only rival federated fundraisers in existence. Many national funds entered the field of workplace charity in the Bay Area in the 1980s and later. In addition, a large number of independent local nonprofits, representing a broad range of causes, also began to participate in Bay Area workplace campaigns on a regular basis. As we see below, however, the participation of a wider and larger group in San Francisco reflects a more complicated relationship between the United Way and its rivals than in Chicago.

Given that a particularistic conception of community has become the dominant model for workplace charity in the Bay Area, the task becomes to account for why this transformation has occurred. To do so, three developments must be explained: the entry of rivals into workplace campaigns, the distribution of contributions to organizational representatives of new communities, and the reorganization of the United Way itself. As before, I emphasize organizational contestations within institutional constraints. In San Francisco, unlike in Chicago, local firms possessed a historical affinity for a decentralized model of philanthropy. But the current situation in San Francisco does not represent the linear unfolding of that cultural logic. Instead, it was determined by the efforts of both the United Way and Alternative Funds to pursue their interests within that specific context. As I have already noted, these interactions unfold in a two-stage process: Alternative Funds must first obtain access to workplace sites, and then once they have access, participating fundraisers compete over charitable contributions.

Gaining Access to Workplace Charity: Gatekeepers in San Francisco

Alternative Funds in the Bay Area followed a similar historical trajectory as those in Chicago in their quest to obtain permission to solicit for workplace contributions. They employed the same twofold sequential strategy, drawing upon two different mechanisms to gain entry. Beginning in the early 1980s, Alternative Funds in the Bay Area began by targeting workplace campaigns in the public sector. There was a precedent, in that one important campaign in the state had already been opened up by another Alternative Fund: the Brotherhood Crusade in Los Angeles, the first Black United Fund to be formed, had successfully sued for access to the Combined Federal Campaign in 1970. Alternative Funds then set their sights on the state of California's workplace campaign, acquiring access through litigation. By the middle of that decade, many public sector campaigns in the Bay Area, including that of the city of San Francisco, all of the county governments in the area, and the University of California at Berkeley, had allowed in competition without undue struggle. United Way rivals then set their sights on "semi-private" campaigns, gaining access to many utilities, school boards, and hospitals (National Committee for Responsive Philanthropy 1986). The leader of one Alternative Fund recounted that the organization had easily joined around thirty public sector campaigns within the first few years of its existence.

As in Chicago, Alternative Funds next turned to the challenge of gaining access to workplace campaigns within the private sector. Here, unlike their counterparts in Chicago, they were assisted in this process by the institutional environment of the local field. In Chicago, the local corporate elites were committed to a centralized vision of philanthropy. In contrast, many gatekeepers in the Bay Area held a decentralized model of philanthropy. Firms in the Bay Area from the 1960s had consistently tended to privilege the desires and demands of donors over the needs of the community as articulated by social service professionals. In all, the Bay Area elite viewed philanthropy as a mechanism for donors (either individuals or firms) to realize their own interests. Therefore, companies' relationships with the United Way in San Francisco were more flexible. Although local corporations might affiliate with the United Way to gather contributions, many were not adverse to and even saw the benefits of an open campaign with multiple participants.

A view of Bay Area corporate philanthropy as centered on donor demands has been expressed by participants in the field. Jean Beaman, a senior UWBA executive for over a decade, explained the relationship between the United Way in San Francisco and local firms. She noted that, for the United Way, "the only way to keep up a relationship with bigger companies was to try and offer more than just health and human services. They weren't really interested in those kinds of things, and that made it really tough for us because that's really what we were supposed to be doing as a United Way." Comments of this nature, expressing frustration with the philanthropic goals of local businesses, were frequently made by UWBA members when asked to describe the nature of the region's corporate community.

In addition, scholars have found that institutional donors in the Bay Area have more innovative patterns of funding than in other large cities (Williams 1990; Tepperman 1995). In his comprehensive survey of philanthropy in the city, for example, Shepherd (1977:1020) determined that corporations and foundations in San Francisco possessed a unique pattern of giving; they "spread the money out more" than elsewhere. These attitudes toward philanthropy reflect the larger culture of the city. In his study of the Bay Area, Manuel Castells (1983) emphasized that community organizations played an important role in San Francisco's decentralized power structure, and consequently, the city "became a space of co-existing interests and cultures" (p. 105).

As with the case of Chicago, the dominance of a particular model of philanthropy can be illustrated through more systematic measures. For one, as discussed in the last chapter, attitudes toward philanthropy are enacted in local corporations' giving programs. Bay Area companies embody the philosophy of strategic philanthropy: only three of the eleven firms head-quartered in San Francisco in 1990 directed their gifts to the community or the United Way. In contrast, two-thirds of those firms in Chicago listed the community or the United Way as recipients. The majority of corporations in the Bay Area send their contributions to a particularly narrow and specific set of interests, such as forestry education or family violence (Public Management Institute 1990; *Fortune* 1995).

Take the example of Levi Strauss & Co™, the fashion retailing company headquartered in San Francisco. Founded in 1853, the privately owned firm employs 1,250 people in the Bay Area and over 11,000 worldwide. The company makes charitable donations through two entities: the corporation itself and the Levi Strauss Foundation (donating over $11 million in 2003). The foundation engages in social change philanthropy in just two areas: HIV/AIDS prevention and economic development and education for youth and women, particularly in those regions where Levi Strauss & Co produces its goods. Strikingly absent from Levi Strauss's charitable program is any discussion of the needs of the local community in which the corporation itself is headquartered (Levi Strauss Corporation 2004).

Perhaps the best illustration of the corporate leaders' view of philanthropy can be found in the past relationship of local firms with the United Way, even before the formation of Alternative Funds. Many Bay area companies historically have not accepted the centrality of the United Way, placing the locus of decision making within the hands of donors. They have expressed this understanding in two ways: first, through their adoption of in-plant federations, and, subsequently, by pressing for the United Way's adoption of a policy of donor choice.

First, as early as the 1950s, a striking number of large firms in the Bay Area had distributed their philanthropic contributions (as well as those of their employees) through in-plant federations, rather than through the United Way. In-plant federations are workplace campaigns that are managed by and within a single company. With the consent of management, a committee of employees decides which nonprofits, typically both United Way and non-United Way entities, will receive charitable funds, based on the perceived interests of the corporation and its employees. A number of Bay Area firms, including United Airlines and Crocker Bank of California, had implemented in-plant federations, and other companies saw its attractions (United Way of the Bay Area 1978; Brilliant 1990). They had, in the words of Sonya Carleton, a senior UWBA executive at the time, "already bailed out of the United Way."

By the mid-1970s, local firms in San Francisco proposed a new mechanism for workplace charity. They began to see in-plant federations as costly and time-consuming, believing that a United Way policy of donor choice would provide the same set of benefits for them but in a more efficient manner. Donor choice shifted the responsibility, organization, and cost of gathering funds from companies to the United Way. Several key firms in the Bay Area, including Pacific Bell and Pacific Gas and Electric, threatened that unless the UWBA provided choice to donors, they would do so themselves by adopting or expanding their in-plant federations. The minutes of a 1978 UWBA board meeting noted, "It was brought out that unless United Way elects to institute a [Donor Choice] program, the larger corporations will be forced to do so" (United Way of the Bay Area 1978). The United Way responded to these threats by implementing a policy of donor choice in 1979. Although the United Way maintained its monopoly, individual employees now were allowed to designate their gift to a single nonprofit in the health and human services, as long as it was located in the larger Bay Area (United Way of the Bay Area 1978).

This picture of workplace charity altered again, however, with the formation of three new Alternative Funds in the 1980s. Encouraged by their success in gaining access to workplace campaigns within the public and semi-private sectors, Alternative Funds in the Bay Area next sought to gain access to private sector firms. United Way rivals sought to convince local corporations of the benefits of an open and competitive employee campaign. Despite the United Way's policy of donor choice, Alternative Funds were initially quite successful in achieving access to the private sector, especially when compared to their compatriots in Chicago. In particular, Alternative Funds were allowed entry by newer companies in the Bay Area, which did not possess long-standing relationships with the United Way. Apple Computer, based in nearby Silicon Valley, was the first Fortune 500 company in the nation to allow federations other than the United Way to solicit employees. By 1989, over fifty private sector campaigns in the greater Bay Area had opened up to United Way rivals, including such local firms as Safeway, Patagonia, ESPRIT, and the Gap (United Way of the Bay Area 1990; Millar 1991; Stanford University 1992).[1]

The United Way and Co-Optation

Within a decade of the appearance of the first Alternative Funds, differences in the institutional environment of the fields of workplace charity in Chicago and in San Francisco affected the initial success of Alternative Funds in the two cities. While Alternative Funds in the Bay Area were succeeding in gaining access to a growing array of private sector workplace campaigns, their counterparts in Chicago had hit a figurative brick wall. However, the ultimate outcome for the field of workplace charity in San Francisco was not so straightforward; it did not entail the inevitable realization of the logic of a supportive institutional environment. Instead, the United Way felt compelled to respond to this dynamic, implementing a new strategy to retain its control of fundraising in private sector workplaces.

For the local United Way in San Francisco, the composition of the field – with a high level of competition and an ambivalent corporate culture – posed an important challenge. The United Way feared that all local firms would allow rivals to participate in open campaigns. Internal reports of the United Way, for example, highlighted the growing access of rivals to workplace campaigns as one of the key challenges faced by the United Way (United Way of the Bay Area 1986, 1987). For the United Way, the negative consequences of an open campaign were tremendous: it estimated that 30 to 40 percent of its market share would be diverted to its rivals (United Way of the Bay Area 1990).

Faced with such a threat, the United Way in San Francisco implemented the strategic response of co-optation in 1991. In organizational theory, the strategy of co-optation is derived from the theoretical framework of resource dependence (Pfeffer and Salancik 1978). Resource dependence theory assumes that organizations cannot generate sufficient resources for survival so they must employ a variety of strategies to ensure revenue and to minimize uncertainty. Co-optation refers to any type of interorganizational linkage that neutralizes the threat of external rivals for resources. In his study of the Tennessee Valley Authority, for example, Philip Selznick (1949) details how the Authority attempted to generate support by incorporating other actors, such as the Department of Agriculture and local colleges and universities, into its planning structures. Organizations, he claims, will co-opt other actors into the decision-making process to minimize the danger they pose or to gain legitimacy from the environment.

Similarly, the United Way in the Bay Area implemented a comprehensive policy of co-optation, called "Project Share" (Robertson 1990). Chapter 5 recounted how local United Ways have put in place a variety of strategies, including the expansion of member agencies, the formation of partnerships, and the adoption of donor choice, to limit the appeal of rival fundraisers. Facing a high level of competition, the UWBA adopted another response, using Project Share to prevent the continuing growth of open workplace campaigns in the Bay Area. The following year, for example, the UWBA's 1992 Annual Report stated, "Through Project Share, we have engaged new groups to be part of our annual fundraising campaign, thereby expanding the 'united' in United Way" (United Way of the Bay Area 1992:1). Similarly, according to Bob Sakamano, an executive of an AF, "Project Share is motivated by a desire to maintain the [United Way] monopoly and, you see, its ultimate goal is to prevent side-by-side campaigns."

To maintain its monopoly, the United Way of San Francisco encouraged almost all of its rival fundraisers and any local nonprofit to enter into a partnership with it. In exchange for withdrawing from all private sector campaigns, these organizations would be given a listing in the United Way's fundraising material and receive any gifts designated to them by donors. By 1992, the United Way in San Francisco had entered into partnerships with a total of 3,500 other organizations: some were rival federated fundraisers, but most were unaffiliated charities (Moore 1993). For partner organizations, Project Share offered a chance for revenue diversification.

The UWBA did not succeed in co-opting all of its competitors into Project Share. Three of the local Alternative Funds – the Bay Area Black United Fund, the California Combined Health Agencies (formerly called CHAD), and the Progressive Way – refused to join. All three had been in existence for ten years or longer and had become the strongest competition to the United Way. They saw no advantage in making such an agreement with the United Way. From the perspective of these holdouts, equal participation in an open campaign would result in greater revenue than participating as a partner in a United Way-only campaign. John Farnsworth, a representative from one of these standout funds, explained, "We looked into it and found that we weren't going to get that much money at all. It would be a step backward for us." A fourth local fund, EarthShare of California, the biggest of all the local funds, was not invited to participate in the joint campaign (Bothwell 1998).

Project Share served to modify the composition of workplace charity in San Francisco so that the field embraced and allowed for a curious mix of both traditional and new conceptions of community. On the one hand, co-optation served to facilitate the presence of communities of purpose. It broadened the scope of recipient nonprofits able to solicit contributions from donors. Previously, the UWBA had limited earmarked contributions to those non-profits within the health and human services. However, with Project Share, the United Way had co-opted many local nonprofits in the Bay Area. Such a sweep meant that these member charities held a wide range of missions, from minority and ethnic concerns, to women's groups, to environmental associations. As a result, donors became able to direct their gifts to recipient organizations based on most any type of identity or interest.

On the other hand, Project Share succeeded in preventing the growth of true competition between the United Way and Alternative Funds. Although many rival organizations were now present in private sector campaigns, the United Way retained control of the fundraising process. Further, the four major Alternative Funds in the Bay Area were not present in Project Share given that they hoped to still gain entry as equal rivals to the United Way. Finally, when donors gave to the United Way, they were still giving to a local and interdependent notion of community. Throughout this period, the United Way had maintained its traditional mode of fund distribution and retained its historical relationship with member agencies. Like the United Way in Chicago, the United Way in San Francisco equated a gift to itself with a gift to the local community, oriented around a singular and shared notion of the common good.

The United Way: From Member Agencies to Grants

Yet, the United Way's proactive maneuvers to maintain its monopoly, although largely successful, had unexpected consequences. Its implementation of the strategies of donor choice and Project Share did prevent true competition by Alternative Funds from increasing further. But the repercussions of these two strategies were rather dire for the United Way. Taken together, and accompanied by an external crisis of legitimacy, they ultimately undermined the traditional organizational structure of the United Way. As a result, the continuing association of the United Way with a community of place would be short-lived.

To begin, the conjunction of the United Way's policies of donor choice and Project Share served to encourage donor designation of gifts. In the Bay Area, the rate of earmarking had risen slowly and gradually to about 20 percent of all gifts in 1987, equivalent to that in Chicago, and had stagnated there for several years. However, the UWBA's implementation of Project Share in 1990 – its co-optation of rival nonprofits – facilitated designation by donors. Previously, employees had been allowed to designate their gift to a local charity. But for the United Way to honor that wish, donors had to give them the name and address of the nonprofit. Now, with Project Share, individuals were not only able to give to a wider range of philanthropic causes, as discussed above, but they were now assisted in that process by the United Way providing them with a list of partners.

In consequence, the rate of earmarking in San Francisco doubled after the start of Project Share, from 23 percent of all gifts to 46 percent of all gifts over the next two years. Earmarked contributions constituted nearly half of all revenue gathered by the United Way of the Bay Area. At the same time, the UWBA experienced a drastic decline in revenue. In 1992, it faced a challenge not of its own making, that of the Aramony scandal at the United Way of America. As with Chicago, this event had damaging consequences for the United Way in San Francisco.[2] A year after the scandal broke, as shown in Figure 5, the UWBA's revenue dropped by almost 9 percent – twice the average of other United Ways (Millar 1994).

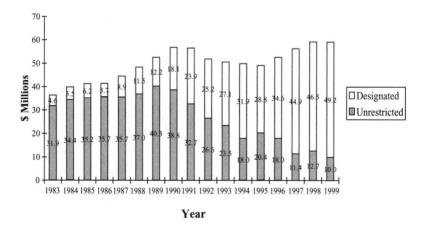

Figure 5 Pattern of Giving to the United Way of the Bay Area

The combination of increased designation and decreased revenue resulted in the donation of less money to the United Way and, more important, less money to member agencies. Between 1992 and 1994, the United Way's pool of unrestricted funds declined from 50 percent to 36 percent of all gifts. With less money under its control, the United Way had fewer dollars to allocate to its member agencies. By 1994, for example, the UWBA's member agencies had suffered an average 49 percent reduction in their share of United Way donations from three years earlier (Moore 1994). This drop in unrestricted revenue made the United Way's historical function as a fund allocator for member agencies impossible to maintain. In 1996, following a three-year planning process, the United Way dissolved its membership of agencies. Its affiliated agencies, including the Salvation Army, the YMCA, and others, were no longer guaranteed the receipt of annual allocations. It adopted a new method of resource allocation called the Community Impact Fund in which the UWBA would dole out unrestricted contributions as grants based on an open and competitive process. Any and all local nonprofits would be allowed to apply for United Way dollars.[3]

By the late 1990s, the fields of workplace charity in Chicago and San Francisco varied in important ways. These differences, however, did not reflect just a divergence in the nature of the institutional environment. Instead, through the UWBA's policies of donor choice and Project Share, many organizations representing new communities of purpose had gained entry to the majority of workplace campaigns in the Bay Area. The United Way in the Bay Area also looked very different from both its historical form and from the United Way/Crusade of Mercy; it had shed its traditional organizational structure by delinking itself from member agencies. Although it would retain a discourse of community to legitimate its grants programs, what it came to mean by community was very different from that of the United Way in Chicago.

Trouble for the United Way

The outcome of this interaction between the institutional environment and the United Way was that a conception of community based on purpose had gained a solid footing within workplace charity in San Francisco. Its eventual

supplanting of a traditional model of community was furthered by two developments within the local field of workplace charity. As in Chicago, the
field of workplace charity was affected not only by the appearance of new
pledge processors but also by the restructuring of the economy. But in the
Bay Area, these changes were more drastic and held more fundamental implications. They led not only to the further decentralization of workplace
charity toward donors and away from any centralized entities but also to the
implementation of a new identity for the United Way.

WORKPLACE CAMPAIGN MANAGERS

The United Way's policy of co-optation had not resulted in the participation
of all rivals in their campaigns. Recall that none of the local Alternative Funds
had entered into a partnership with the UWBA. The Bay Area Black United
Fund, the California Combined Health Appeal, EarthShare of California,
and the Progressive Way continued to seek to participate alongside the
United Way in private sector campaigns. They hoped to continue their track
record of success in gaining separate entry on their own terms. But by the
1990s, they faced what they called a "quagmire," an inability to convince
many firms of the merits of their inclusion. Although they experienced some
success on a firm-by-firm basis, they were not maintaining the historical pattern of growth of the 1980s. Said one head of a Bay Area Alternative Fund,
"We worked to get into the private sector, [but] we ran into a real leveling
off of the growth curve."

Alternative Funds saw their difficulty as arising out of Project Share.
Project Share allowed the United Way to claim to local firms that it provided an efficient mechanism by which donors could give to communities of
purpose. The United Way also could maintain its monopoly while allowing
companies to enact or realize their decentralized view of philanthropy in
workplace charity. Consider the opinion of Barbara Sanchez, a staff member
at another rival nonprofit, who proclaimed that the United Way's partnerships "allow the UWBA to go to a corporation and say, no you don't need to
include other fundraisers. Look, we represent those causes as well."

As a result, as in Chicago, some of the local Alternative Funds turned to an
alternative route by which to gain access to workplace campaigns. They chose
to compete with the UWBA for the ability to serve as fiscal agents. By 2000,

several different Alternative Funds had successfully bid to manage the city of San Francisco's workplace campaign, the Combined Federal Campaign for the greater Bay Area, and those of several private sector firms, including one of the largest banks in the region, the Wells Fargo campaign.

Perhaps more important, and in contrast to Chicago, Bay Area Alternative Funds were not the only actors to seek management of workplace campaigns. A small but growing number of for-profit companies, typically Internet companies, also competed to serve as fiscal agents (Greene 2000). The practice of e-philanthropy – the management of philanthropy and volunteerism through Internet Web sites – was extended to workplace charity. This new technology enabled fundraising (the solicitation and distribution of donors' gifts to nonprofits) to be done over the Internet, rather than via paper or personal networks, and, consequently, relatively cheaply. Concurrently, there was a growing awareness that workplace charity could be a site in which profit could be made and e-philanthropy extended into this arena. The UWBA, for example, recognized over forty on-line fundraising competitors. One of the United Way's main rivals was Charitableway.com, launched in October 1999, by an ex-Microsoft executive with over $43 million in venture capital. Charitableway managed campaigns for workplaces and included more than 630,000 charities as potential recipients (Wallace 2004). It soon was joined by other companies, including Corematter (formerly known as allcharities.com) which, by 2000, had became the pledge processor for a number of high-profile firms in the Bay Area, including NEC and Chlorox.

Because these fiscal agents included both Alternative Funds and for-profit entities, their implications for workplace charity were more fundamental than in Chicago. The appearance and success of for-profit pledge processors resulted in new communities of purpose being able to gain access to workplace charity in a wider range of firms – extending beyond United Way's Project Share partners to include the abstaining Alternative Funds, as well as other independent nonprofits. As with the case of Chicago, when one of these new actors successfully bid to manage a campaign, all participants received an equal voice and presence in a campaign. In contrast, when the United Way acted as the fiscal agent, it attempted to equate a workplace gift with a contribution to the United Way.

Yet, these new pledge processors also put in question the necessity of Alternative Funds. By allowing hundreds of thousands of independent nonprofits, representing a wide range of issues and causes, to participate in a workplace campaign, federated fundraisers were rendered unnecessary and, hence, potentially obsolete. One leader of the Alternative Fund movement called for-profit fiscal agents the "the wave of the future" and noted that "the real competition, henceforth, for federated groups is not the United Way, it is the private sector." Similarly, one United Way staff member claimed that "what they have reduced the United Way to is one book on a shelf of 900,000 books."

The growth of for-profit competitors also had repercussions for the United Way. Facing substantive rivalry over pledge processing within the private sector, the United Way of the Bay Area devolved its fundraising activities into a separate entity. Established in 1993 and made a distinct entity in 2000, PipeVine was a nonprofit organization that competed along with Alternative Funds and firms to manage workplace campaigns. For a set percentage of all donations, PipeVine offered to collect, report, and process a firm's pledged funds through its online giving system, as well as provide an "extensive database of nonprofit organizations" to company participants and conduct verification of recipient nonprofits' 501(c)(3) status. By 2000, PipeVine had twenty-two corporate clients, in addition to those affiliated with the United Way, and processed $92 million in pledges from over 400,000 donors.[4]

THE RESTRUCTURING OF THE LOCAL ECONOMY

As struggles occurred over access to fundraising sites, the workplace itself was changing. As in Chicago, the local economy in the Bay Area was being restructured, but this transformation was taking place on a wider, more fundamental scale in San Francisco. San Francisco, perhaps more than anywhere in the nation, exemplifies the large-scale transformation of the American economy from a manufacturing base to a service-based one (Harvey 1989). The Bay Area has shifted from an industrial and defense-based economy to a predominantly knowledge and technology-based economy of computers, electronics, and telecommunications (Bay Area Economic Forum 1999).

The restructuring of the economy altered the character of the institutional environment of workplace charity in two ways. First, the emergence of a new economy diminished the already limited amount of support for the United

Way among corporate gatekeepers. As new firms appeared, they held no history of affiliation with United Way. Changes in the Bay Area economy, according to one senior United Way executive, have entailed the "increase in the number of companies with no tradition of philanthropy." Or, as the head of a national-level Alternative Fund states: "The other thing that's really been a boon to us is the development of the high-tech industry which tends to be a very much younger workforce. They typically do not have workplace giving campaigns already in place. These companies are sort of starting up and so, they might be interested in one or more of the specific causes represented by United Way rivals."

Accompanying the rise of a new economy has been the emergence of a new culture of philanthropy. Although local firms had historically embraced a decentralized model of philanthropy, now a more radical and intensified version was adopted by corporate actors in the Bay Area. This new type of altruism, often called venture philanthropy, was developed in Silicon Valley in the 1980s and emerged from the entrepreneurial culture of the new economy (Billitteri 2000b). The Bay Area currently possesses a number of foundations and organizations dedicated to the application of venture philanthropy, as do other regions of the country with technology-driven economies (Kirsner 1999). This form of philanthropic giving, by transposing the principles of venture capital to philanthropy, changes the nature of the relationship between donors and recipients: donors no longer view contributions as gifts, but as investments (Letts, Ryan, and Grossman 1997). In order to obtain a "return," venture philanthropists typically make large investments, they are involved with grantees for long periods of time, and they focus on the long-term needs and growth of recipient organizations (Billitteri 2000b). This vision of philanthropy was increasingly adopted by local firms in the Bay Area and extended to workplace charity.

Soliciting for Charitable Contributions

Together, these two developments – the restructured economy and the growth of venture philanthropy – served to further decentralize the field of workplace charity. They not only put in question the institutionalized and central role of the United Way but also the necessity and desirability of any type of intermediary entity, whether the United Way or Alternative Funds. Unlike the case of Chicago, federated fundraisers could no longer claim to offer a convenient service to gatekeepers. Now, workplace charity became increasingly organized around a direct relationship between individual donors and individual nonprofit organizations. In the process, a new conception of community, oriented around multiple and shared purposes, has come to dominate not only workplace charity but also the local United Way.

Not surprisingly, the United Way of the Bay Area has been forced to address the decentralization of workplace charity. Located between donors and recipient organizations, the UWBA sought to justify its intermediary position by the late 1990s. By altering its discourse and organizational practices, the United Way in San Francisco aimed to convince donors of the merit of a charitable contribution to it, rather than to independent nonprofits or to Alternative Funds. To that end, like the United Way in Chicago, the United Way in San Francisco has implemented a strategy of differentiation. As I noted in the last chapter, a strategy of differentiation occurs when an organization proposes a criterion for judgment, attempting to convince others not only of the suitability of that criterion but also of the organization's superiority over its rivals when judged by that criterion.

However, the specific scale of evaluation is subject to some degree of proactive orchestration on the part of nonprofit organizations. In Chicago, as we have seen, the United Way claimed that it best allowed donors to make a gift to the local community of Chicago. In San Francisco, the United Way had also adopted a discourse of community, but the meaning of community differed markedly from that found in Chicago. Instead of positioning itself in opposition to organizations representing communities of purpose, the United Way in San Francisco instead presented itself as the *facilitator* of those new communities. It claimed to constitute the best means by which donors could contribute to their own specific and particular understanding of community, whether it is based on gender, race, sexual orientation, or even place. So, in the words of one United Way staff member, "We do what contributors value."

This strategy of differentiation is based on a particular view of donors. Representatives from the United Way expressed a strong belief that Bay Area donors not only desire control but also identify with particularistic causes and communities. One executive, David Rodriguez, told me, "Frankly, I think every strategy [of the United Way] is being built around donor choice. So, I guess in terms of priorities, it's at the top." When donors do attach conditions to their contributions, they are understood to disavow any affinity to a traditional, place-based conception of community. A 1993 internal United Way memo concluded that the United Way faced "a multiplicity of competing community agendas" (United Way of the Bay Area 1993). Or take the opinions of two senior and long-time managers at the United Way of the Bay Area: in the course of my interviews, one told me that the "sense of community is different around here," and another expressed exasperation that "multiple communities exist [in the Bay Area]; there is not a sense of a single community. It's tough to bring together everyone."

As a result, the United Way has positioned itself as best able to help donors realize these specific philanthropic goals. By 2000, the goal of the UWBA was that "when donors think of building their communities, they identify the United Way as a partner and speak proudly of its leadership" (United Way of the Bay Area 2000b). One senior UWBA executive summarized the difference between her United Way and the traditional United Way as being that "we engage donors, instead of educating them." To differentiate itself, the UWBA claimed that it could act as an objective assessor of nonprofits serving a specific, purpose-based community. Unlike other rival organizations, it would let donors know which nonprofits would provide the best return on their investments. In that same year, the president of the UWBA stated, "We'd like to position the United Way as a source of credible evaluative information that helps a donor meet their charitable goal" (Greene 2000). To that end, the UWBA implemented several new charitable programs that served to legitimate its place between donors and nonprofit organizations. These programs took two distinct forms, depending on who was perceived to be the donor.

THE COMMUNITY IMPACT FUND

The Community Impact Fund (CIF) was created by the UWBA in 1996, when it dismantled the traditional method of allocating funds to member agencies and began to distribute competitive grants to nonprofit organizations. The Community Impact Fund was the new name for a gift to the United Way itself. The CIF targeted donors within large workplaces, who typically made small contributions and with whom the United Way could not have a personalized relationship. With the Community Impact Fund, the UWBA maintained an emphasis on a place-based conception of community, but now there were several substantive differences between its new vision of community and that used in the past and employed elsewhere by other United Ways. These differences include the definition of community, the mode of determination of community needs, and the selection of recipient organizations.

First, the local community was no longer understood as constituting a single cause (transcending the distinct and varying interests of its different members) but rather as composed of several different causes. The needs of San Francisco constituted the aggregate of the needs of a variety of local populations, each with its own challenges and issues. The UWBA identified eight issue areas to which applicants' programs needed to be directed: Families and Children, Community Service & Volunteerism, Education, Disaster and Emerging Readiness, Job and Workforce Development, Health, Homelessness & Housing, and HIV/AIDS (United Way of the Bay Area 2000c).

Unlike the United Way in Chicago, the perceptions of donors were central to this conception of community. In Chicago, the needs of the community are measured and determined by the United Way itself through scientific methods. In the Bay Area, in contrast, these specific issue areas were selected not only in response to the United Way's assessment of recipients' needs in the Bay Area but also to tap donors' concerns. One senior volunteer said, "By focusing the campaign around these Impact Issues we will be able to respond more effectively to donor needs and interests" (United Way of the Bay Area 1998b:10). One representative clarified how the Community Impact Fund was meant to involve donors. He stated, "We are trying to demonstrate to the new donor, that we are not your parents' United Way. The days of simply giving to an institution that did some stuff that you knew nothing about are over." In fundraising material, donors are encouraged to give to the Community Impact Fund through a designated contribution to the issue area closest to their own area of concern.

The UWBA claimed that the Community Impact Fund offered the most efficient way for donors to address their specific community concern. With its new method of resource allocation, the UWBA employed a new criterion for selecting beneficiaries, that of accountability. Thus, the United Way evaluated the outcomes of agency programs, attempting to ensure that grants to these nonprofits were "money well spent." CEOs of participating firms, for example, received a thank-you card that stated the "Community Impact Fund provides funding to programs with a proven success rate" (United Way of the Bay Area 2000c).

Donor Advisement Programs

For the United Way of the Bay Area, the Community Impact Fund has been supplemented by the growth of several new programs, collectively known as donor advisement, which are viewed by many United Way staff as the future of the UWBA. Together, they are aimed at acquiring large gifts from elite givers – typically senior management. Again, as in Chicago, the United Way has turned to resource diversification in response to the restructuring of the local economy. As large firms have declined in number and size, there has been a realization within the United Way that its traditional mode of fundraising will no longer be adequate. As June Havelock, a long-time executive, told me, as "the workplace changes, the UWBA should offer multiple strategies and channels to help people meet their charitable goals. . . . We're going to have to do alternative methods of raising funds. It's not just going into a company and passing out forms and getting people to complete their forms and doing payroll deduction and stock dividends."

With these new programs, the United Way in San Francisco became focused on a new resource provider – the elite giver. The current president of the UWBA has been quoted as saying that the United Way's "fund-raising is not employer-based" (Futcher 2000:B1). The United Way saw its new customer as "the most generous donor, the social/civic minded core customer, those who give $1,000 or more" (United Way of the Bay Area 1998a:3). A 1998 report on the future of the UWBA concluded, "Experience has shown focused fund raising efforts with top givers is a more efficient use of resources than 'shotgun' solicitation efforts of the past. Going forward, UWBA is committed to developing programs with top givers that encourage individual recognition and involvement instead of facelessly collecting contributions and expecting an almost automatic annuity from donors" (United Way of the Bay Area 1998a:1).

The challenge for the UWBA is that, unlike in Chicago, elite givers in the Bay Area do not tend to give to the United Way or to its historical vision of a community of place. The growth of venture philanthropy, as discussed above, has led donors to expect to be able to control the donative transfer. In response, the United Way has developed a series of customized projects around the specific interests of the elite giver. Underlying each of them is the claim that the United Way will allow donors to give to a particular community or cause in the most efficient and effective way possible. As with the Community Impact Fund, the UWBA will engage in the labor necessary to determine which nonprofit organizations will allow donors to best meet their goals. The UWBA president noted that "the value United Way adds is that, because we are committed to measurable outcomes and have a knowledge base of what really works and what are the indicators of success, we could create portfolios that represent the best of breed among programs in a given geographic area or around a given issue" (as quoted in Greene 2000). The goal, according to one senior executive, is to get "top of the line awareness for any senior executive who has a lot of money that he wants to pour into the money, and who wants to find the best partner for the best, most comprehensive solutions. That is my . . . our goal."

For example, elite givers can give to the UWBA through a program called "Jointly Invested Philanthropy," in which the United Way provides research on "special interest giving opportunities and outstanding nonprofit programs in areas of donors' interests" (United Way of the Bay Area 2000a). By 2000, gifts to Jointly Invested Philanthropy totaled over $13 million. Or leadership givers may donate to one of the UWBA "Collaborative Projects," in which the United Way brings together multiple partners, including private (individual and corporate) and public funders and nonprofit agencies to meet community needs (United Way of the Bay Area 2000c).

The UWBA also has adopted many of the techniques of other vehicles of elite philanthropy, which represent a fundamental departure from the traditional workplace-based methods of the United Way. In 2000, for example, the UWBA began a program to raise funds through a planned giving program. Donors were encouraged to recognize the United Way as a recipient in their wills (United Way of the Bay Area 2001). In the next year, the UWBA initiated a charitable investment fund similar to that offered by Fidelity Investment's Charitable Gifts Fund. Donors would be able to receive a tax exemption on their gift and have their gifts earn interest while they decided which cause or organization their money will support. The UWBA also holds an endowment to which elite givers may donate, as do many other United Ways (Foote 1991).

As with the United Way in Chicago, leadership giving constitutes a growing portion of the UWBA's total revenue; from 1997–2000, the total amount increased by 22 percent. By 1999, leadership giving constituted 33 percent of the overall UWBA campaign, totaling just over $19 million (United Way of the Bay Area 2000a). Although successful in terms of raising significant funds, the move toward elite giving entails possible future challenges for the United Way. As the UWBA has turned away from mass fundraising within the workplace, it has left behind Alternative Funds and entered into competition with a new set of organizations: community foundations (Billitteri 2000a) and financial services firms like Fidelity that offer donor-advised funds. To compete with these organizations, the UWBA claims that its superiority for the elite giver lies in its ability to act as a "community catalyst," forging collaborations and partnerships with actors from the private, public, and nonprofit sectors. One staff summarized the unique appeal of the United Way as being that "we use our access to a lot of high-level decision makers in the community, the businesses, the agencies, as our leverage to try and achieve those kinds of community goals that maybe a lot of agencies have but we can be the ones to facilitate it, organize it, construct it." When asked what separated the UWBA from local community foundations, one executive responded that "community foundations are just up there, maybe deciding where funds go. In contrast, we're out there, rubbing shoulders with everyone involved, down in the trenches, talking with government officials, designing programs, all of it. The community foundation doesn't do any of that."

But, if the United Way envisions its future as serving as a "community catalyst" to realize the interests of elite givers, a potential conflict exists between these two goals. The demands of elite donors are not always synonymous with the concerns of institutional funders and partners, such as government agencies or other nonprofit actors. As one senior United Way staff summarized, "Often times what the donor perceives to be the problem, the United Way, claiming ourselves to be the community expert, it isn't or the way you want to approach it, isn't the solution." Moving forward, it is difficult to tell how the UWBA will resolve this potential dilemma. It seems likely that given the United Way's increasing dependence on elite givers, it will continue to develop in ways that serve to fulfill donors' understandings of community, irrespective of the actual needs of the local Bay Area or the concerns of potential partners in the public and nonprofit sectors.

Conclusion

In all, the ultimate outcome for workplace charity in the Bay Area has been that donors, almost regardless of their own understandings of collectivity, are now giving within fundraising appeals and opportunities that represent and encourage a particularistic conception of community. Communities of purpose are present in workplace charity in a variety of forms: as independent nonprofits, as designated organizations, and as Alternative Funds. The United Way itself has been reoriented around this new conception of community. Driven by the need to legitimate its existence in a decentralized field of workplace charity, the United Way of the Bay Area has organized itself around donors' multiple and varied understandings of community.

CHAPTER 8

Community, Charitable Giving, and the Nonprofit Sector

This book has examined how workplace charity has been affected by the appearance of Alternative Funds and how their presence speaks to the question of community. In workplace charity, the meaning of community has multiplied in form, expanding beyond a community of place to include multiple communities of purpose. I have shown that the outcome of this competition has not been straightforward; that is, one vision of community has not come to triumph over another. For workplace charity, community is not in decline, as posited by some scholars, but neither has traditional community been replaced by a new vision of community based on a shared identity or interest. Instead, community has played out in different ways across different sites.

To explain this variation, the specific logic of community in workplace charity has been shown to result from the intersection between the institutional environment and the strategic maneuvers of nonprofit organizations. To develop this thesis, I have focused on four major aspects of the field of workplace charity: nonprofit organizations represent shifting under-standings of community in the larger society; these charities have sought to gain access to workplace campaigns so as to solicit funds; their effect on workplace giving has been determined largely by gatekeepers; and the or-ganizations themselves are capable of proactive tactics to further their own ends.

The idea of community has been variously represented in workplace charity, reflecting particular visions of community present in the wider soci-ety. Historically, the United Way has held a monopoly over workplace charity. The United Way embodies a traditional vision of community based on place and propinquity. It was formed during the Progressive era, when a belief in the benefits of rationality was accompanied by the spirit of welfare capitalism. When donations to individual nonprofits were replaced by a single and more efficient federated fundraiser, the concept of community was proposed as a new recipient of charitable gifts. The United Way, then the Commu-nity Chest, claimed to facilitate the vitality of a local, geographically based place – a town or city – by assessing its needs and distributing funds accord-ingly to member agencies.

But while the United Way enjoyed a long monopoly, it now faces compe-tition from Alternative Funds – federated fundraisers representing coalitions of charities sharing a similar mission or cause. The presence of Alternative Funds has expanded and multiplied the models of community present in workplace charity. Alternative Funds represent the growth in American so-ciety of collective identities, new modes of facilitating the public good, and altered scales of community. These Alternative Funds emerged out of a set of particular historical moments, reflecting both broader cultural shifts and new resource flows in the nonprofit sector. Although some Alternative Funds represent long-standing alternatives to a community of place, the majority of Alternative Funds emerged from the tremendous expansion of nonprof-its oriented around the New Social Movements of the 1960s and 1970s. These charities turned to workplace charity – taking the form of Alternative Funds – as a result of decreasing levels of government revenue and a growing awareness of workplace giving as a site of resource diversification.

I then asked whether and how the presence of Alternative Funds has altered workplace charity. Alternative Funds possess the potential to fun-damentally change the structure and meaning of workplace charity. When they are present alongside the United Way in a workplace campaign, a wider variety of nonprofits, serving a broader assortment of recipients, can benefit from workplace funds. The act of giving is also transformed when Alternative Funds are present. It gains new meanings as donors possess the ability to direct their contributions to issues and organizations of their own choice.

However, the potential impact of rivalry on workplace giving has not been as transformative in practice. Instead, significant cross-sectional variation exists across different sites of workplace charity. Alternative Funds are present in only a limited number of cities, and they tend to be able to solicit funds in certain types of workplace campaigns more than others. Even in those places where Alternative Funds do pose a significant rivalry to the United Way, their emergence has had different outcomes. In Chicago, for example, workplace charity has remained defined and structured by a traditional vision of community based on place. In contrast, in San Francisco, the field has been reorganized around a multiplicity of communities of purpose.

These uneven outcomes represent two different points of contestation and conflict. First, the formation of Alternative Funds does not necessarily mean that they will be able to solicit donors in the workplace. Alternative Funds must first gain entry to workplace campaigns – they must be allowed access by campaign gatekeepers. Here, the institutional environment matters: firms extend the understandings that govern their own philanthropic practices to that of their employees. In places where corporate philanthropy is still governed by professionals and the goal of community welfare, Alternative Funds have found it difficult to gain access. In locales where corporate philanthropy has been decentralized toward firms' own goals, Alternative Funds are more likely to obtain permission to solicit workers. When both federated fundraisers are present, Alternative Funds and United Ways advance their own conception of community over that of others in order to gather resources and legitimacy. In all, the logic of community takes on different meanings across different locales.

More generally, the book's thesis and empirical findings prompt a consideration of the complex relationship among organizations, the nonprofit sector, and community. Three points seem worthy of emphasis: charitable giving as a social relationship, the consequences of competition for the nonprofit sector, and an organizationally mediated approach to community.

An Institutional Approach to Philanthropy

By analyzing how and through what processes community is realized in workplace charity, this book speaks to the literature on philanthropy. Typically, the degree and direction of private giving are explained by a focus on individual characteristics. To account for patterns of giving, this micro-level approach to altruism analyzes either donors' demographic characteristics or their subjective motivations. Accordingly, this literature would predict that the outcome regarding community in workplace charity is determined by the demands and desires of individuals in the workplace. However, my analysis shows that the logic of community across locales has little to do with individuals' characteristics. In actuality, donors' choices in the workplace – whether or not they give to communities of place or of purpose – reflect the larger composition and dynamics of the larger field.

My theoretical argument has two parts. The first recognizes that donors are located in relation to fundraising organizations. Nonprofits serve as the mechanisms through which individuals make charitable contributions. In workplace charity, the presence or absence of different types of federated fundraisers serves to structure the choices that individuals have; that is, whether they are able to donate to communities of place and/or purpose. For this step in the analysis, I join an emerging body of research on philanthropy that stresses the institutionally mediated nature of altruism (Ostrander and Schervish 1990; Schervish 1995; Sokolowski and Wokciech 1996; Wolfe 1998). These scholars have focused on the dyadic relationship between donors and nonprofit organizations. They have shown that fundraisers possess specific types of collection regimes that structure the opportunities for altruism, which are irreducible to individual-level characteristics (Titmuss 1997[1970]; Chaves 1999; Sargent 1999; Healy 2000, 2004). Charitable giving is "structured, promoted, and made logistically possible by organizations and institutions with a strong interest in producing it" (Healy 2004:387).

However, it is not enough to simply state that donors are embedded in institutional relations with fundraisers that structure the opportunities or constraints faced by donors. A second analytic step is necessary. This step involves moving beyond the dyadic relationships between donors and fundraisers to also take into account the institutional context of fundraisers themselves. It is not only that donors face opportunities and constraints from fundraisers; it is also that fundraisers face opportunities and constraints posed by the larger institutional relationships in which they themselves are enmeshed.

More specifically, fundraisers do not act in isolation but instead are located in an organizational field. An organizational field comprises all those actors involved in the production of a single product or service: "those organizations that, in the aggregate constitute a recognized area of institutional life; key suppliers, resource and product consumers, regulatory agencies, and other organizations" (DiMaggio and Powell 1991:64). Members of an organizational field constitute a network of social relations governed by the distribution of resources and power and by a shared logic (Bourdieu 1977, 1990; Fligstein 1990, 2001; DiMaggio and Powell 1991; Friedland and Alford 1991; Galaskiewicz and Bielefeld 1998). This theoretical framework brings a historically grounded concern for the composition and dynamics of the field to understanding why and how its members act in the ways that they do. Actors are not free to pursue their self-interest in an unfettered manner, but are constrained and shaped by the logic of the field.

Similarly, the structure and dynamics of the field of workplace charity determine the variable and changing meaning of community across different sites and locales. Differences in nonprofits' relationships with donors can be seen to result from variation in the configuration and historical interactions of multiple actors within the field (Bourdieu 1977, 1990; Fligstein 1990, 2001; DiMaggio and Powell 1991; Friedland and Alford 1991; Galaskiewicz and Bielefeld 1998). The composition of the organizational field provides the external pressures and constraints within which fundraising organizations emerge, determining the opportunities and constraints available to funders. It is this dynamic between nonprofits and their organizational fields, rather than donors' demands, which explains variation in nonprofits' presence in workplace charity and, as a result, variation in the conceptions of community available to individual givers.

Competition and the Nonprofit Sector

The findings of the book possess relevance for a better understanding not only of donors in the nonprofit sector but also of recipient organizations. In addition to shifting levels of government funding and increasing commercialization, competition has emerged as a salient and pressing issue for nonprofits. Competition refers to the simultaneous demand by two or more actors for limited environmental resources. The last three decades have witnessed a dramatic rise in the number of nonprofit organizations, increasing from 300,000 in 1967 to over 1 million by 1997 (Weisbrod 1998).

Recent literature has identified the consequences of competition for the nonprofit sector (Steinberg 1987; Thorpe and Brecher 1988; Alexander 1998; Schlesinger 1998; Tuckman 1998; Weisbrod 1998). This research has analyzed how nonprofits attempt to gather contested and limited goods in a crowded field by using a variety of strategies. Nonprofits may diversify into less crowded funding arenas (Alexander 1998; Froelich 1999), they may form partnerships with other actors (Gronbjerg 1993; Galaskiewicz and Bielefeld 1998), or they may differentiate themselves from rivals (Barman 2002). By employing a comparative and historical approach to the emergence of competition in workplace charity, this book is able to place these and other tactics within a continuum. My analysis of federated fundraisers in workplace charity allowed me to identify a range of organizational responses to rivalry. Three overarching types of reactions to competition were implemented by participants in workplace charity: organizations altered their own structure and practices, they modified the fundraising arena, and they diversified their revenue stream.

In the first type of strategic response, nonprofits change their own organizational activities. Organizations engage in "work" on themselves to better position themselves in a crowded field. A case example here is the strategy of differentiation. Differentiation takes place when a nonprofit presents itself to donors as superior to its competitors. In my study, I found that both the United Ways in Chicago and San Francisco portrayed themselves to contributors as preferable to other potential recipients. However, they employed different criteria by which to assert their superiority: whereas the United Way in Chicago asserted that it best facilitated a community of place, the United Way in San Francisco posited that it best assisted donors' giving to their selected communities of purpose.

Nonprofits may instead react to rivalry by changing the composition of their environment. For one, charities can alter the nature of their relationship with competitors. Co-optation, for example, occurs when a focal organization seeks to eliminate or reduce the amount of competition that it faces. The United Way of the Bay Area, for instance, entered into an agreement with several of its rivals whereby the partner nonprofits no longer gathered funds as independent entities but became affiliated with the focal organization. Another example here is that of mapping (Alexander 1998). Nonprofits engage in mapping when they implement new activities that mimic those of their rivals. Mapping takes place when nonprofits attempt to reduce the previously unique or distinct attraction of their competitors by offering similar programs. Many United Ways mapped their rivals when they implemented a policy of donor choice. Mapping tends to occur when nonprofits are larger or stronger than their rivals. Hence, the activities and practices of competitors can be incorporated into the focal organization without fear of a loss of mission and meaning.

The last type of strategic response, diversification, involves the most forceful and proactive maneuver on the part of nonprofits. Here, charities decide to no longer compete with rivals for a particular kind of resource, but instead move their fundraising efforts to a new venue with less or no rivalry. Faced with competition from Alternative Funds for small donations, the United Way/Crusade of Mercy engaged in revenue diversification by focusing on the solicitation of larger gifts from workplace management. Diversification is employed by nonprofit organizations when new resources appear to be easily accessible.

Contrary to the premises of organizational theory, which stresses the forces of inertia over adaptation (Hannan and Freeman 1977), organizations in the nonprofit sector are capable of strategically reacting to, varying, and minimizing the scope of rivalry in a variety of ways. These tactics differ in the extent to which they end up altering the organization itself and the degree that they change the nature of an organization's fundraising arena.

An Organizational Approach to Community

By analyzing the case of workplace charity, the book approaches the debate over community from an organizational perspective. It analyzes how nonprofits, representing different understandings of collectivity and the public good, entered into the field of workplace charity and vied for resources and legitimacy. In so doing, the book has made two contributions to the literature on community. First, it has expanded our knowledge on how communities become translated into organizational form. Alternative Funds represent the organizational outcome of an interpretive view of community based on a shared interest and identity. By recognizing this emergent conception of community, rather than emphasizing the decline of a traditional view of community, the book asks where, why, and how this new model of collectivity, generated out of changing mechanisms of belonging, translates from the wider society and into the nonprofit sector. My empirical analysis of the case of workplace charity suggests that this translation is not automatic or immediate. New forms of community have been created and have become viable in American society due to historical changes in the nation's political and social culture since the 1960s. But the book concludes that whether or not these social groups enter the nonprofit sector is not a straightforward process. Instead, their presence as organizations is determined by the structure of and interactions between actors in that field. The question of whether or not communities enter the nonprofit sector as organizations is determined not by the demands of donors or the but by strength and size of the nonprofit community.

Second, I have argued that the competition between organizations in workplace charity – that is, contestations between the United Way and Alternative Funds – represents something much larger and more significant than simply fighting among organizational rivals for charitable donations. Instead, this contestation represents a series of struggles between two different institutionalized conceptions of community. As I have elucidated, this battle over workplace donations has resonance for a long-standing and larger debate about the vitality of the American nonprofit sector and the health of civic society more generally. Although some authors have asserted a decline in nonprofit organizations as a mode of civic engagement, my research on workplace charity suggests that these debates are framed by a singular conception of community and, thereby, overlook important changes and dynamics. This debate rests upon a traditional model of community, one based on place. Conversely, I have claimed that the debate over community in the United States should be seen not as a matter of the decline or the persistence of community but instead as a matter of shifting and competing conceptions of community. Alongside the traditional vision of community based on place, communities have arisen based on shared purpose. By overemphasizing the decline of one form of community, that body of scholarship overlooks the rise of the other.

In workplace charity, we can see what happens when we recognize the existence of both visions of community. The contestations over community between United Ways and Alternative Funds result in different forms of community and different patterns of giving becoming dominant in different American cities. The book finds that the state of community is not one of decline or rebirth, but instead is more complicated. One form of community has not come to triumph or banish another vision of community. Moreover, these conflicts over community are resolved in ways that do not reflect how individuals embedded in the local arena of workplace charity imagine and understand community. The meaning of community in workplace charity, in other words, does not constitute the expression or realization of the donors' preferences or clients' characteristics. Instead, the ultimate predominance of one conception of community over another largely is driven by the model of philanthropy held by another group of actors in workplace charity, those of corporate gatekeepers, as mediated by the work of nonprofits. Ultimately, the meaning of community in this one arena of contemporary society occurs almost incidentally to the wishes of those who give and the needs of those who receive.

Reference Matter

Notes

1. This figure for 2001 represents the last year for which data on both United Ways and Alternative Funds are available.

2. As a term, the United Way (also previously known as the Community Chest, the Red Feather Appeal, and/or the United Fund) encompasses three distinct but interrelated entities. First, it refers to each of the over 2,000 local United Ways that raise funds in their community. Each United Way is an autonomous actor, independently managed by a board of directors and accountable to its community. "United Way" is also used to denote the United Way of America, an independent trade association that provides policy guidance, training, and literature for local United Ways in return for a small percentage of their annual revenue. Finally, "United Way" is often employed to describe the concept of federated fundraising in the workplace, and it tends to encompass the totality of local United Ways and the United Way of America.

3. I use the term "Alternative Fund" with some hesitation. Based on my interviews with representatives with United Way rivals, I have found that not all like or employ this term to describe themselves. Nonetheless, I use it to describe this group of voluntary associations as it clearly and succinctly describes their role in workplace charity.

4. Community studies, for example, have consisted of ethnographic examinations of one town; most social scientists are familiar with Middletown, Yankee City, Crestwood Heights, and other exemplars of the genre (Lynd and Lynd 1929; Warner and Lunt 1941; Seeley, Sim, and Loosley 1956).

5. Here, Weber's distinction between the types of social relationships is useful: he distinguishes between "communal" ties, based on affectual or traditional feelings, and "associative" ties, based on mutual pursuit of rational interests and typically occurring in the market (1978:40).

6. Yet, if place and propinquity are the necessary prerequisites of community, they do not always produce community. Social interactions need not produce shared

values, as demonstrated by Janowitz's (1952) analysis of suburban communities of "limited liability" and Nina Eliasoph's (1998) study of voluntary associations.

7. Not all theorists have been so insistent on the decline of community with modernity. Durkheim (1964[1893]), for example, was more hopeful. In the transition from a mechanical to organic solidarity, he saw space for collective behavior. The contractual relations that dominate modern society are still dependent on shared understandings – thus, they are moral in nature. Similarly, for more contemporary dissenting views on the implications of individualism for community, see Giddens 1991 and Lichterman 1996.

8. In calling attention to the role of symbolic boundaries, this literature draws from scholarship in the Durkheimian and Weberian tradition (Durkheim 1954[1912]; Weber 1978), one that identifies classification as a constitutive element of social life (Levi-Strauss 1962; Douglas 1966; Zerubavel 1997). Categories serve to divide the social world into unified and distinct groups (Bourdieu 1984; Bourdieu and Wacquant 1992; Lamont 1992).

9. Two different techniques were employed to select the cases under analysis. The selection of the case of Chicago emerged from preliminary research that I conducted on the United Way for the greater Chicago area. The city of Chicago represented a case of a city where workplace charity remains oriented around a community of place. The technique of purposive sampling was used to select the other case study: a city in which workplace charity is organized around communities of purpose. Through interviews with participants in the field of workplace charity, it became apparent which cities displayed this pattern of giving. The case of San Francisco was selected because of my prior knowledge of the region and because of difficulties gaining access to the other United Ways.

10. For the United Way in San Francisco, in exchange for receiving access to the organization, I volunteered on a part-time basis, assisting staff members responsible for the allocation of unrestricted funds.

11. The composition of the sample of respondents for the two cases differed given that much of the events in the case of San Francisco occurred in the 1970s and 1980s, whereas salient events in Chicago occurred in the 1990s. Therefore, for the case of San Francisco, I interviewed twelve current United Way of the Bay Area staff, three former staff members, three current board members, three other corporate elites, and representatives from two former member agencies. I attempted to contact corporate elites and board members involved with the United Way of the Bay Area in the 1970s, but I was not able to do so due to the death or illness of potential informants. For the case of Chicago, I interviewed ten United Way/Crusade of Mercy current and former staff members, four current and former members of the board of directors, two long-time volunteers, five corporate elites, and representatives of four member agencies. Because many potential respondents were not interested in talking to an outside observer, I used the method of snowball sampling to determine my sample. However, let me note that I conscientiously tried to gather data from a heterogeneous

sample of respondents. In both cases, I made sure to include networks of respondents who held a range of positions and contrasting views on the role of the United Way.

CHAPTER 3

1. As a result, although some scholars have recently argued that new modes of association, derived from New Social Movements and citizen advocacy, primarily occur at the national level (Minkoff 1995; Skocpol 1999), the composition of Alternative Funds supports other literature that finds that new modes of voluntary activity have also emerged at the local level (Cohen and Arato 1994; Foley and Edwards 1996; Wuthnow 1998).

2. However, some scholars have challenged the claim of uniqueness for New Social Movements, subsuming these collective actions into the larger category of social movements (D'Anieri, Ernst, and Kier 1990; Plotke 1990). Some authors have pointed out that all social movements rely on collective identity (Tucker 1991; Calhoun 1995). Others have challenged the claim of historical newness for New Social Movements, showing that social movements with similar orientations, organizational forms, and goals arose in the nineteenth and early twentieth century; examples here include the suffragette, abolitionist, and temperance movements (Buechler 1990; Taylor and Whittier 1992). Here, I maintain the division between the collective identities generated out of New Social Movements and those of other origins to emphasize the specificity of this particular vision of community as opposed to others that have emerged within workplace charity.

3. The National Committee for Responsive Philanthropy recognized sixteen Black United Funds as being in existence in 2003 (National Committee for Responsive Philanthropy 2004).

4. All data in this chapter on the revenue of Alternative Funds are derived from a survey of Alternative Funds that I conducted in 2000, as well as information gathered from www.guidestar.org and by the National Committee for Responsive Philanthropy (2003).

5. The term "second wave" to describe the women's movement of the 1960s and early 1970s is used by observers to distinguish it from the "earlier period of feminist organizing in the nineteenth century" (DeVault 1996:29).

6. Thus, various scholars have shown how collective identities are not automatic; instead, these communities rely on actors and organizations that construct and promote a collective and shared identity out of divergent interests. See, for example, Seidman (1993) and Gamson (1996).

7. Of course, a select number of religiously oriented nonprofits, such as the Salvation Army, Lutheran Social Services, and Catholic Social Services, traditionally have received funding from the United Way. The justification here has been that they provide services to the entire population of the local community.

8. To identify the mission of those nonprofits participating in social action funds, I employed the Internet to locate the Web sites for those funds and to obtain a list of member agencies. I then coded these member agencies according to their primary mission, as specified by the Alternative Fund.

9. The National Committee for Responsive Philanthropy, in contrast, identifies forty-nine Social action funds (National Committee for Responsive Philanthropy 2003).

10. Data taken from the *Yearbook of International Organizations* (1996), as cited in Simmons (1998).

11. Dick Leary, executive director of International Services of America, as quoted in National Committee for Responsive Philanthropy (1986:59).

12. An additional type of Alternative Fund is not included in this book, but is worthy of note. Arts funds are made up of arts-oriented nonprofits that have joined together to facilitate the process of fundraising in their local community. According to their trade association, sixty-two Arts funds exist across the United States. Arts funds have been excluded from this analysis given the specific origins of their income. For Arts funds, revenue raised in the workplace constitutes less than one-quarter of all dollars raised in 2001 (Americans for the Arts 2002). In contrast, nearly all other Alternative Funds receive the majority of their funds from workplace donations.

CHAPTER 4

1. Charles Craig of the New Jersey Black United Fund, as cited in National Committee for Responsive Philanthropy (1986:5).

2. Katy Lowery of the Cooperating Fund Drive, as quoted in National Committee for Responsive Philanthropy (1986:42).

3. Or, as Brilliant (1990) notes, if these member agencies were already affiliated with a local United Way, they sought to expand their share of funding.

4. A dichotomous dependent variable (with a value of 0 or 1) is employed because there was little variation in the value of the dependent variable across those cases with Alternative Funds. If a city possessed one Alternative Fund, it almost always possessed several other Alternative Funds (these usually were a Health fund, a Social action fund, and a Black United Fund). The only exceptions here are the largest cities, including New York City, Philadelphia, Los Angeles, and Seattle, where a greater number of Alternative Funds are found.

5. See Barman (forthcoming) for further details regarding the quantitative analysis and results.

CHAPTER 5

1. United Way rivals and critics have sought to use the law to prevent a United Way monopoly in workplace charity, but have failed. In 1978, four United Ways in northern California were sued by the Combined Health Agencies Drive for monopoly

of payroll deductions and interference with CHAD's relationships with businesses. The case was decided in favor of the United Way in 1978 (Brilliant 1990).

2. Alternative Funds may benefit from, but also encourage, employee pressure on corporations to incorporate other funds in addition to the United Ways into their workplace campaigns. Many Black United Funds, for example, have organized and assisted African-American employees toward this end. Chrysler™, for instance, was sued by workers in 1977 when African-American employees wanted the right to contribute through payroll deduction to the United Black Community Fund of St. Louis (Brilliant 1990).

3. The irony, as Muirhead (1999) points out, is that corporate philanthropy has essentially come full circle in terms of its focus. From its inception until the 1953 court ruling, firms' charitable gifts necessarily had to be business-related. It is only now, a half-century later, that firms are again donating based on their own bottom line.

CHAPTER 6

1. Data on the fundraising levels of national Alternative Funds in the Chicago area are unavailable because those organizations collate contributions according to corporations, rather than geographical location.

2. The United Way/Crusade of Mercy also distributes a small portion of its general funds as grants to member and nonmember agencies (United Way/Crusade of Mercy 2001).

3. During the period under study, the United Way/Crusade of Mercy was a separate fund distribution entity from many of the suburban United Ways (called the United Way of Suburban Chicago), but it has since merged with those organizations to form a single entity.

4. Recently, it has grown even more, merging with those remaining independent suburban United Ways to form a single fundraising entity.

5. The United Way of Chicago also implemented a variety of other responses – minorities were added to the organization's staff, and the allocation to the Chicago Urban League, a high-profile minority-based nonprofit, was significantly increased (United Way of Chicago 1992).

6. In 2003, the Public Interest Fund of Illinois joined with the Illinois Women's Funding Federation to form Community Shares of Illinois.

7. These firms were headquartered in the Bay Area in 1994 (*Fortune* 1995). The philanthropic goals of these firms were taken from the Public Management Institute (1990).

8. To have a comparable sample size to that of San Francisco, I randomly sampled eleven of the Fortune 500 firms headquartered in the Chicago area.

9. Prior studies have shown the importance of business coalitions for the economic, political, and social vitality of a region (Judd and Parkinson 1990; Galaskiewicz 1991; Kanter 2000).

10. The UW/CM's turn to leadership giving reflects the growth of this trend among the system of United Ways. Leadership gifts of $1,000 or more increased from 13 percent of all gifts to United Ways in 1993 to 25 percent in 1998. The United Way of America has developed policy guidelines concerning leadership giving and has encouraged the "locals" to expand this resource base (Billitteri 2000b).

CHAPTER 7

1. Their growing access to both public and private sectors was reflected in the level of fundraising by local Alternative Funds. By the mid-1980s, San Francisco Alternative Funds were, compared to other cities across the country, the most successful in gathering workplace gifts. In 1984, CHAD raised $560,000 (National Committee for Responsive Philanthropy 1986), the Bay Area Black United Fund gathered a total of $300,000 in the 1989 campaign (Moore 1990), and the Environmental Federation of California accumulated $700,000 in that same year (Stanford University 1992). Although still only a fraction of the UWBA's total revenue at the time, it is important to point out that the annual revenue of these Alternative Funds surpassed that of most other Alternative Funds in the nation, both then and now.

2. The UWBA faced another concurrent challenge. As respondents told me, its decision to halt funding for the Boy Scouts because of its policy of discrimination against gay members received a mixed reaction (Moore 1994).

3. In the first year, the United Way received applications from 5,000 local nonprofits. It ended up de-funding 100 member agencies and funding 100 new and mostly small and lesser known nonprofits (United Way of the Bay Area 1996, 2000c). Even more impressively, the UWBA did not eliminate its donative transfers only from new or small member agencies. Instead, the UWBA severely decreased or cut funding for its large, traditional, and legitimacy-granting member agencies. The Girl Scouts and the local Urban League, for example, each had their allocations cut by more than $300,000 (Epstein 1996).

4. Ultimately, however, there was less profit to be extracted from pledge processing than many actors had initially thought (Greene 2000). Many of the for-profit entities would soon close, and PipeVine itself experienced a "mysterious collapse" as millions of dollars went missing (Wallace 2004).

References

Abbott, Andrew. 1988. *The System of Professions: An Essay on the Division of Expert Labour*. Chicago: University of Chicago Press.

Abzug, Rikki. 1996. "The Evolution of Trusteeship in the United States: A Round-up of Findings." *Nonprofit Management & Leadership* 7:101–111.

Aldrich, Howard. 1979. *Organizations and Environments*. Englewood Cliffs, NJ: Prentice-Hall.

Alexander, Victoria. 1996. *Museums and Money*. Bloomington: Indiana University Press.

———. 1998. "Environmental Constraints and Organizational Strategies." In *Private Action and the Public Good*, edited by Walter W. Powell and Elizabeth S. Clemens, 272–290. New Haven: Yale University Press.

Alperson, Myra. 1995. *Corporate Giving Strategies That Add Business Value*. New York: Conference Board.

American Association for Organizing Charity. 1917. *Financial Federations: The Report of a Special Committee*. New York: American Association for Organizing Charity.

American National Red Cross. 1949. *The Case for Freedom in Welfare Fund Raising*. Washington, DC: American National Red Cross.

Americans for the Arts. 2002. *United Arts Funds Fiscal Year 2001*. Washington, DC: Americans for the Arts.

Anderson, Benedict. 1983. *Imagined Communities: Reflections on the Origin and Spread of Nationalism*. London: Verso.

Andrews, F. Emerson. 1950. *Philanthropic Giving*. New York: Russell Sage Foundation.

Armstrong, Elizabeth. 2002. *Forging Gay Identities*. Chicago: University of Chicago Press.

Ashforth, Blake E. and Barrie W. Gibbs. 1990. "The Double-Edge of Organizational Legitimacy." *Organization Science* 1:177–94.

Astin, A.W., L.J. Sax, and J. Avalos. 1999. "Long Term Effects of Volunteerism during the Undergraduate Years." *Review of Higher Education* 22:187–202.

Barley, Stephen and Gideon Kunda. 1992. "Design and Devotion: Surges of Rational and Normative Ideologies of Control in Managerial Discourse." *Administrative Science Quarterly* 37(3):363–399.

Barman, Emily. 2002. "Asserting Difference: The Strategic Response of Nonprofits to Competition." *Social Forces* 80(4):1191–1222.

Barry, John W. and Bruno V. Manno, eds. 1997. *Giving Better, Giving Smarter: Renewing Philanthropy in America*. Washington, DC: National Commission on Philanthropy and Civic Renewal.

Bay Area Committee for Responsive Philanthropy. 1979. *Small Change from Big Bucks: A Report and Recommendations on Bay Area Foundations and Social Change*. San Francisco: Bay Area Committee for Responsive Philanthropy.

Bay Area Economic Forum. 1999. *The Bay Area: Winning in the New Global Economy*. San Francisco: Bay Area Economic Forum.

Bell, Colin and Howard Newby. 1971. *Community Studies*. London: Unwin.

Bellah, Robert N., Richard Madsen, William M. Sulliver, Ann Swidler, and Steven M. Tipton. 1980. *Habits of the Heart*. Berkeley: University of California Press.

Bender, Thomas. 1982. *Community and Social Change in Urban America*. Baltimore: Johns Hopkins University Press.

Ben-Ner, Avner and T. Van Hoomissen. 1992. "An Empirical Investigation of the Joint Determination of the Size of the For-Profit, Non-Profit and Voluntary Sectors." *Annals of Public and Cooperative Economics* (63):391–415.

Berger, Peter and Richard Neuhaus. 1977. *To Empower the People: The Role of Mediating Structures in Public Policy*. Washington, DC: American Enterprise Institute.

Berman, Mark, ed. 1994. *The Future of Workplace Giving*. New York: Conference Board.

Berry, Jeffrey. 1997. *The Interest Group Society*, 3rd.ed. New York: Longman.

Bielby, William T. and Denise D. Bielby. 1999. "Organizational Mediation of Project-Based Labor Markets: Talent Agencies and the Careers of Screenwriters." *American Sociological Review* 64:64–85.

Bielefeld, Wolfgang. 2000. "Metropolitan Nonprofit Sectors: Findings from NCCS Data." *Nonprofit and Voluntary Sector Quarterly* 29(2):297–314.

Bielefeld, Wolgang and John Corbin. 1996. "The Institutionalization of Nonprofit Human Service Delivery: The Role of Political Culture." *Administration and Society* (28):362–389.

Billitteri, Thomas J. 2000a. "United Ways Seek a New Identity." *The Chronicle of Philanthropy*, March 9.

———. 2000b. "Venturing a Bet on Giving." *The Chronicle of Philanthropy* XII(16):1–7,10, 12.

Black United Fund of Illinois. 1998. *Helping Hands: A Publication of the BUFI*. Chicago: Black United Fund of Illinois.

Blau, Peter J. 1970. "A Formal Theory of Differentiation in Organizations." *American Sociological Review* 35(2):201–218.

Bloomgarden, Henry S. 1958. *Before We Sleep*. New York: Putnam.

Blum, Debra and Susan Gray. 1998. "Big Business Means Big Philanthropy." *Chronicle of Philanthropy*, July 16.

Boli, John and George M. Thomas. 1999. *Constructing World Culture: International Non-Government Organizations since 1875*. Stanford: Stanford University Press.

Booth, Alan, Douglas Higgins, and Robert Cornelius. 1989. "Community Influences on Funds Raised by Human Service Volunteers." *Nonprofit and Voluntary Sector Quarterly* 18(1):81–92.

Bordt, Rebecca. 1997. *The Structure of Women's Nonprofit Organizations*. Bloomington, IN: Indiana University Press.

Boris, Elizabeth T. 1999. "The Nonprofit Sector in the 1990s." In *Philanthropy and the Nonprofit Sector*, edited by Charles T. Clotfelter and Thomas Ehrlich, 1–33. Bloomington, IN: Indiana University Press.

Bothwell, Robert. 1998. *Federated Giving: Recent History, Current Issues*. Washington, DC: National Committee for Responsive Philanthropy.

Bourdieu, Pierre. 1977. *Outline of a Theory of Practice*. Cambridge: Cambridge University Press.

———. 1984. *Distinction: A Social Critique of the Stratification of Taste*. Cambridge, MA: Harvard University Press.

———. 1990. *The Logic of Practice*. Cambridge, MA: Polity Press.

Bourdieu, Pierre and Loic J.D. Wacquant. 1992. *An Invitation to Reflexive Sociology*. Chicago: University of Chicago Press.

Boyd, Nan Alamilla. 2003. *Wide Open Town: A Queer History of San Francisco*. Berkeley, CA: University of California Press.

Boyte, Harry C. 1980. *The Backyard Movement: Understanding the New Citizen Movement*. Philadelphia: Temple University Press.

———. 2004. *Everyday Politics*. Philadelphia: University of Pennsylvania Press.

Bradshaw, Pat, Vic Murray, and Jacob Wolpin. 1996. "Women on Boards of Directors: What Difference Do They Make?" *Nonprofit Management and Leadership* 6(3):241–254.

Branch, Shelly. 2001. "Philip Morris's Ad on Macaroni and Peace – Kosovo Tale Narrows Gap between Philanthropy, Publicity." *Wall Street Journal*, July 24.

Bremner, Robert H. 1960. *American Philanthropy*. Chicago: University of Chicago Press.

Brilliant, Eleanor. 1990. *The United Way: Dilemmas of Organized Charity*. New York: Columbia University Press.

———. 2000a. *Private Charity and Public Inquiry*. Bloomington, IN: Indiana University Press.

———. 2000b. "Women's Gain: Fund Raising and Fund Allocation as an Evolving Social Movement Strategy." *Nonprofit and Voluntary Sector Quarterly* 29(4):554–570.

Brint, Steven. 2001. "Gemeinschaft Revisited: Rethinking the Community Concept." Sociological Theory 19:1–23.

Browning, Rufus, Dale Marshall, and David Tabb. 1984. *Protest Is Not Enough: The Struggle of Blacks and Hispanics for Equality in Urban Politics*. Berkeley: University of California.

Brulle, Robert J. 2000. *Agency, Democracy, and Nature: The U.S. Environmental Movement from a Critical Theory Perspective*. Cambridge, MA: MIT University Press.

Buechler, Steven M. 1990. *Women's Movements in the United States*. New Brunswick, NJ: Rutgers University Press.

Buenker, John D. 1988. "Sovereign Individuals and Organic Networks: Political Culture in Conflict during the Progressive Era." *American Quarterly* 40:187–204.

Burlingame, Dwight F. and Dennis R. Young, eds. 1996. *Corporate Philanthropy at the Crossroads*. Bloomington, IN: Indiana University Press.

Calhoun, Craig. 1994. "Social Theory and the Politics of Identity." In *Social Theory and the Politics of Identity*, edited by Craig Calhoun, 9–36. Cambridge: Blackwell.

———. 1995. "'New Social Movements' of the Early Nineteenth Century." In *Repertoires and Cycles of Collective Action*, edited by Mark Traugott, 173–215. Durham, NC: Duke University Press.

Camarillo, Albert. 1991. "Mexican Americans and Nonprofit Organizations: An Historical Overview." In *Hispanics and the Nonprofit Sector*, edited by Herman E. Gallegos and Michael O'Neill, 15–32. New York: Foundation Center.

Capek, Mary Ellen S. 1998. *Women and Philanthropy: Old Stereotypes, New Challenges*, vol. 2. San Francisco: Women's Funding Network.

Carnegie, Andrew. 1962. *The Gospel of Wealth and Other Timely Essays*, edited by Edward C. Kirland. Cambridge, MA: Belknap Press of Harvard University Press.

Carpenter, Dave. 2003. "Big Shoulders to Big Services." *Northwest Indiana Times*, November 30.

Carson, Emmett D. 1983. "The National Black United Fund: From Movement for Social Change to Social Change Organization." *New Directions for Philanthropic Fund-Raising* 1(Fall):53–71.

———. 1999. "The Role of Indigenous and Institutional Philanthropy in Advancing Social Justice." In *Philanthropy and the Nonprofit Sector in a Changing America*, edited by Charles T. Clotfelter and Thomas Ehrlich, 248–274. Bloomington, IN: Indiana University Press.

Carter, Richard. 1961. *The Gentle Legions*. New York: Doubleday

Castells, Manual. 1983. "Urban Poverty, Ethnic Minorities and Community Organization: The Experience of Neighborhood Mobilization in San

Francisco's Mission District." In *The City and the Grassroots: A Cross-Cultural Theory of Urban Social Movements*, 106–137. Berkeley, CA: University of California.

Cerulo, Karen A. 1997. "Identity Construction: New Issues, New Directions." *Annual Review of Sociology* 23:385–409.

Chambre, Susan M. 1995. "Creating New Nonprofit Organizations as Response to Social Change: HIV/AIDS Organizations in New York City." *Policy Studies Review* 14:117–127.

Chaves, Mark. 1999. "Financing American Religion." In *Financing American Religion*, edited by Mark Chaves and Sharon L. Miller, 169–188. Walnut Creek, CA: AltaMira Press.

Child, John. 1972. "Organizational Structure, Environment, and Performance: The Role of Strategic Choice." *Sociology* 6:1–22.

"Charities: All for One, One for All." 1949. *Newsweek*, November 21(34):25–26.

Clapp, Raymond. 1926. *Study of Volume and Cost of Social Work 1924*. Cleveland: Welfare Federation of Cleveland.

Clarke, Lee and Carroll Estes. 1992. "Sociological and Economic Theories of Markets and Nonprofits: Evidence from Home Health Organizations." *American Journal of Sociology* 97(4):945–69.

Clotfelter, Charles. 1997. "The Economics of Giving." In *Giving Better, Giving Smarter: Working Papers of the National Commission on Philanthropy and Civic Renewal*, edited by John W. Barry and Bruno V. Manno, 31–51. Washington, DC: National Commission on Philanthropy and Civic Renewal.

Cmiel, Kenneth and Susan Levy. 1980. *Corporate Giving in Chicago 1980*. Chicago: Donors Forum of Chicago.

Cohen, Anthony P. 1985. *The Symbolic Construction of Community*. Tavistock: Ellis Horwood.

Cohen, Jean. 1985. "Strategy or Identity: New Theoretical Paradigms and Contemporary Social Movements." *Social Research* 52:663–716.

Cohen, Jean and Andrew Arato. 1994. *Civil Society and Political Theory*. Cambridge: MIT Press.

Coleman, James. 1988. "Social Capital in the Creation of Human Capital." *American Journal of Sociology* 94(Supplement):S95–120.

Combined Federal Campaign. 2004a. "Combined Federal Campaign (CFC) Results." Washington, DC: Combined Federal Campaign. Retrieved November 6, 2004, from http://www.opm.gov/cfc/html/2002-Summary-Totals.pdf.

———. 2004b. "U.S. Office of Personnel Management." Washington, DC: Combined Federal Campaign. Retrieved July 27, 2004, from http://www.opm.gov/cfc/html/cfc_hist.htm#recent.

Community Chests and Councils, Inc. 1937. *Yesterday and Today with Community Chests*. New York: Community Chests and Councils, Inc.

Community Chests and Councils of America. 1938. *Experiments with More Inclusive Federations*. New York: Community Chests and Councils, Inc.

Community Health Charities. 2001. "Working for a Healthy California." Sacramento, CA: Community Health Charities.

Community Health Charities of Illinois. n.d. "Community Health Charities of Illinois: Representing the Premier Health Care Agencies of Illinois." Chicago: Community Health Charities of Illinois.

Conley, Dalton. 2000. "The Racial Wealth Gap: Origins and Implications for Philanthropy in the African American Community." *Nonprofit and Voluntary Sector Quarterly* 29(4):530–540.

Consulting Network. 2000. *Employee Workplace Campaigns at the Crossroads: Recommendations for Revitalization*. Alexandria, VA: America's Charities and Consulting Network.

Cook, Dick. 1985. *Study of United Way Donor Option Programs*. Washington, DC: National Committee for Responsive Philanthropy.

Corbin, John J. 1999. "A Study of Factors Influencing the Growth of Nonprofits in Social Services." *Nonprofit and Voluntary Sector Quarterly* 28(3):296–314.

Cordes, Joseph J., Jeffrey R. Henig, Eric C. Twombly, with Jennifer Sauders. 1999. "The Effects of Expanded Donor Choice in United Way Campaigns on Nonprofit Human Services Providers in the Washington, D.C. Metropolitan Area." *Nonprofit and Voluntary Sector Quarterly* 28:127–151.

Cordes, Joseph J. C. Eugene Steuerle, and Eric Twombly. 2004. "Dimensions of Nonprofit Entrepreneurship: An Exploratory Essay." Pp. 115–151 in *Public Policy and the Economics of Entrepreneurship*, edited by Douglas Holtz-Eakin and Harvey S. Rosen. Cambridge, MA: The MIT Press.

Cortes, Michael. 1991. "Philanthropy and Latino Nonprofits: A Research Agenda." In *Hispanics in the Nonprofit Sector*, edited by Herman E. Gallegos and Michael O'Neill, 139–160. New York: Foundation Center.

Crown, Judith and Greg Hinz. 1999. "Who Stole Chicago?" *Crain's Chicago Business*, May 3.

Cutlip, Scott. 1965. *Fund Raising in the United States*. New Brunswick, NJ: Rutgers University Press.

D'Anieri, Paul, Clair Ernst, and Elizabeth Kier, "New Social Movements in Historical Perspective." *Comparative Politics*, 22:4 (July) 1990: 445–459.

Davis, King E. 1975. *Fund Raising in the Black Community: History, Feasibility, and Conflict*. Metuchen, NJ: Scarecrow Press.

DeLeon, Richard. 1992. Left Coast City: Progressive Politics in San Francisco, 1975–1991. Lawrence, KS: University of Kansas.

Delgado, Gary. 1986. *Organizing the Movement*. Philadelphia: Temple University Press.

———. 1997. *Beyond the Politics of Place: New Directions in Community Organizing*, 2nd. ed. Berkeley, CA: Chardon Press.

D'Emilio, John. 1992. Sexual Politics, Sexual Communities: The Making of a Homosexual Minority in the United States, 1940–1970. Chicago: University of Chicago Press.

"Detroit Gathers Charity 'Drives' Under One Roof." 1949. *Saturday Evening Post* 222 (October 1):10–12.

DeVault, Marjorie. 1996. "Talking Back to Sociology: Distinctive Contributions of Feminist Methodology." *Annual Review of Sociology* 22:29–50.

Devine, Edward T. 1921. "Welfare Federations." *Survey*, July 16:495–499.

Dickey, Marilyn. 1998a. "Alternative Funds Make Slow Progress in Quest to Solicit Corporate Workers." *Chronicle of Philanthropy*, May 21.

———. 1998b. "Companies Make a Big Push to Get Employees to Donate and Volunteer." *Chronicle of Philanthropy*, July 16.

DiMaggio, Paul J., and Walter W. Powell. 1991. "The Iron Cage Revisited: Institutional Isomorphism and Collective Rationality." In *The New Institutionalism in Organizational Analysis*, edited by Walter W. Powell and Paul J. DiMaggio, 63–82. Chicago: University of Chicago Press.

Dinerman, Beatrice. 1965. *The Dynamics of Priority Planning: A Study of Decision Making in Welfare*. Los Angeles: Ford Foundation and Research Department, Welfare Planning Council.

Do Unto Others. 2004. "DUO." Corte Madera, CA: Do Unto Others. Retrieved June 7, 2004, from www.duo.org.

Dobbin, Frank. 1994. *Forging Industrial Policy: The United States, Britain and France in the Railway Age*. Cambridge: Cambridge University Press.

Domhoff, G. William. 1998. *Who Rules America?*, 3rd ed. Mountain View, CA: Mayfield Publishing Company.

Douglas, Mary. 1966. *Purity and Danger*. London: Routledge and Kegan Paul.

Drake, Jeniece M. 1998. "The Way It Used to Be..Now!" *N'Digo*, December 16:4–5.

Duis, Perry. 1976. *Chicago: Creating New Traditions*. Chicago: Chicago Historical Society.

Dunham, Arthur. 1958. *Community Welfare Organization. Principles and Practice*. New York: Thomas Y. Crowell.

Durkheim, Emile. 1954[1912]. *The Elementary Forms of Religious Life*. London: Allen and Unwin.

———. 1964[1893]. *The Division of Labour in Society*. New York: Free Press.

———. 1970[1897]. *Suicide: A Study in Sociology*. New York: Free Press.

Earth Share of America. 2004. "About Us." Washington, DC: Earth Share of America. Retrieved November 10, 2004, from http://www.earthshare.org/about_us/aboutus.html.

Edwards, Richard. 1999. "International Development NGOs: Agents of Foreign Aid or Vehicles for International Cooperation?" *Nonprofit and Voluntary Sector Quarterly* 1:25–37.

Elazar, Daniel. 1984. *American Federalism: A View from the States*, 3rd. ed. New York: Harper & Row.

Elias, Norbert. 1991. *The Society of Individuals*, translated by E. Jephcott. Oxford: Basil Blackwell.

Eliasoph, Nina. 1998. Avoiding Politics: How Americans Produce Apathy in Everyday Life. Cambridge: Cambridge University Press.

Environmental Fund of Illinois. n.d. "Illinois Is Your environment – Keep It Healthy and Green." Unpublished material. Chicago: Environmental Fund.

Epstein, Cynthia Fuchs. 1992. "Tinker-bells and Pinups: The Construction and Reconstruction of Gender Boundaries at Work." In *Cultivating Differences: Symbolic Boundaries and the Making of Inequality*, edited by Michele Lamont and M. Fournier, 232–256. Chicago: University of Chicago Press.

Epstein, Edward. 1996. "United Way Cuts Gifts to Big Groups." *San Francisco Chronicle*, May 16:A1.

Espiritu, Yen Le. 1992. *Asian American Panethnicity: Bridging Institutions and Identities*. Philadelphia: Temple University Press.

Etzioni, Amitai. 1995. *The Spirit of Community: Rights, Responsibilities and the Communitarian Agenda*. London: Fontana Press.

Evans, Sara. 1979. *Personal Politics*. New York: Knopf.

Fairfax, Jean E. 1995. "Black Philanthropy: Its Heritage and Its Future." In *Cultures of Giving II: How Heritage, Gender, Wealth, and Values Influence Philanthropy*, edited by Charles H. Hamilton and Warren F. Ilchman, 9–22. San Francisco: Jossey-Bass.

Ferman, Barbara. 1991. "Chicago: Power, Race, and Reform." *Big City Politics in Transition* 38:47–63.

Ferree, Myra Marx and Patricia Yancy Martin, eds. 1995. *Feminist Organizations: Harvest of the Women's Movement*. Philadelphia: Temple University Press.

Fink, Justin. 1990. "Philanthropy and the Community." In *Critical Issues in Philanthropy*, edited by Jon Van Til et al., 133–164. San Francisco: Jossey Bass.

Fiorina, Morris. 1999. "Extreme Voices: A Dark Side of Civic Engagement." In *Civic Engagement in American Democracy*, edited by Theda Skocpol and Morris Fiorina, 395–426. New York: Russell Sage Foundation.

Fischer, Claude. 1984[1976]. *The Urban Experience*. San Diego: Harcourt, Brace and Jovanovich.

Fligstein, Neil. 1990. *The Transformation of Corporate Control*. Cambridge, MA: Harvard University Press.

———. 2001. *The Architecture of Markets*. Princeton, NJ: Princeton University Press.

Foley, Michael W. and Bob Edwards. 1996. "The Paradox of Civil Society." *Journal of Democracy* 7:38–52.

Foote, Joseph. 1991. "The Great Divide." *Foundation News*, January/February: 16–21.

"The Fortune 500." 1975. *Fortune* 41(5):23–38.

"The Fortune 500." 1995. *Fortune* 131(9):31–45.

Foundation Center. 1990. *The Foundation Directory*. New York: Foundation Directory.

Fowler, Robert Booth. 1995. "Community: Reflections on Definition." In *New Communitarian Thinking*, edited by Amitai Etzioni, 88–98. Charlottesville, VA: University Press of Virginia.

Freeman, Jo. 1975. *The Politics of Women's Liberation*. New York: David McKay.

Freudenberg, Nicholas and Carol Steinsapir. 1992. "Not in Our Backyards: The Grassroots Environmental Movement." In *American Environmentalism: The US Environmental Movement, 1970–1990*, edited by Riley E. Dunlap and Angela Mertig, 27–35. Philadelphia: Taylor & Francis.

Friedland, Roger and Robert Alford. 1991. "Bringing Society Back In: Symbols, Practices and Institutional Contradictions." In *The New Institutionalism in Organizational Analysis*, edited by Walter W. Powell and Paul J. DiMaggio, 232–263. Chicago: University of Chicago Press.

Froelich, Karen A. 1999. "Diversification of Revenue Strategies: Evolving Resource Dependence in Nonprofit Organizations." *Nonprofit and Voluntary Sector Quarterly* 28:246–268.

Frumkin, Peter. 2002. *On Being Nonprofit: A Conceptual and Policy Primer*. Cambridge, MA: Harvard University Press.

Futcher, Jane. 2000. "United Way Chief Notes Individuals." *Marin Independent Journal*, October 21:B1–B2.

Galaskiewicz, Joseph. 1985. *Social Organization of an Urban Grants Economy*. New York: Academic Press.

———. 1989. "Corporate Contributions to Charity: Nothing More than a Marketing Strategy?" In *Philanthropic Giving: Studies in Varieties and Goals*, edited by Richard Magat, 246–260. New York: Oxford University Press.

———. 1991. "Making Corporate Actors Accountable: Institution-Building in Minneapolis-St. Paul." In *The New Institutionalism in Organizational Analysis*, edited by Walter W. Powell and Paul J. DiMaggio, 293–310. Chicago: University of Chicago Press.

Galaskiewicz, Joseph and Wolfgang Bielefeld, eds. 1998. *Nonprofit Organizations in an Age of Uncertainty: A Study of Organizational Change*. New York: Aldine de Gruyter.

Gamm, Gerald and Robert Putnam. 1999. "The Growth of Voluntary Associations in America, 1840–1940." *Journal of Interdisciplinary History* 29:511–557.

Gamson, Joshua. 1996. "The Organizational Shaping of Collective Identity: The Case of Lesbian and Gay Film Festivals in New York." *Sociological Forum* 11(2): 231–261.

Gamson, William. 1992. *Talking Politics*. New York: Cambridge University Press.

Geertz, Clifford. 1973. *The Interpretation of Cultures*. New York: Basic Books.

Giddens, Anthony. 1991. *Modernity and Self-Identity*. Stanford: Stanford University Press.

Gieryn, Thomas F. 1983. "Boundary-Work and the Demarcation of Science from Non-Science: Strains and Interests in Professional Ideologies of Scientists." *American Sociological Review* 48(6):781–795.

Giving USA. 2005. Indianapolis, IN: Giving USA Foundation.

Glaser, John S. 1994. *The United Way Scandal: An Insider's Account of What Went Wrong and Why*. New York: John Wiley & Sons, Inc.

Glaser, Barry G. and Strauss Anselm L. 1967. *The Discovery of Grounded Theory*. Chicago: Aldine.

Global Impact. 2005a. "About Global Impact." Alexandria, VA: Global Impact. Retrieved January 20, 2005, from http://www.charity.org/about_us/about_global_impact.html.

———. 2005b. "What is Workplace Giving." Alexandria, VA: Global Impact. Retrieved February 10, 2005, from http://www.charity.org/workplace_giving/what_is_workplace_giving.html.

Goode, William J. 1957. "Community within a Community: The Professions." *American Sociological Review* 22:194–200.

Greene, Stephen. 2000. "In Silicon Valley, United Way Sees Role as Program Evaluator." *Chronicle of Philanthropy*, August 24.

Griswold, Wendy. 1992. "The Writing on the Mud Wall: Nigerian Novels and the Imaginary Village." *American Sociological Review* 57(6):709–724.

Gronbjerg, Kristen. 1993. Understanding Nonprofit Funding: Managing Revenues in Social Services and Community Development Organizations. San Francisco: Jossey-Bass.

Gronbjerg Kirsten and Laurie Paarlberg. 2001. "Community Variations in the Size and Scope of the Nonprofit Sector." *Nonprofit and Voluntary Sector Quarterly* 30(4):684–706.

Gronbjerg, Kristen, Lori Harmon, Aida Olkkonen and Asif Raza. 1996. "The United Way System at the Crossroads: Community Planning and Allocation." *Nonprofit and Voluntary Sector Quarterly* 25(4):428–452.

Habermas, Jurgen. 1989. *The Structural Transformation of the Public Sphere*. Cambridge, MA: MIT University Press.

Haider, Donald. 1995. *Case Study of the United Way System of Metropolitan Chicago: Grappling with Change*. Evanston, IL: Center for Urban Affairs and Policy Research.

———. 1997. "Do Trust and Efficiency Still Sell?" In *Giving Better, Giving Smarter: Working Papers of the National Commission on Philanthropy and Civic Renewal*, edited by John W. Barry and Bruno V. Manno, 147–168. Washington, DC: National Commission on Philanthropy and Civic Renewal.

Hall, Peter Dobkin. 1989. "Business Giving and Social Investment in the United States." In *Philanthropic Giving: Studies in Varieties and Goals*, edited by Richard Magat, 221–245. New York: Oxford University Press.

———. 1992. *Inventing the Nonprofit Sector*. Baltimore: Johns Hopkins University Press.

———. 1999. "Vital Signs: Organizational Population Trends and Civic Engagement in New Haven, Connecticut, 1850–1998." In *Civic Engagement in American Democracy*, edited by Theda Skocpol and Morris Fiorina, 211–248. New York: Russell Sage Foundation.

Han, Shin-Kap. 1994. "Mimetic Isomorphism and Its Effect on the Audit Services Market." *Social Forces* 73(2):637–663.

Hannan, Michael T. and John Freeman. 1977. "The Population Ecology of Organizations." *American Journal of Sociology* 82:929–64.

Harder, W. Paul, Madeleine Kimmich, and Lester Salamon. 1985. *The San Francisco Bay Area in a Time of Government Entrenchment*. Washington, DC: Urban Institute Press.

Harvey, David. 1989. *The Condition of Postmodernity*. Cambridge, MA: Blackwell Books.

Hatfield, Larry D. 1970. "11 Health Groups to Rival Crusade." *San Francisco Sunday Examiner and Chronicle*, December 27:A4.

Hawes, J.M. 1991. *The Children's Rights Movement*. Boston: Twayne.

Hawley, Amos. 1971. *Urban Society: An Ecological Approach*. New York: Ronald Press.

Heald, Morrell. 1970. *The Social Responsibilities of Business*. Cleveland: Case Western University Press.

Health Charities of Florida. 2003. "Pure and Simple." Crawfordville, FL: Health Charities of Florida. Retrieved November 4 2003, from www.healthcharitiesfla.org.

Healy, Kieran. 2000. "Sacred Markets and Secular Ritual in the Organ Transplant Industry." *American Journal of Sociology* 105 (6):1633–1657.

———. 2004. "Altruism as an Organizational Problem: The Case of Organ Procurement." *American Sociological Review* 69:387–404.

Hillery, George. 1955. "Definitions of Community: Areas of Agreement." *Rural Sociology* 20:11–123.

Himmelstein, Jerome. 1997. *Looking Good and Doing Good*. Bloomington, IN: University of Indiana Press.

Hirsch, Paul M. 1972. "Processing Fads and Fashions: An Organizational-Set Analysis of Cultural Industry Systems." *American Journal of Sociology* 77(January):639–659.

Hispanic United Fund. 2006. "Our Mission." Corte Madera, CA: Hispanic United Fund. Retrieved February 24, 2006 from http://www.hispanicunitedfund.org/mission.html.

Hodgkinson, Virginia and Murray Weitzman. 1994. *Giving & Volunteering in the United States*. Washington, DC: Independent Sector.

————. 1997. *Nonprofit Almanac 1996–97: Dimensions of the Independent Sector*. San Francisco: Jossey-Bass Publishers.

Hoge, Dean, Charles Zech, Patrick McNamara, and Michael J. Donahue. 1996. *Money Matters: Personal Giving in American Churches*. Louisville, KY: Westminster John Knox Press.

Hughes, Allison. 1994. *Corporate Impact on the Community: A Study of Charitable Contribution Patterns for Corporations with Local, Non-Local Domestic and Foreign Headquarters in Three U.S. Cities*. Economics Honors Thesis, Harvard University.

Hummon, David. M. 1990. *Commonplaces – Community Ideology and Identity in American Culture*. Albany, NY: State University of New York Press.

Independent Sector. 2001. *The Nonprofit Almanac IN BRIEF*. Washington, DC: Independent Sector.

Iriye, Akira. 2002. Global Community: The Role of International Organizations in the Making of the Contemporary World. Berkeley, CA: University of California Press.

James, Estelle. 1987. "The Nonprofit Sector in Comparative Perspective." In *The Nonprofit Sector: A Research Handbook*, edited by Walter W. Powell, 397–415. New Haven, CT: Yale University Press.

Janowitz, Morris. 1952. *The Community Press in an Urban Setting*. Chicago: University of Chicago Press.

Jasper, James M. and Dorothy Nelkin. 1992. *The Animal Rights Crusade: The Growth of a Moral Protest*. New York: Free Press.

Jencks, Christopher. 1988. "Who Gives to What?" In *The Nonprofit Sector: A Research Handbook*, edited by Walter W. Powell, 321–339. New Haven, CT: Yale University Press.

Jenkins, J. Craig. 1988. "Nonprofit Organizations and Public Advocacy." In *The Nonprofit Sector: A Research Handbook*, edited by Walter W. Powell, 296–320. New Haven, CT: Yale University Press.

Jenkins, J. Craig and Abigail Halcli. 1999. "Grassrooting the System? The Development and Impact of Social Movement Philanthropy, 1953–1990." In *Philanthropic Foundations: New Scholarship, New Possibilities*, edited by Ellen Condliffe Lageman, 229–256. Bloomington, IN: Indiana University Press.

Johnson, Elmer W. 1999. *Chicago Metropolis 2020: Preparing Metropolitan Chicago for the 21st Century*. Chicago: The Commercial Club of Chicago and the American Academy of Arts and Sciences.

Johnston, Hank, Enrique Larana, and Joseph R. Gusfield. 1994. "Identities, Grievances, and New Social Movements." In *New Social Movements: From Ideology to Identity*, 3–35. Philadelphia: Temple University Press.

Judd, Dennis and Michael Parkinson, eds. 1990. "Leadership and Urban Regeneration: Cities in North America and Europe" *Urban Affairs Annual Reviews* 37.

Kanter, Rosabeth Moss. 2000. "Business Coalitions as a Force for Regionalism." In *Reflections on Regionalism*, edited by Bruce Katz, 154–182. Washington, DC: Brookings Institute Press.

Karl, Barry. 1987. *The Rise of a Gay and Lesbian Movement*. Boston: Twayne Publishers.

Katz, Michael B. 1986. *In the Shadow of the Poorhouse: A Social History of Welfare in America*. New York: Basic Books.

Kaufman, Jason. 2003. *For the Common Good? American Civic Life and the Golden Age of Fraternity*. New York: Oxford University Press.

Keller, Suzanne. 2003. *Community: Pursuing the Dream, Living the Reality*. Princeton, NJ: Princeton University Press.

Kirsner, Scott. 1999. "Nonprofit Motive." *Wired* 7.09. Retrieved February 24, 2005, from http://www.wired.com/wired/archive/7.09/philanthropy.html.

Kraft Foods, Inc. 2005a. "Contributions and Community." Retrieved September 26, 2005, from. http://kraft.com/responsibility/cc_employeefund.aspx.

Kraft Foods, Inc. 2005b. "Contributions and Community." Retrieved September 26, 2005, from http://kraft.com/responsibility/cc_kraft_cares.aspx.

Kuhn, Thomas. 1970. *The Structure of Scientific Revolutions*. Chicago: University of Chicago Press.

Kusmer, Kenneth L. 1973. "The Functions of Organized Charity in the Progressive Era: Chicago as a Case Study." *The Journal of American History* 60:657–678.

Lamont, Michele. 1992. *Money, Morals, and Manners: The Culture of the French and American Upper-Middle Class*. Chicago: University of Chicago Press.

Lasch, Christopher. 1979. *The Culture of Narcissism: American Life in an Age of Diminishing Expectations*. New York: Norton.

———. 1991. *True and Only Heaven: Progress and Its Critics*. New York: Norton.

Lauffer, Armand. 1997. *Grants, Etc.* Thousand Oaks, CA: Sage Publications, Inc.

Lawler, Edward T. 1994. "Total Quality Management and Employee Involvement: Are They Compatible?" *Academy of Management Executive* Jan: 68–76.

Lears, Jackson. 1991. *No Place of Grace: Antimodernism and the Transformation of American Culture, 1880–1920*. New York: Pantheon.

Leebron, Harvey. 1924. *The Financial Federation Movement*. Chicago: Chicago Council of Social Agencies.

Lenkowsky, Leslie. 2002. "Foundations and Corporate Philanthropy." In *State of Nonprofit America*, edited by Lester Salamon, 355–386. Washington, DC: Brookings Institution Press.

Letts, Christine, William Ryan, and Allen Grossman. 1997. "Virtuous Capital: What Foundations Can Learn from Venture Capitalists." *Harvard Business Review*, March-April.

Levi-Strauss, Claude. 1962. *The Savage Mind*. Chicago: University of Chicago Press.

Levi Strauss Corporation. 2004. "Social Responsibility/Giving Guidelines." San Francisco: Levi Strauss Corporation. Retrieved November 1, 2004, from http://www.levistrauss.com/responsibility/foundation/guidelines.htm.

Levy, Reynold. 1999. *Give and Take: A Candid Account of Corporate Philanthropy*. Boston: Harvard Business School Press.

Lichterman, Paul. 1996. *The Search of Political Community*. Cambridge: Cambridge University Press.

Lincoln, James R. 1977. "The Urban Distribution of Voluntary Organizations." *Social Science Quarterly* 58:472–480.

Litwak, Eugene and Lydia F. Hylton. 1962. "Interorganizational Analysis: A Hypothesis on Coordinating Agencies." *Administrative Science Quarterly* 6:395–420.

Lubove, Roy. 1965. *The Professional Altruist*. Cambridge, MA: Harvard University Press.

Lynd, Robert S. and Helen Merrell Lynd. 1929. *Middletown: A Study in Contemporary American Culture*. New York: Harcourt, Brace, and Company.

Maas, Peter. 1960. "Where Does Your Charity Dollar Go?" *Look*, March 15:40–46.

Marx, Jerry. 1997. "Corporate Philanthropy and the United Way: Challenges for the Year 2000." *Nonprofit Management and Leadership* 8:19–30.

Matthews, Glenna. 1997. "Forging a Cosmopolitan Civic Culture: The Regional Identity of San Francisco and Northern California" In *Many Wests: Place, Culture, and Regional Identity*, edited by Michael Steiner, 211–234. Lawrence, KS: University Press of Kansas.

Mayer, Harold M., Richard C. Wade, and Glen E. Holt. 1969. *Chicago: Growth of a Metropolis*. Chicago: University of Chicago Press.

McAdam, Douglas. 1999[1982]. *Political Process and the Development of Black Insurgency*. Chicago: University of Chicago Press.

McCarthy, John and Meyer Zald. 1977. "Resource Mobilization and Social Movements." *American Journal of Sociology* 82:1212–1242.

McCarthy, Kathleen D. 1982. *Noblesse Oblige: Charity and Cultural Philanthropy in Chicago, 1849–1929*. Chicago: University of Chicago Press.

———. 1987. "Charting the Research Agenda: An Historian's Perspective." In *Setting the Research Agenda in Philanthropy and Voluntarism: Eight Discussion Papers*, edited by Charles T. Clotfelter, 23–31. Durham, NC: Duke University, Center for the Study of Philanthropy and Voluntarism.

———. 1991. "The Gospel of Wealth: American Giving in Theory and Practice." In *Philanthropic Giving: Studies in Varieties and Goals*, edited by Richard Magat. 46–62. New York: Oxford University Press.

McElroy, Katherine M. and John J. Siegfried. 1986. "The Community Influence on Corporate Contributions." *Public Finance Quarterly* 14(4): 394–414.

McLaughlin, Paul and Marwan Khawaja. 2000. "The Organizational Dynamics of the U.S. Environmental Movement: Legitimation, Resource Mobilization, and Political Opportunity." *Rural Sociology* 65:422–439.

McRoberts, Omar. 2003. *Streets of Glory: Church and Community in a Black Urban Neighborhood.* Chicago: University of Chicago Press.

Melucci, Alberto. 1980. "The New Social Movements." *Social Science Information* 19:199–226.

Menard, Scott. 1995. *Applied Logistic Regression Analysis.* Thousand Oaks, CA: Sage.

Meyer, Eugene, Mrs. 1945. "Judgment Day for the Private Welfare Agency." *Public Opinion Quarterly* 9:338–345.

Meyer, John W. and Brian Rowan. 1977. "Institutionalized Organizations: Formal Structure as Myth and Ceremony." *American Journal of Sociology* 83:340–363.

Middleton, Melissa. 1987. "Nonprofit Board of Directors: Beyond the Governance Function." In *The Nonprofit Sector: A Research Handbook*, edited by Walter W. Powell, 141–153. New Haven, CT: Yale University Press.

Millar, Bruce. 1991. "United Way's Rivals Gain Ground." *The Chronicle of Philanthropy* IV(4):1, 24–25.

———. 1994. "A Warning for United Way Leaders." *The Chronicle of Philanthropy*, April 5:27–28.

Milosky, Carl. 1979. "Not for Profit Organizations and Community: A Review of the Sociological Literature." *PONPO Working Paper No. 6.* New Haven, CT: Yale University Press.

Minkoff, Debra. 1995. *Organizing for Equality: The Evolution of Women's and Race-Ethnic Organizations in America, 1955–1985.* New Brunswick, NJ: Rutgers University Press.

———. 1997. "Producing Social Capital: National Social Movements and Civil Society." *American Behavioral Scientist* 40(5):606–619.

Monroe, Kristen. 1996. *The Heart of Altruism: Perceptions of a Common Humanity.* Princeton, NJ: Princeton University Press.

Moore, Kelly. 1996. "Organizing Integrity: American Science and the Creation of Public Interest Organizations, 1955–1975." *American Journal of Sociology* 6:1592–1627.

Moore, Teresa. 1993. "United Way Agencies to Receive Less Money." *San Francisco Chronicle*, June 3:A19.

———. 1994. "Revamp for Bay United Way." *San Francisco Chronicle*, September 7:A1.

Morris, Aldon. l984. *The Origins of the Civil Rights Movement: Black Communities Organizing for Change.* New York: Free Press.

Mount, Joan. 1996. "Why Donors Give." *Nonprofit Management and Leadership* 7:3–14.

Mowat, Lynn. 1948. "The Chest at the Crossroads." *The Community* 1948(6): 106–108.

Muirhead, Sophia A. 1999. *Corporate Contributions: The View from 50 Years*. New York: Conference Board.

Munemitsu, Sally and Thomas W. Knowlton. 2004. *Rediscovering a Strategic Resource: Your Employees*. New York: TCC Group.

Murphy, Tara. 2001. "Sears Takes It to the Next Level." *Forbes*, December 11.

Musick, Marc A., John Wilson, and William B. Bynum Jr. 2000. "Race and Formal Volunteering: The Differential Effects of Class and Religion." *Social Forces* 78:1539–1571.

National Committee for Responsive Philanthropy. 1986. *Charity in the Workplace*. Washington, DC: National Committee for Responsive Philanthropy.

———. 1998. *Charity in the Workplace*. Washington, DC: National Committee for Responsive Philanthropy.

———. 2003. *Giving at Work*. Washington, DC: National Committee for Responsive Philanthropy.

Nisbet, Robert. 1953. *Community and Power*. New York: Oxford University Press.

Norton, William. 1923. *Financial Federations*. New York: Survey.

———. 1927. *The Cooperative Movement in Social Work*. New York: MacMillan.

Oakes, Leslie S., Barbara Townley and David J. Cooper. 1998. "Business Planning as Pedagogy: Language and Control in a Changing Institutional Field." *Administrative Science Quarterly* 43:257:92.

Oboler, Suzanne. 1995. *Ethnic Labels, Ethnic Lives: Identity and the Politics of (Re)Presentation in the United States*. Minneapolis: University of Minnesota Press.

Offe, Claus. 1985. "New Social Movements: Challenging the Boundaries of Institutional Politics." *Social Research* 52(4):817–868.

Oliver, Christine. 1991. "Strategic Responses to Institutional Processes." *Academy of Management Review* 16:145–179.

Orsi, Robert. 1985. *The Madonna of 115th Street: Faith and Community in Italian Harlem, 1880–1950*. New Haven, CT: Yale University Press.

Oster, Sharon. 1995. *Strategic Management for Nonprofit Organizations*. Oxford: Oxford University Press.

Ostrander, Susan. 1995. *Money for Change: Social Movement Philanthropy at Haymarket People's Fund*. Philadelphia: Temple University Press.

Ostrander, Susan and Paul Schervish. 1990. "Giving and Getting: Philanthropy as Social Relations." In *Critical Issues in American Philanthropy: Strengthening Theory and Practice*, edited by Jon Van Til, 67–98. San Francisco: Jossey-Bass.

Otto, Freda Hinsche. 1994. "The Democratization of Workplace Giving: The Emergence of Alternative Funds and Its Effect on Employee Giving." PhD diss., University of Southern California.

Padilla, Felix. 1985. *Latino Ethnic Consciousness: The Case of Mexican Americans and Puerto Ricans in Chicago*. Notre Dame: University of Notre Dame.

Pampel, Fred. 2000. *Logistic Regression: A Primer*. Thousand Oaks, CA: Sage Publications, Quantitative Applications in the Social Sciences.

Paprocki, Steven. 1988. *On the Effects of Different Types of Workplace Campaigns on Employees' Total Giving and Giving to United Way*. Washington, DC: National Committee for Responsive Philanthropy.

Park, Robert E. 1959. *Human Communities*. Glencoe, IL: Free Press.

Paxton, Pamela. 1999. "Is Social Capital Declining in the United States? A Multiple Indicator Assessment." *American Journal of Sociology* 88–127.

Perlmutter, Felice Davidson, ed. 1988. *Alternative Social Agencies: Administrative Strategies*. New York: Haworth Press.

Perlmutter, Felice Davidson and Vicki W. Kramer. 2001. "Progressive Social Change Funds: Strategies for Survival." Washington, DC: Aspen Institute Nonprofit Sector Research Fund Working Paper Series.

Persons, Frank. 1922. *Central Financing of Social Agencies*. Columbus: Columbus Advisory Council.

Pfeffer, Jeffrey and Anthony Leong. 1977. "Resource Allocations in United Funds: Examination of Power and Dependence." *Social Forces* 55(3):775–790.

Pfeffer, Jeffrey and Gerald Salancik. 1978. *The External Control of Organizations: A Resource Dependence Perspective*. New York: Harper and Row.

Piliavin, Jane and Hong-Wen Charng. 1990. "Altruism: A Review of Recent Research." *Annual Review of Sociology* 16:27–65.

Pitney Bowes. 2005. "Pitney Bowes Annual Report 04." Stamford, CT: Pitney Bowes, Retrieved February 25, 2006, from http://media.corporate-ir.net/media _files/nys/pbi/reports/AR_2004.pdf.

Plotke, David. "What's so New about New Social Movements?" *Socialist Review* 20(1): 81–102.

Podgorski, Al and Nancy Stuenkel. 1994. "Civics 101." *The Chicago Sun-Times*, October 30:1.

Polivy, Deborah Kaplan. 1982. "A Study of the Admissions Policies and Practices of Eight Local United Way Organizations." *Working Paper No. 49*. New Haven, CT: Yale University Program on Non-Profit Organizations.

———. 1985. "Increasing Giving Options in Corporate Charitable Payroll Deduction Campaigns: Who Benefits?" *ISPS Working Paper No. 2083*. New Haven, CT: Yale University Institute for Social and Policy Studies.

———. 1988. "The United Way: Understanding How It Works is the First Step to Effecting Change." In *Community Organizations: Studies in Resource Mobilization and Exchange*, edited by Carl Milofsky, 157–169. New York: Oxford University Press.

Polletta, Francesca. 1998. " 'It Was Like a Fever . . . ' Narrative and Identity in Social Protest." *Social Problems* 45(2): 137–159.

Polletta, Francesca. 2002. *Freedom is an Endless Meeting: Democracy in American Social Movements*. Chicago: University of Chicago Press.

Powell, Walter W. and Rebecca Friedkin. 1987. "Organizational Change in Nonprofit Organizations." In *The Nonprofit Sector: A Research Handbook*, edited by Walter W. Powell, 180–194. New Haven, CT: Yale University Press.

"Practical Methods of Making Adjustment." 1932. *Bulletin* 65(Feb 15):3–5.

Pride Foundation. 2004. "Pride Foundation Programs." Seattle: Pride Foundation, Retrieved November 10, 2004, from http://www.pridefoundation.org/programs/.

Procter, Arthur W. and Arthur A. Schuck. 1926. *The Financing of Social Work*. New York: AW Shaw Company.

Public Interest Fund of Illinois. 2000. "Your Payroll Deduction Choice at Work." Champaign, IL: Public Interest Fund of Illinois, Retrieved March 30, 2000, from www.pifi.org.

Public Management Institute. 1990. *Corporate 500: The Directory of Corporate Philanthropy 1990*. San Francisco, CA: Public Management Institute.

Putnam, Robert. 1993. *Making Democracy Work: Civic Traditions in Modern Italy*. Princeton, NJ: Princeton University Press.

———. 1995. "Bowling Alone: America's Declining Social Capital." *Journal of Democracy* 6:65–78.

———. 2000. *Bowling Alone: The Collapse and Revival of American Community*. New York: Simon & Schuster.

Quandt, Jean. B. 1970. *From the Small Town to the Great Community: The Social Thought of Progressive Intellectuals*. New Brunswick, NJ: Rutgers University Press.

Rabinowitz, Alan. 1990. *Social Change Philanthropy in America*. Westport, CT: Quorum Books.

Ratcliff, Richard E., Mary Elizabeth Gallagher, and Kathryn Strother Ratcliff. 1979. "The Civic Involvement of Bankers: An Analysis of the Influence of Economic Power and Social Prominence in the Command of Civic Policy Positions." *Social Problems* 26:298–303.

Reid, Elizabeth. 1999. "Nonprofit Advocacy and Political Participation." In *Nonprofits and Government: Collaboration and Conflict*, edited by Elizabeth T. Boris, 291–325. Washington, DC: Urban Institute Press.

Reinhold, Richard. 2000. "Chicago's Place in the Metropolitan Area Economy: Why the City Still Matters." *Illinois Labor Market Review* 6(2).

Renz, David O. 1999. "The Case of Kansas City." In *Philanthropy and the Nonprofit Sector in a Changing America*, edited by Charles T. Clotfelter and Thomas Erlich, 315–346. Bloomington, IN: Indiana University Press.

Rheingold, Howard. 1993. *The Virtual Community: Homesteading on the Electronic Frontier*. New York: Harper.

Riesman, David. 1950. *The Lonely Crowd: A Study of the Changing American Character*. New Haven: Yale University Press.

Rimmerman, Craig A. 2002. *From Identity to Politics: The Lesbian and Gay Movements in the United States*. Philadelphia: Temple University Press.

Roberts, Jerry. 1977. "United Way Criticized by State Donor Group." *San Francisco Chronicle*, September 13:12.

Robertson, Alonza. 1990. "United Way Calling for Peace Pact with 'Rival' Charities." *San Francisco Chronicle*, September 10:A9.

Roof, Wade Clark and William McKinney. 1987. *American Mainline Religion. Its Changing Shape and Future*. New Brunswick, NJ: Rutgers University Press.

Rose-Ackerman, Susan. 1988. "United Charities: An Economic Analysis." In *Community Organizations: Studies in Resource Mobilization and Exchange*, edited by Carl Milofsky, 136–156. New York: Oxford University Press.

Rudolph, Lewis. 1993. "Paradigm Shifts: United Ways in Search of Renewal." Unpublished report. Alexandria, VA: United Way of America.

Ryan, John, James Hawdon, and Allison Branick. 2002. "The Political Economy of Diversity: Diversity Programs in Fortune 500 Companies." *Sociological Research Online* 7:1.

Saiia, David, Archie B. Carroll, and Ann K. Buchholtz. 2003. "Does Philanthropy Begin at Home? The Strategic Motivations Underlying Corporate Giving Programs." *Business & Society* 42(2):169–201.

Salamon, Lester. 1987. "Partners in Public Service: The Scope and Theory of Government-Nonprofit Relations." In *The Nonprofit Sector: A Research Handbook*, edited by Walter W. Powell, 99–117. New Haven, CT: Yale University Press.

———. 1999. *America's Nonprofit Sector: A Primer*, 2nd. ed. New York: Foundation Center.

Salamon, Lester and Helmut Anheier. 1996. *The Emerging Nonprofit Sector: An Overview*. Manchester: Johns Hopkins Non-Profit Sector Series.

Sandel, Michael. 1996. *Democracy's Discontent: America in Search of a Public Philosophy*. Cambridge, MA: Harvard University Press.

Sanders, Marion. 1958. "Mutiny of the Bountiful." *Harper's Magazine* 217(December):23–31.

Sargeant, Adrian. 1999. "Charitable Giving: Towards a Model of Donor Behaviour." *Journal of Marketing Management* 15(4):215–238.

Schervish, Paul G. 1995. "Passing It On: The Transmission of Wealth and Financial Care." In *Care and Community in Modern Society: Passing on the Tradition of Service to Future Generations*, edited by Paul G. Schervish, Virginia A. Hodgkinson and Margaret Gates and Associates, 109–133. San Francisco: Jossey-Bass Publishers.

Schlesinger, Mark. 1998. "Mismeasuring the Consequences of Ownership: External Influences and the Comparative Performance of Public, For-Profit, and Private Nonprofit Organizations." In *Private Action and the Public Good*, edited by Walter W. Powell and Elizabeth S. Clemens, 85–113. New Haven: Yale University Press.

Schneider, John C. 1996. "Philanthropic Styles in the United States: Towards a Theory of Regional Differences." *Nonprofit and Voluntary Sector Quarterly* 25(2):190–209.

Schudson, Michael. 1998. *The Good Citizen: a History of American Civil Life*. New York: Free Press.

Scott, W. Richard. 1997. *Organizations: Rational, Natural, and Open Systems.* Englewood Cliffs, NJ: Prentice Hall.

Scott, W. Richard and John Meyer. 1991. "The Organization of Societal Sectors: Propositions and Early Evidence." In *The New Institutionalism in Organizational Analysis*, edited by Walter W. Powell and Paul J. DiMaggio, 108–142. Chicago: University of Chicago Press.

Sears, Roebuck and Co. 2004. "Sears Annual Report 2003." Chicago, IL: Sears, Roebuck, and Co., Retrieved February 25, 2006 from http://adp.mobular.net/adp/24/13/18/.

Seeley, John W., Buford H. Junker and R. Wallace Jones. 1957. *Community Chest.* New Brunswick, NJ: Transaction Publishers.

Seeley, John R., Alexander Sim, and Elizabeth W. Loosley. 1956. *Crestwood Heights: A Study of the Culture of Suburban Life.* New York: Basic Books.

Seidman, Steven. 1993. "Identity Politics in a 'Postmodern' Gay Culture: Some Historical and Conceptual Notes." In *Fear of a Queer Planet*, edited by Michael Warner, 105–142. Minneapolis: University of Minnesota Press.

Selznick, Philip. 1949. *TVA and the Grass Roots.* Berkeley, CA: University of California Press.

———. 1992. *The Moral Commonwealth: Social Theory and the Promise of Community.* Berkeley, CA: University of California Press.

Shao, Stella. 1995. "Asian American Giving: Issues and Challenges (A Practitioner's Perspective)." In *Cultures of Giving II: How Heritage, Gender, Wealth, and Values Influence Philanthropy*, edited by Charles H. Hamilton and Warren F. Ilchman, 53–64. San Francisco: Jossey-Bass.

Shepherd, Jack. 1977. "Passing the Buck: Philanthropy in San Francisco." 1977. *Research Papers: Volume II Philanthropic Fields of Interest.* Washington DC: Department of the Treasure.

Silvergleid, Jordan E. 2003. "Effects of Watchdog Organizations in the Social Capital Market." *New Directions for Philanthropic Fundraising* 41:7–26.

Simmons, P. J. 1998. "Learning to Live with NGOs." *Foreign Policy* 112:82–96.

Sinclair, Michelle and Joseph Galaskiewicz. 1997. "Corporate-Nonprofit Partnerships: Varieties and Covariations." *New York Law School Law Review* 41:1059–1090.

Sklar, Martin J. 1988. *The Corporate Reconstruction of American Capitalism, 1890–1916: The Market, the Law, and Politics.* Cambridge: Cambridge University Press.

Skocpol, Theda. 1999. "Advocates without Members: The Recent Transformation of American Civic Life." In *Civic Engagement in American Democracy*, edited by Theda Skocpol and Morris Fiorina, 461–509. New York: Russell Sage Foundation.

Skocpol, Theda, Ziad Munson, Andrew Karch, and Bayliss Camp. 2002. "Patriotic Partnerships: Why Great Wars Nourished American Civic Voluntarism." In *Shaped by War and Trade: International Influences on American Political Development*, edited by Ira Katznelson and Martin Shefter, 134–180. Princeton, NJ: Princeton University Press.

Smith, David Horton. 1977. "The Role of the United Way in Philanthropy." *Research Papers* 2:1353–1381.

Smith, Steven R. 1999. "Government Financing of Nonprofit Activity." In *Nonprofits and Government: Collaboration and Conflict*, edited by Elizabeth T. Boris and C. Eugene Steuerle, 177–210. Washington, DC: Urban Institute Press.

Smith, Steven R. and Mark Lipsky. 1993. *Nonprofits for Hire: The Welfare State in the Age of Contracting*. Cambridge, MA: Harvard University Press.

Smith, Zay N. 1992. "Charity Scandal Cuts Donations." *The Chicago Sun-Times*, March 2:3.

Social and Economic Justice Fund. 2001. "The Social and Economic Justice Fund." Oakland, CA: Social and Economic Justice Fund.

Sokolowski, S. Wojciech. 1996. "Show Me the Way to the Next Worthy Deed: Towards a Microstructural Theory of Volunteering and Giving." *Voluntas* 7(3):259–278.

Sontheimer, Morton. 1952. "Charity's Civil War." *Cosmopolitan*, October:36–37.

Spangle, Michael and David Knapp. 1996. "Ways We Talk about the Earth: An Exploration of Persuasive Tactics and Appeals in Environmental Discourse." In *Earthtalk: Communication Empowerment for Environmental Action*, edited by Star A. Muir and Thomas L. Veenendall, 3–26. Westport, CT: Praeger.

Stanford University. 1992. "Philanthropy and Competition in the Workplace: Fundraising at Hewlett-Packard." Unpublished paper. Stanford, CA: Stanford University.

Stein, Maurice. 1960. *The Eclipse of Community: An Interpretation of American Studies*. Princeton, N.J., Princeton University Press.

Steinberg, Richard. 1987. "Nonprofit Organizations and the Market." In *The Nonprofit Sector: A Research Handbook*, edited by Walter W. Powell, 118–140. New Haven: Yale University Press.

Steinberg, Richard and Mark Wilhelm. 2005. "Religious and Secular Giving, By Race and Ethnicity." *New Directions for Philanthropic Fundraising* 48:57–66.

Suttles, Gerald D. 1972. *The Social Construction of Communities*. Chicago: University of Chicago Press.

Taylor, Verta and Nancy E. Whittier. 1992. "Collective Identity in Social Movement Communities: Lesbian Feminist Mobilization." In *Frontiers of Social Movement Theory*, 104–129. New Haven, CT: Yale University Press.

Tepperman, Jean. 1995. "Eye on San Francisco." *Foundation News & Commentary*, Jan/Feb:29–32.

Thompson, James D. 1967. *Organizations in Action: Social Science Basis of Administrative Theory*. New York: McGraw-Hill.

Thorpe, Kenneth and Charles Brecher. 1988. "The Social Role of Nonprofit Organizations: Hospital Provision of Charity Care." *Economic Inquiry* 29:472–84.

Titmuss, Richard. 1997[1970]. *The Gift Relationship: From Human Blood to Social Policy*, edited by Ann Oakley and John Ashton. New York: The New Press.

Tocqueville, Alexis de. 1840, 1844. *Democracy in America*. New York; Schocken.

Tolbert, Pamela and Lynne Zucker. 1998. "The Institutionalization of Institutional Theory." In *Handbook of Organization Studies*, edited by Stewart R. Clegg et al., 175–190 London: Sage Publications.

Tonnies, Ferdinand. 1957. *Community & Society*, translated and edited by Charles Loomis. East Lansing, MI: Michigan State University.

Touraine, Alain. 1985. "An Introduction to the Study of Social Movements." *Social Research* 52:749–87.

Trattner, Walter. 1974. *From Poor Law to Welfare State: A History of Social Welfare in America*. New York: Free Press.

Trolander, Judith 1973. "The Response of Settlements to the Great Depression." *Social Work* September:92–102.

Tucker, Kenneth H. 1991. "How New are the New Social Movements?" *Theory, Culture & Society* 8:75–98.

Tuckman, Howard P. 1998. "Competition, Commercialization, and the Evolution of Nonprofit Organizational Structures." *Journal of Policy Analysis and Management* 17:175–94.

United Bay Area Crusade. 1969. "Minutes of January 28th Meeting of the United Bay Area Crusade Board of Directors." Unpublished document. San Francisco: UBAC.

United States Census Bureau. 1980. *1980 Census of Population and Housing*. Washington, DC: U.S. Census Bureau.

———. 1982. *State and Metropolitan Area Data Book*. Washington, DC: U.S. Census Bureau.

———. 1990. *1990 Census of Population and Housing*. Washington, DC: U.S. Census Bureau.

———. 2000. *2000 Census of Population and Housing*. Washington, DC: U.S. Census Bureau.

United Way/Crusade of Mercy. 2003. *United Way/Crusade of Mercy Annual Report*. Chicago: United Way/Crusade of Mercy.

United Way/Crusade of Mercy. 1998a. *Civic Committee Report*. Unpublished document. Chicago: United Way/Crusade of Mercy.

———. 1998b. *Donor's Guide*. Chicago: United Way/Crusade of Mercy.

———. 1997a. *Group Discussions with Donors and Non-Donors of United Way*. Unpublished paper.

———. 1997b. *The Way Ahead: United Way/Crusade of Mercy Strategic Outline*. Unpublished paper.

———. 1999. *UW/CM Pledge Card*. Chicago: United Way/Crusade of Mercy.

———. 2000. *United Way/Crusade of Mercy Annual Report*. Chicago: United Way/Crusade of Mercy.

———. 2001. *United Way/Crusade of Mercy Annual Report*. Chicago: United Way/Crusade of Mercy.

United Way Historical Summary. n.d. Unpublished paper.

United Way Metro Chicago. 2003. *What Matters at United Way*. Chicago: United Way Metro Chicago.

United Way of Chicago. 1990. *History of United Way of Chicago*. Unpublished Paper.

———. 1992. A History of the United Way of Chicago, 1930–1990. Chicago: United Way of Chicago.

———. 2002. The Way We Care: 2001–2002 Annual Report to Metropolitan Chicago. Chicago: United Way of Chicago.

United Way of America. 1963. *Directory*. Alexandria, VA: United Way of America.

———. 1971. *Measurements of Campaign Performance*. Washington, DC: United Way of America.

———. 1975. *Directory*. Washington, DC: United Way of America.

———. 1977. *People and Events: A History of the United Way*. Washington, DC: United Way of America.

———. 1978. *Donor Preference Policies and Practices*. Washington, DC: United Way of America.

———. 1980. *Listening to the Community: 1979 United Way National Marketing Survey*. Washington, DC: United Way of America.

———. 1982. *Donor Option*. Washington, DC: United Way of America.

———. 1984. *Needs Assessment and Evaluation Practices of United Ways*. Alexandria, VA: United Way of America.

———. 1988. *Competitive Marketing: A Guide for United Ways and Other Nonprofits*. Alexandria, VA: UWA Strategic Planning and Market Research Division.

———. 1999. "Donor Preference Policies and Practices." Unpublished document.

———. 2004. "2000–01 CAMPAIGN RESULTS (Highlights)." Alexandria, VA: United Way of America, Retrieved September 2, 2004, from http://national. unitedway.org/aboutuwa/publications/2000campaignresults/2000results.cfm.

United Way of the Bay Area. 1978. "Minutes of June 14th Meeting of United Way of the Bay Area Board of Directors. Unpublished document. San Francisco: United Way of the Bay Area.

———. 1986. *Donor Option and Designations . . . A Perspective*. San Francisco: United Way of the Bay Area.

———. 1987. *Widening the Circle of Commitment*. San Francisco: United Way of the Bay Area.

———. 1990. "Statement of Strategic Direction." Unpublished document. San Francisco: United Way of the Bay Area.

———. 1992. *UWBA Annual Report*. San Francisco: United Way of the Bay Area.

———. 1993. *United Way Strategic Plan*. San Francisco: United Way of the Bay Area.

———. 1996. *UWBA Annual Report*. San Francisco: United Way of the Bay Area.

———. 1998a. *UWBA Report to the Community*. San Francisco: United Way of the Bay Area.

———. 1998b. *Vision 2001*. San Francisco: United Way of the Bay Area.

———. 2000a. *Campaign Advisor Handbook*. San Francisco: United Way of the Bay Area.

———. 2000b. *Communications Platform*. San Francisco: United Way of the Bay Area.

———. 2000c. *Community Impact Fund Report*. San Francisco: United Way of the Bay Area.

———. 2000d *Thank you Card*. San Francisco: United Way of the Bay Area.

———. 2001. *Annual Report*. San Francisco: United Way of the Bay Area.

———. 2002. *Annual Report*. San Francisco: United Way of the Bay Area.

Useem, Michael. 1988. "Market and Institutional Factors in Corporate Contributions." *California Management Review* 30:77–88.

Van Maanen, John and Stephen R. Barley. 1984. "Occupational Communities: Culture and Control in Organizations." *Research in Organizational Behavior* 6:287–365.

Wallace, Nicole. 2004. "Donation-Processing Charity Lost at Least $17.7-Million in Gifts." *Chronicle of Philanthropy*, March 4.

Walter, Kate. 1997. "Nurturing Charitable Causes through Fundraising Campaigns." *HRMagazine*, October.

Walton, R.E. 1985. "Toward a Strategy for Eliciting Employee Participation Based on Policies of Mutuality." In *HRM Trends & Challenges*, edited by R.E. Walton and P.R. Lawrence, 35–65. Cambridge, MA: Harvard Business School Press.

Warner, Amos G. 1894. American Charities: A Study in Philanthropy and Economics. Boston: Cromwell.

Warner, Lloyd and Paul S. Lunt. 1941. *The Social Life of a Modern Community*. New Haven: Yale University Press.

Warren, Roland L. 1967. "The Interorganizational Field as a Focus of Investigation." *Administrative Science Quarterly* 12:143–44.

Watson, Frank Dekker. 1922. *The Charity Organization Movement in the United States*. New York: Arno Press.

Waugh, Dexter. 1977. "New Potshots at United Way." *San Francisco Examiner & Chronicle* September 11:A6.

Webber, Melvin M. 1963. "Order in Diversity: Community without Propinquity." In *Cities and Space*, edited by Lowdon Wingo, 25–54. Baltimore: Johns Hopkins University Press.

Weber, Max. 1978. *Economy and Society. An Outline of Interpretive Sociology*, edited by Guenter Roth and C. Wittich. Berkeley, CA: University of California.

Weisbrod, Burton. 1988. *The Nonprofit Economy*. Cambridge, MA: Harvard University Press.

———. 1997. "The Future of the Nonprofit Sector." *Journal of Policy Analysis and Management* 16:541–55.

Weiss, Penny A. and Marilyn Friedman, eds. 1995. *Feminism and Community*. Philadelphia: Temple University Press.

Wellman, Barry. 1979. "The Community Question: The Intimate Networks of East Yorkers." *The American Journal of Sociology* 84(5):1201–1231.

Wellman, Barry, ed. 1999. *Networks in the Global Village: Life in Contemporary Communities*. Boulder, CO: Westview Press.

Wenocur, Stanley. 1974. "Confederation Adaptability to External Change Pressures." PhD diss., University of California.

———. 1975. "A Political View of the United Way." *Social Work* May:223–228.

Wenocur, Stanley and Michael Reisch. 1989. *From Charity to Enterprise: The Development of American Social Work in a Market Economy*. Chicago: University of Illinois Press.

Wenocur, Stanley, Richard V. Cook, and Nancy L. Steketee. 1984. "Fund-Raising at the Workplace." *Social Work* Spring:55–60.

White, Arthur H. 1989. "Patterns of Giving." In *Philanthropic Giving: Studies in Varieties and Goals*, edited by Richard Magat, 65–71. New York: Oxford University Press.

Wiewel, Wim and Albert Hunter. 1985. "The Interorganizational Network as a Resource: A Comparative Case Study on Organizational Genesis." *Administrative Science Quarterly* 30:482–496.

Williams, Raymond. 1983. *Keywords*. London: Fontana.

Williams, Roger M. 1990. "Pluralism at Work." *Foundation News*, May/June:60–67.

Wirth, Louis. 1938. "Urbanism as a Way of Life."*American Journal of Sociology* 44:3–24.

Witty, Cathie J. 1989. "Workplace Giving: Employee Attitudes, Perceptions, and Behavior." *Working Paper No. 9*. San Francisco: University of San Francisco.

Wolch, Jennifer R. and R.K. Geiger. 1983. "The Urban Distribution of Voluntary Resources: An Exploratory Analysis." *Environment and Planning A* 15:1067–1082.

Wolf, Deborah Goleman. 1979. *The Lesbian Community*. Berkeley, CA: University of California Press.

Wolfe, Alan. 1998. "What is Altruism?" In *Private Action and Public Good*, edited by Walter W. Powell and Elisabeth S. Clemens, 36–46. New Haven, CT: Yale University Press.

Wolpert, Julian. 1993. *Patterns of Generosity in America*. New York: Twentieth Century Fund Press.

Wuthnow, Robert. 1988. *The Restructuring of American Religion*. Princeton, NJ: Princeton University Press.

———. 1994. *Sharing the Journey: Support Groups and America's New Quest for Community*. New York: Free Press.

————. 1998. *Loose Connections: Joining Together in America's Fragmented Communities*. Cambridge, MA: Harvard University Press.

Ylvisaker, Paul N. 1987. "Foundations and Nonprofit Organizations." In *The Nonprofit Sector: A Research Handbook*, edited by Walter W. Powell, 360–379. New Haven, CT: Yale University Press.

Young, Dennis and Lester Salamon. 2002. "Commercialization, Social Ventures, and For-Profit Competition." In *The State of Nonprofit America*, edited by Lester Salamon, 423–446. Washington, DC: Brookings Institution Press.

Zerubavel, Eviatur. 1997. *Social Mindscapes: An Invitation to Cognitive Sociology*. Cambridge, MA: Harvard University Press.

Index